Dialogues among Civilizations and Cultures

Iranians in the Minds of Americans

DIALOGUES AMONG CIVILIZATIONS AND CULTURES

Additional books and e-books in this series can be found on Nova's website under the Series tab.

DIALOGUES AMONG CIVILIZATIONS AND CULTURES

IRANIANS IN THE MINDS OF AMERICANS

EHSAN SHAHGHASEMI

nova science publishers
New York

Copyright © 2019 by Nova Science Publishers, Inc.

All rights reserved. No part of this book may be reproduced, stored in a retrieval system or transmitted in any form or by any means: electronic, electrostatic, magnetic, tape, mechanical photocopying, recording or otherwise without the written permission of the Publisher.

We have partnered with Copyright Clearance Center to make it easy for you to obtain permissions to reuse content from this publication. Simply navigate to this publication's page on Nova's website and locate the "Get Permission" button below the title description. This button is linked directly to the title's permission page on copyright.com. Alternatively, you can visit copyright.com and search by title, ISBN, or ISSN.

For further questions about using the service on copyright.com, please contact:
Copyright Clearance Center
Phone: +1-(978) 750-8400   Fax: +1-(978) 750-4470   E-mail: info@copyright.com.

NOTICE TO THE READER

The Publisher has taken reasonable care in the preparation of this book, but makes no expressed or implied warranty of any kind and assumes no responsibility for any errors or omissions. No liability is assumed for incidental or consequential damages in connection with or arising out of information contained in this book. The Publisher shall not be liable for any special, consequential, or exemplary damages resulting, in whole or in part, from the readers' use of, or reliance upon, this material. Any parts of this book based on government reports are so indicated and copyright is claimed for those parts to the extent applicable to compilations of such works.

Independent verification should be sought for any data, advice or recommendations contained in this book. In addition, no responsibility is assumed by the Publisher for any injury and/or damage to persons or property arising from any methods, products, instructions, ideas or otherwise contained in this publication.

This publication is designed to provide accurate and authoritative information with regard to the subject matter covered herein. It is sold with the clear understanding that the Publisher is not engaged in rendering legal or any other professional services. If legal or any other expert assistance is required, the services of a competent person should be sought. FROM A DECLARATION OF PARTICIPANTS JOINTLY ADOPTED BY A COMMITTEE OF THE AMERICAN BAR ASSOCIATION AND A COMMITTEE OF PUBLISHERS.

Additional color graphics may be available in the e-book version of this book.

Library of Congress Cataloging-in-Publication Data

ISBN: 978-1-53615-172-5

Published by Nova Science Publishers, Inc. † New York

CONTENTS

Introduction		**vii**
Chapter 1	The "Great Satan" versus "The Axis of Evil"	**1**
	Introduction	*1*
	Cross Cultural Schemata	*2*
	Iranians in the Minds of Americans	*8*
	Analysis	*35*
Chapter 2	American Missionary Life and Work in Iran	**39**
	Introduction	*39*
	Hardships and Deaths	*48*
	Health Care and Relief Service	*51*
	Education	*55*
	Evangelization	*61*
	Intercultural Communication Strategy	*67*
	Political Strategy	*70*
	Discussion	*73*
Chapter 3	Iran and United States in Historical Context	**77**
	Introduction	*77*
	Earliest Contacts	*78*
	American Legation in Tehran	*82*
	The Constitutional Revolution	*84*

	World War I	87
	World War II	91
	The Coup	94
	The Islamic Revolution	100
	Discussion	104
Chapter 4	Studying American Cross Cultural Schemata	**107**
	Introduction	107
	Social Cognition	109
	Schemata	111
	Cross Cultural Schemata	114
	Method and Procedure	116
Chapter 5	Findings	**119**
	Demographics	120
	American Cross Cultural Schemata of Iranians	123
	Sources of Cross Cultural Schemata	124
	Other Factors	155
Chapter 6	Cross Cultural Schemata	**159**
	Neutral	161
	Negative	173
	Positive	205
	No Cross Cultural Schemata	222
	No Comment or Not Applicable	225
	Mixed and Contradictory Cross Cultural Schemata	226
Conclusion		**241**
Bibliography		**245**
About the Author		**263**
Index		**265**

INTRODUCTION

In 2007 I passed a course entitled "Intercultural Communication" with Professor Saied Reza Ameli in which he encouraged us to work on the concept of schemata. I worked on another subject, but when I saw the results of the works of my classmates, I developed an interest into this subject. Later in 2007 after I befriended late Professor D. Ray Heisey of Kent State University, I proposed him we study cross cultural schemata Iranian and American people had of each other. After we published this article in *Intercultural Communication Studies* in 2009, I decided to work more on this subject. This was the reason I later decided to do my dissertation on this subject. I was highly motivated and determined, but, had I knew hardships and difficulties, I would have been working on a different project. Nevertheless, there were many people who reached out and helped me very much. I am thankful to all of them.

First of anything, I would like to thank my wife Sima, whose support and patience helped me a lot during three years of hard work. I also thank Professor Saied Reza Ameli of University of Tehran who took a lot of time and helped me with his deep knowledge of the field of intercultural communication. Professor Ameli was supervisor of my dissertation and before that, he had supervised my thesis between 2006 and 2008. I would like to thank Professor Hamid Abdollahyan, Professor Foad Izadi, and Professor Ali Rabiei who accepted to be advisers of my dissertation.

Professor Hamid Abdullahyan helped a lot in methodology section and I used his own method of sampling; Professor Foad Izadi have prominent works on Iran's portrayal in the U.S.'s media, and Professor Ali Rabei helped me with designing the structure of my dissertation. I thank Professor Alireza Dehghan of University of Tehran, Professor Hassan Bashir of Imam Sadeq University, and Professor Mahmoud Shahabi of Allameh TabaTabaei University who accepted to referee my dissertation and incorporating their valuable comments enriched my work. I need to express my appreciation to Professor D. Ray Heisey of Kent State University who helped me formulate this research design, and also I should mention Professor Michael H. Prosser, Emeritus Professor at University of Virginia and a founder of the field of Intercultural Communication whose comments was very helpful at all stages of my project.

I had the privilege of brief consultations with Professor Mohsen Mobasher from University of Houston-Downtown, Professor Flora Keshishian from St. John's University, Professor Heleen Murre-van den Berg from Leiden Institute for Area Studies, Professor Arthur Asa Berger at San Francisco State University, and Professor Ervand Abrahamian from City University of New York who themselves have done related research and were kind enough to share with me their findings, thoughts and suggestions. I also thank Loosineh Markarian, an Iranian Armenian scholar and activist from University of Denver for giving me information about different Christian sects in contemporary Iran.

This book is a report on a cross-country online survey and without the help of many people in Iran or abroad, there was no possibility of fulfilling this task. Some people were even kind enough to borrow me password of their email accounts and during one month or more I was able to log in their emails and send emails to the American citizens. Others helped me by forwarding the link of my questionnaire to other American citizens. I therefore thank Goudarz Mirani, Zahra Emamzadeh, Hossein Hassani, Mojtaba Hajijafari, Hesam Mahmoudi, Nasrin Shahghasemi, Mohsen Shahghasemi, Hamed Shahghasemi, Omid Shahghaesmi, Nasim Shahghasemi, Ali Shahghasemi, Ghasem Hosseini, Akram Goshtasbi, Mostafa Ahmadzadeh, Taher Khadiv, Negahdar Hosseinpour, Somayeh

Dalvand, Zohreh Taher, Manijeh Akhavan, Bijan Tafazzoli, Mehrdad Bina, Maysami Shirzadifard, Kristina Robertson, Danielle (Fisher) Heacox, Hojat Shahghasemi, Dan Crystal, Laurie Shanderson, Mark Pezzo among others. I am very grateful to friends at Nova Publishing who accepted to publish this book.

The original work included many tables, formula, graphs and diagrams. I have converted it into a more accessible text; I have also included many direct accounts of my respondents to give the reader more tangible and immediate access to the respondents' image of Iranian citizens. I have also made changes in the conclusion section to make it more readable by international audience. I hope this is a beginning of a series of further research on this subject. Maybe after a threshold, this subject finds louder voice in the media and eventually becomes a political priority.

Chapter 1

THE "GREAT SATAN" VERSUS "THE AXIS OF EVIL"

INTRODUCTION

In the second decade of the new millennium, the emergence of DAESH in tens of countries including Western countries again brought up Iran-U.S confrontations to the global debates. Both countries have been a threat to each other for about four decades. U.S. has included Iran in the so called "Axis of Evil," while the Iranian Islamic government has repetitiously called the U.S. "Great Satan," and "Global Arrogance."

This is despite the fact that these two countries have had a very long and friendly relations, at both political and cultural levels. Moreover, there has been many geographical and even cultural similarities between both countries. If Iran were superimposed over a map of North America, it would extend north to south from Reno, Nevada, to Monterey, Mexico, and west to east from San Diego, California, to Amarillo, Texas. In fact, the terrain, climate, and latitude of Iran bear considerable resemblance to corresponding features of the American southwest and northwestern Mexico. Iran, however, is much more arid with more extremely hot and barren areas, especially in its central and eastern deserts (Ward, 2009, p. 5). Both countries have inescapable shared interests in Middle East and other regions and at times these shared interests have forced both countries to cooperate indirectly – and sometimes directly.

The continuous clandestine war between these countries has over shadowed cultural relationships and perceptions and a brief search into op-ed articles and even in the academic resources shows that only a handful of the publications consider "culture" as a central point in studying Iran-U.S. relations. People of both countries, therefore, have learned to see each other through the lens of politics. Image of Iranian people in the minds of Americans has changed during the last decades. Unfortunately, it was only after the Iranian revolution and ensuing hostilities that polling institutes and academics turn to seriously measure American's view towards Iran. And, this is even more unfortunate that these studies rarely concerned perceptions American people have of Iranian people –and not government. In fact, the number of surveys with this subject, as we will see later in this book, is few. Therefore, I decided to take up this task and see how U.S. Americans see Iranian people. In order to do so, I decided to use cross cultural schemata as a theoretical lens.

CROSS CULTURAL SCHEMATA

The globalization process as we know it has brought great changes to the human life. Increasingly, not only people know much more about other people in every corner of the world, but also they have to construct reliable images of them, because mass migration and other phenomena have increased the possibility that we encounter members of every group from every part of the world. As boom in the media industry is both driving force of globalization and the outcome of it, these media increasingly play important role in determining how images of the world, including people of difference, take shape. There are other means like tourism and mass migration which are both results of globalization, but, the research have shown the role of media is overwhelming.

Before the media become pervasive, "cross cultural schemata" (we will come back to this term again) were created by voyages of exploration and discovery, by the establishment of new trade routes to exotic areas of the world, and by encounters with new cultures and people in the context of pilgrimage or military activity (Shackley, 2006, p. 2). The openness of the nature of narrative, however, let people to blend realities with fictions.

Writing and traveling have always been closely connected. The traveler's tale is as old as fiction itself: one of the very earliest extant stories, composed in Egypt during Twelfth Dynasty, a thousand years before the odyssey, delineates a shipwrecked sailor alone on an incredible island. The biblical and classical traditions are both rich in examples of travel writing, literal and symbolic (Hulme & Youngs, 2002) and the schemata were mainly transmitted or fixated by the way of written tales. The atmosphere of the old folk-tales surrounding the hero's encounters with *exotic* people such as the Lotus-eaters and the Laestrygonians, with carnivorous monsters and with being divine and semi-divine was rampant (Heubeck & Hoekstra, 1990). Homer's Odyssey is a good example of an 8th BC view on the world. To travel through it is to discover a succession of characters embodying the "Other" and the *exotic* (Saïd, 2011, p. 164).

Another example from the ancient time is Gilgamesh. The Epic of Gilgamesh is an account about the deeds of a famous hero-king of ancient Mesopotamia and is full of adventures and encounters with strange creatures, men and gods alike *(Kovacs, 1989)*. This text from Sumer is believed to be as old as 2500 BC *(Tigay, 1982)*. Other epics from other cultures like Panchatantra of ancient India and the Mayan epics of Mesoamerican civilization are rich with talking animals and exotic customs and people.

Herodotus's work is still known to be the best source for understanding the realities of early travel. He travelled as far as Egypt, sailing up the Nile to Thebes and the First Cataract. He described Egyptians, Greeks and circum-Mediterranean world, but he mixed scientific observation with tales and fables (Shackley, 2006). He also gave a negative image of the Persians. The Persians exerted a remarkable hold over the Greek imagination and Greek literature overflows with references to all kinds of diverse Persian exotica: Persian-sounding (but fake) names, references to tribute, to *proskynesis* (obeisance), law, impalement, the King's Eye, good roads, eunuchs, gardens, drinking, and gold (Llewellyn-Jones & Robson, 2010, p. 46).

Xenophon's four novellas in the *Cyropaedia* are another good example. Intriguingly, the wide range of stock characters found in Xenophon's novellas seem to be exotic – an indolent king, a frightened eunuch, a cruel despot, a brave warrior, a grief-stricken father, a devoted slave, and a beautiful but chaste woman. Today we believe that most possibly Xenophon drew on Ctesias' *Persica*as for his novellas, although Xenophon's own sojourn within the Persian Empire, as well as his own active imagination, can account for much of what else is contained in the *Anabasis* and the *Cyropaedia* (Llewellyn-Jones & Robson, 2010).

Like the representation industry of the modern days, stories of exotic people in distant regions had elements of the reality. Crusade times for example brought about a series of narratives about Muslims. The earliest western images of the Muslims had been fabricated out of fear and ignorance and had demonized Muslims as fabulous monsters with the heads of dogs *(Marr, 2006)*. The crucible of the Crusades with its ideological rivalry developed derogatory images of Islam that were little more than "tenacious fictions and mythical legends which took on literary lives of their own" *(Marr, 2006, p. 90)*. In the ninth book of his historia ecclesiastica, Orderic Vitalis included an account of the crusade which he based on a considerable degree upon historical books of that time. Orderic had probably never met a Muslim. Yet, in a blistering attack, he vilifies Muslims as the embodiment of all the vices most abhorred by Christians *(Shatzmiller, 1993)*. He described them as "foreigners," "creatures of another race," "raging idolaters against Christ," "adulterers" and "Bastards." He calls them "stupid and barbarian" possessing no moral sense, they oppress the weak and the poor with the excesses of their "pagan tyranny." They act solely out of the animal instinct of rage and fear and in war with Christians, they behave like "cruel monsters" "howling and gnashing their teeth" *(Shatzmiller, 1993, pp. 101-102)*. The medieval art also included paintings of Muslims as monsters, as Strickland *(2003)* has discussed in detail some of them. Yet, the conflict between Islam and Christendom, from the time of the Crusades, was mainly concerned with

Turks, less with Arabs, and hardly at all with Persians. Persia seemed to have vanished, at least from the consciousness of Europeans (Frye, 2003). On the other side, I must say, there was the same distorted images being fabricated against the crusaders.

Throughout seventeenth and eighteenth-century the exotic influence continued, but it was to be tamed; changed into recognizably English middle-class ways of thinking and coordinated with the worldview of the time. English readers could usually think they were superior to any of the outlandish behavior or ways of life they read in books. Therefore, although the fascination with the exotic, seen in travelers' stories over the centuries from Mandeville to Raleigh, is a common theme, now the concern was not simply to document but to accommodate experience within recognizable bounds (Carter & McRae, 2001). Even stories of Othello's in the work of Shakespeare is accused of becoming code for the implausibility and willful deception of travelers' tales (Kinney, 2012).

A fashion for exotic places and people, closely related to the Gothic, led to such outrageous works as *Vathek* (1786) by William Beckford. This Arabian tale is about a cruel man, Caliph Vathek, palaces for the indulgence of the five senses, child sacrifice, and considerable excesses of excitement. Its exaggerations are tempered with a degree of twentieth-century wastelands in solitude. The creature's own point of view is given full voice in the epistolary form of the novel, balancing with pathos the horror which other narrative voices describe (Carter & McRae, 2001). In the Sixteen, Seventeen and Eighteen centuries the extent of exaggeration by the travelers was so high that Irish writer and clergyman Jonathan Swift wrote *Gulliver's Travels* (1726, amended 1735), in which Lemuel *Gulliver*, first a Surgeon, and then a Captain of Several Ships visits different places. This classic of English literature is both a satire on human nature and a parody of the travelers' tales genre (Andersen, 2012). Some scholars have recently investigated lies and parodies of traveler's tales in centuries of exploration (see for example Cooke (2013) and Cohen (2008)).

The French soldiers of Napoléon Bonaparte barely stopped travelling, covering huge distances over many years from capped Alpine passes to hot plains of Castile, from the vineyards of Italy and Rhineland to deserts of

Egypt and North Africa. Some fought beneath the Pyramids, others in the sugar-islands of the Caribbean. And if it all ended disastrously in the snows of Russia, those who returned to France came back with a wealth of *travelers' tales* about *exotic* landscapes and cultured capital cities, strange diets and novel crops. A whole generation of young French people who would in other circumstances have ventured little beyond the confines of their native place was suddenly exposed to the wonders of an entire continent (Forrest, 2006). The emergence of fantasy writing, set in other worlds or expressing other realities, became a popular genre of the second half of the nineteenth century. Of course, the exotic had been a theme in literature from Mandeville to Beckford, and the Romantics had brought many oriental elements into their writings. The bestselling book of its day, *Lalla Rookh* (1817) by Thomas Moore (1779–1852), was a series of Oriental tales inverse, anticipating Edward Fitzgerald's *The Rubaiyat of Omar Khayyam* (1859) in its appeal (Carter & McRae, 2001).

The invention of anthropology as a new science and method systematized but not healed the way people of difference were presented to the more prosperous world. It could be said that anthropology formally came into the being with the works of Franz Boas in United States and Bronislaw Malinowski in the Britain in the late 19th and early 20th centuries. Prior to Malinowski, most anthropologists collected data on primitive societies by relying either on missionaries or colonial agents (Llobera, 2003). The most important criticism against anthropology is "cultural evolutionism." Trying to account for the vast diversity of human cultures, the first group of early anthropologists suggested that all societies pass through a series of distinct evolutionary stages. This theory placed Euro-American cultures at the top of the evolutionary ladder and less developed cultures on the lower rungs (Ferraro & Andreatt, 2011). This ladder of civilization simply looked like all ladders: those who were on the lower rungs were supposed to climb the ladder to become a *civilized* man like the anthropologist himself.

After the WWII a wave of decolonization started. Though some of these countries fell in the hands of tyrants after their eventual and sometimes bloody emancipation, for the first time scholars from previous colonies started to question not only what colonizers did to their people, but also the way Western scholars, writers and artists presented them to the Westerners. It was in 1978 that Edward Said famously formulated a theory that scholars could use to explain the negative, exotic, and often erotic vision of the East routinely promoted in the West. His book *Orientalism* described a method by which Western colonialist discourse had represented the 'colonies' and cultures of the Middle Eastern world as a way of justifying and supporting the West's imperialist enterprise. Put more succinctly, Orientalism is an idiosyncratic European means of representing Otherness (Llewellyn-Jones & Robson, 2010).

Do the so-called globalization and democratization of the media help people to have a better perception and less biased perspective of each other? Theoretically, the answer is yes. Yet, the reality is not so much compromising. Ameli (2012) has conducted an intensive study on 6 decades of Western academic products and after analyzing 18,225 articles, 2,477 dissertations and 3,170 books produced in the Western Academia has come to the conclusion that pessimism against Muslims and Islamic world has been on the raise particularly after 11/9 and 7/7. Moreover, a 2006 epic movie named *300* shows how we should still be pessimist about the way media reveal the world to us. The film *300* derives its title from the number of Spartan warriors who, led by their indomitable king, Leonidas, held the narrow pass at Thermopylae on the northern coast of Greece against the massive forces of the Persian Army assembled by King Xerxes. This small but elite band of Spartans held the Persian invaders at the "Hot Gates" for three bloody days in the late summer of 480 BC, just long enough for the city-states of Ancient Greece to form a coalition and mobilize their forces to repel the overwhelming enemy assault from the East (Cyrino, 2010). The movie was widely criticized of being political and ideological (Hassler-Forest, 2010). Another accusation is *300*'s so-called facile embrace of racism towards modern Iran, the geographical, ethnic, and cultural descendant of ancient Persia. Some of the Persians in *300* are depicted as deformed or monstrous, sometimes even barely recognizable as human beings, and others are depicted as stereotypical and banal representatives of Western orientalism- effeminate, decadent, exotic

(Lauwers, Dhont, & Huybrecht, 2012, p. 80). Despite wide critical receptions by commentators, the general public in the West and particularly U.S. welcomed the movie. Snyder's *300* reaped an astonishing and record-breaking $71 million on its opening weekend, with the largest-ever box-office total in March history and the third-highest for any R-rated film, leading one film critic to note: "The industry was stunned by the magnitude of the Spartan victory." The film continued to earn an amazing domestic box-office total of $211 million and soon proved its global popularity with a worldwide total gross of $456 million (Cyrino, 2010, p. 20). Once again, I do not insist that this kind of image making is particular to Western cultures. I am myself from Middle East and I have witnessed similar image makings of Westerners and Christians.

IRANIANS IN THE MINDS OF AMERICANS

As I mentioned earlier, there are plenty of studies on how American people view Iran. But, only few of them have been conducted with an intercultural approach; most of them merely see Iran as a political entity and try to understand what American public think of this entity. One reason for this can be that doing research on intercultural perceptions needs funds and governmental bodies which are naturally political are less willing to support these subjects. Another reason could be that political authorities are less likely to be knowledgeable! They have no time to read much about things beyond politics and in fact many of them have publications that are written by ghost authors.

Anyway, as texts are very important means in shaping a culture's imagination, in this sections I have included travel writings and memoirs by American travelers, missionaries and politicians who have travelled to Iran, or have described *Iranians* in one way or the other. These people wrote marvelous books and their accounts of Iran and Iranians in their era has been a great contribution in documenting Iranian life, society, economy and politics of the time.

Smith and Dwight who were the first known Americans visiting Iran wrote a book about their life and mission in Iran in the year 1830 (more about this mission can be found in chapter 2). They were sent to evaluate a possible mission to Iran. Their account of Iranians who, at that time, were called "Persians" was not an integrated one. They frequently provided negative and positive -at times exaggerated- account of Persians. Examples follow:

> We had not yet learned how to manage the inhospitality which the Persians have been taught, by their government and their religion, to practise toward foreigners, nor indeed were we acquainted with its nature; and, being too fatigued to proceed farther, we accepted a dark corner in a stable filled with horses, cows, and asses, and almost suffocating us by its stench. (Smith & Dwight, 1834, p. 313)
>
> The Persians have almost always been a subject race, and now the citizen and the peasant hold a less honourable rank than the nomad. Between seven and eight hundred thousand of the inhabitants of Persia still live in tents, and, while not one of them is of the Persian language, they furnish the flower of her army and the pride of her nobility. Turkish, Arabic, Kurdish, and Loorish are their native tongues. (Smith & Dwight, 1834, p. 334)
>
> The manners of the Persians toward *foreigners* differ from those of the Turks even more than their form of intercourse with each other. The Turkish gentleman receives you sitting, coolly put his hand upon his breast for a salutation, asks You to sit as if the invitation in any form was an act of condescension, and a few common-place questions, with long intervals of silence filled up by pipes and coffee, complete the ceremonies of your reception. The Persian not only honours you by rising, but, putting you at once into the position of his lord, and assuming the attitude of your slave, he forces you into his own seat, if it happen to be the most honourable. An active conversation, enlivened by inquisitive thought, and polished with a profusion of compliment succeeds, and you leave him with the feeling that he has improved upon the politeness of the politest nation of Europe. (Smith & Dwight, 1834, p. 336)
>
> Such civility highly prepossesses the *traveller,* at first, in favour of the society of the nation which exercises it, and makes the *missionary* hope that his instructions may be received with as much deference as his

person. Experience soon convinces both, however, that if the Persian excels in politeness, he is forced to it as a mask to cover his deceitfulness. The commonest man is found almost as dexterous in plot and intrigue as if he were practiced in managing the diplomacy of Europe; and allurements of the Persian's civility are soon eclipsed by painful experience of his unequalled duplicity. The traveller finds his hospitality converted into a money-making speculation. (Smith & Dwight, 1834, p. 336)

The Persian, of Aderbaijan (sic) especially, differs also from the Turk in his readiness to admit European innovations. (Smith & Dwight, 1834, p. 337)

The Persians are comparatively tolerant, also, of a discussion of the merits of Mohammedanism, and many will argue with all the technical coolness of a dialectician. Most of the higher class of the nobility, and the learned profession, indeed, pay little regard even to the external forms of religion, and are at heart infidels or sceptics. (Smith & Dwight, 1834, p. 340)

You must not understand that all Persians are inclined to freethinking. The mass of the people are not only very sincere in their faith, but have decidedly an appearance of greater strictness in the observance of their rites than even the Turks. (Smith & Dwight, 1834, p. 340)

In 1833 Justin Perkins and his wife were sent to Urmia, where they opened a school in 1835. In his 1843 book *A Residence of Eight Years in Persia among the Nestorian Christians with Notices of the Muhammedans*, he devoted a chapter to describe Persians:

And the waning zeal of the Persians in regard to their *places* of worship is perhaps no more than a fair index of the decline of their attachment to the worship itself. The Persians may in general be said to be enterprising and imitative, though not very inventive. . . The Persians of Azerbijan (sic) are regarded as the finest race of men in the empire. They are far more athletic and manly than the inhabitants further south. They furnish the best of the king's troops, -most of them, indeed, on whom he places much reliance are collected from this, his native and favorite province. They are also a very fine looking people, being probably a mixed race, combining, perhaps, Georgian beauty with Tartar size and Persian gracefulness. Like all Persians, they have bright, inquisitive minds, very social dispositions and affable, insinuating manners. The inhabitants of Persia doubtless surpass all other nations in external ease and artificial politeness; and it is with great propriety that they are often styled "the French of Asia." But, sad to tell, Persian politeness is little more than *external*. Their real character is that of treachery and falsehood in the extreme. The prevalence of *lying* among them is universal,-so much so, that the practice is hardly regarded as a sin, or a disgrace, in the general estimation. It is therefore necessary, however painful, while you listen to their smooth compliments and their loud professions of friendship, to keep in mind that their hearts are preeminently deceitful, and "the poison of asps is under their tongues." And the general degradation of their morals is appalling. Almost all the sins forbidden in the decalogue,(sic) are fearfully prevalent among them; and to these many add the yet more abominable sin of Sodom, They are, as a people, however, by no means destitute of kindness and hospitality,- particularly towards strangers. (Perkins J., 1843, pp. 149-150)

Asahel Grant and his wife visited Iran in 1835. Grant wrote a book about his mission but he was not so much interested in making sociological assertions about Iranian people, or maybe he was just prudent in making generalizations about people who were still not well known to him. In his book of more than 340 pages, he only once tries to describe the traits of Persian people: "At half-past twelve I found myself in the presence of the Patriarch of the East, the spiritual head of the Nestorian Church, who gave me a cordial welcome, but without that flow of heartless compliment and extravagant expression of pleasure which is so common in the mouth of a Persian" (Grant, 1841, pp. 80-81).

Southgate (1840, pp. 9-10) who was an American missionary in Iran described Persians of the city of Tabriz:

> It is this peculiarity of the Persian character — their great accessibleness and their love for knowledge — which is the grand encouragement to efforts for their improvement. In both respects, as in most others, they are the very opposite of the Turks. Instead of being

difficult of approach, they court the society of a foreigner. They converse with him with the utmost cordiality, they demean themselves towards him with affability and deference, they honour him with the same terms of respect which they address to each other, even to the salutation of peace, (Selam Aleikum,) which a Turk seldom utters to a man of another religion. The Persian invites the foreigner to his house, and receives him with a cordiality and politeness that puts him at once at his ease. . . I speak now of the Persians of the city, and of well-bred Persians generally, who are not of the religious orders. The only additional qualification which I believe my remarks require, is, that the politeness of Persians is, in numberless instances, the product of pure selfishness, induced merely by a desire to gain some favour or advantage. Their love of knowledge, too, has a considerable drawback in their extreme volatility of character, which renders their pursuit of it liable to great fluctuations. Some of the earliest pupils of the German missionaries, who commenced their studies with boundless enthusiasm, gave up in despair when they found that they could not compass the attainment of all human learning in two or three months.

James Layman Merrick who was an American missionary in Persia wrote a poem titled "farewell to Persia" in which he expressed his positive view on Persia as a land and a culture:

> Farewell to the land of the Lion and Sun,
> The kingdom where Magi of old,
> Marked courses which bodies celestial do run,
> And sought nature's laws to unfold.
> Where Zerdusht on altars of earth lit his fire,
> To honor the monarch of day.
> And taught that the spirit of man should aspire
> To blend in Divinity's ray.
> . . .
> The land where apostles and martyrs have prayed,
> And many blest Him who can save,
> Where powers of darkness their engines arrayed
> To batter the truth to the grave.
> Farewell to the land, my adopted for years,

> Ere Providence led from the West,
> Endeared to my hearth by prayer, labor and tears,
> Where I had expected to Rest. . . . (1847, pp. 186-187)

Samuel Goodrich's *A History of All Nations,* a popular textbook published in 1851,explained that while Asians on the whole were "slavish ... superstitious ... [and] treacherous," their arts compared favorably with those of Europe. He wrote "All the efforts of European art and capital have been unequal fully to imitate the carpets of Persia . . ." (Iriye, 2002, p. 411).

James Basset, an American Presbyterian missionary wrote in 1886:

> The cost of living in the country has greatly increased in the course of a few years. The increasing wants of the rich impel to greater extortion, and while a few people are growing richer, the peasants are growing poorer, if that be possible, and the whole country is falling into a financial stress, the only remedy for which, in the ordinary course of things, is a reduction of the population by war and famine. There is an utter want either of capacity, or of a disposition to improve the country. The intentions of the Shah may reasonably be supposed to be good toward his own subjects, but the universal prevalence of greed and dishonesty nullifies every good device. (Bassett, 1886, p. 260)

Samuel Greene Wheeler Benjamin who was the first American minister to Tehran wrote about Persians: "No country has more attractive legends than Persia; and to judge from them we cannot avoid the conclusion that no nation now existing has such a continuous vitality as the old land of Cyrus and Xerxes" (Benjamin, 1887, p. 1). Elsewhere he wrote: "The Persians are a quick-witted, lively, agreeable people, handsome, and of mercurial disposition. They are easy-natured, but their passions are quickly aroused, in which respect they resemble the Latin races" (Benjamin, 1886, p. 43). He added "All wealthy Persians keep open house. That is, a gentleman who is travelling always finds ready welcome and unstinted hospitality at houses of the same rank. This is essential in a country so poorly provided with accommodations for travellers, and does not necessarily imply a generosity superior to our own. Likewise the poor can always obtain bread or a dish of pillau or rice in the kitchen of a wealthy Persian. This is in accordance with the inculcations to charity in the Koran, and is a means of preventing such extreme cases of suffering as we often see among our own poor" (Benjamin, 1886, pp. 51-52).

William Ambrose Shedd who was born in 1965 in Urmia said of his dealings with the Turks as an American missionary: "The Turkish officials are less ceremonious than the Persians and usually less affable. The most important Turk I met, when we passed out after paying our respects, said to another caller, 'These people are our enemies, nichtwahr?' He spoke German" (Shedd M. L., 1922, p. 161). He also said "the Persians don't lack ability to see what should be done, but they do lack the resolution to put it through at the expense of their personal advantage or personal work" (Shedd M. L., 1922, p. 214).

Robert E. Speer in the early 20th century admires Iranians: "one would bespeak for the kindly and lovable people of Iran and for its government a full and intelligent sympathy and best wishes for a future of true prosperity" (Coan, 1939, p. XVI).

Dr. John G. Wishard who was Director of the American Presbytery Hospital in Tehran in late 19th and early 20th centuries wrote in 1908:

> This is especially true of Persia when we remember her long and honourable history, her learning and civilisation, that date back almost to the beginning of time and that have been hidden for centuries from the Western World. The recent potentially mighty changes in the political, social, and economic life of the nation have served to call the attention of readers anew to that interesting land where some of the sweetest poets have sung; from whence have sprung some of the world's greatest armies -the land of the Fire- Worshipper and the Sun. It is especially interesting to us as the place from which the white race sprang. Its name is known in the Persian language as Iran, pronounced E-ron, which is from Arya, hence the Aryan races. (Wishard, 1908, pp. 9-10)
>
> The upper-class Persians, of whom this man was a sample, are nearly always kind and hospitable to travellers and strangers. There is a Persian motto that says, "If you want to know a man, travel with him, or seek

lodgings at his house." As well as being hospitable, the Persians are often very agreeable travelling companions. It is the sort of thing that appeals to their nomadic natures, and they are at their best out in the open air, mounted on a good horse, making a journey. (Wishard, 1908, p. 184)

The Persian language has been called the French of the East. It is rich in polite and poetic phrases, lends itself readily to diplomatic use, and is not unpleasant to the ear of a Westerner. Many of the idioms, so pleasing to the Persian, cannot be readily translated into English. (Wishard, 1908, p. 154)

The attitude of the Persians toward Europeans has been quite as polite as that of many Europeans towards them; but, notwithstanding unpleasant incidents that are bound to arise, for many years to come, the deep-rooted prejudice against the Christian is certainly becoming less. (Wishard, 1908, p. 170)

Girls are often married at an early age, not infrequently when they are mere children. Every doctor in Persia who has had much experience could tell most dreadful and harrowing stories of the suffering these early marriages have caused. I have seen children brought to the hospital that the mere mention of their husbands' names would cause outbursts of shrieks, lest they might be compelled to return to them. It is needless for me to state here that these early marriages on the part of girls means a weakened race. Many of these children are married, often at the age of twelve, to men old enough to be their grandfathers, and this means a large number of widows. As many of these widows are left without means of support, there is only one road open for them, and that road Ieadet (sic) to destruction. Most of them are almost compelled to become plural wives, or, what is worse, temporary ones, the Persian law sanctioning either arrangement. Divorce is common and is no disgrace for the man. Not so for the woman, however, for, if she belongs to the upper classes, it is hardly probable that her second marriage will be that of the first wife of a man equal to her by birth and social standing. (Wishard, 1908, p. 244)

Nearly all the Persians are lovers of peace and good-fellowship, notwithstanding their tempers, which so frequently cause them to make exhibitions of themselves. (Wishard, 1908, p. 277)

The vitality of Mohammedanism in Persia seems much less strong than in Turkey. (Wishard, 1908, p. 155)

After being expelled from Iran under the pressure of Russia and Britain, William Morgan Shuster wrote:

> I shall never forget my emotions as we left the busy streets of Teheran and came out upon the more quiet highroad. Memories of the preceding eight months crowded fast upon me. One cannot leave forever the scene of a frustrated ambition without a pang at the mere physical realization that it is all over. I had been ambitious to serve the Persian people. When the inhabitants of Teheran learned the day on which we were going they sent several of their deputies to me to say that a great crowd of them wished to come and say farewell. I requested that no such demonstration should be made, and when word of it reached the Cabinet, the police notified the leaders of the different societies that no gathering of the kind would be permitted. (Shuster, 1912, p. 226)

In 1924 after a hard travel from U.S. to Turkey, Iraq and finally Iran (Bakhtiari), three American film makers named Merian C. Cooper, Ernest Schoedsack, and Marguerite Harrison filmed 50,000 Bakhtiari people and hundreds of thousands of livestock on a harrowing trek across the Karun River and over the Zagros Mountains to get to highlands where there was enough grass for their herds. Filmmakers had racist tendencies; they called Bakhtiari people "the Forgotten People" among whom some are "white and fair." It seems Cooper and his colleagues wanted to show that they had discovered a group of Arian people. They also claimed they were showing the life of Aryans in 3000 years ago. Cooper later directed *King Kong* (1933) and became more famous. He had a wonderful and rather strange life (Maghsoudlou, 2009).

Abraham Valentine Williams Jackson who was an American scholar whose work on grammar of Avestan language is still known as the most reliable work wrote in 1920:

> Persia has always been a land of poetry, nor has the lyric quality ever been lost from the voice of her people. The guide who leads the traveler's cavalcade across the mountains, and the master of the caravan, as he

heads the long camel train that winds its slow way among the hills, can each troll snatches of verse from poets centuries old. (Saleh, 1976, p. 70)

In 1925, Dr. Arthur Chester Millspaugh wrote:

> the continuous existence of Persia as a nation, from remote antiquity to the present time, the architectural grandeur exemplified by the ruins of Susa and Persepolis and by many other monuments and antiquities, as well as the poetry of Ferdosi, Sa'adi, Hafez, Omar Khayyam, to say nothing of such minor poets as Omar Khayyam, the persistence through the centuries of beautiful and artistic work in textiles, silver, brass, and pottery, and the persistent progressive moment with the maintenance of nationality all illustrate the extraordinary vitality and power of recuperation possessed by the Persian people. Standing between the East and the West, invaded by East and the West and invading both, the Persians have always had a rare capacity to drawing on the special gifts of other peoples without losing their own characteristics and integrity. (Millspaugh, 1925, p. 25)

After travelling to Iran, American journalist Vincent Sheean wrote in 1927:

> ... A people with the noble past and the extraordinary gifts of the Persians can never truly be said to have succumbed to time: resuscitation is a permanent probability just around the corner. In my own brief experience in the country I came to believe that this resuscitation could not be long delayed; there will arise a generation in Persia which will not be content with the vanities of political intrigue or with that most destructive of all vanities, the Vanitas Vanitatum idea ... In our time the true health of Persia is to be sought through the program of its least-heeded voices, the teachers and the women ... A few ideas are worth a hundred thousand rifles. The education which will liberate and reestablish Persia is now only beginning and we are not likely to see a distinctly regenerative accomplishment until it has gone much further. But it is at least a great deal to be able to say that it is under way, and that our own time may yet see a Persia worthy of its ruins. (Saleh, 1976, p. 73)

Professor Arthur Upham Pope in 1938 wrote:

> [T]he peculiar genius of Persia found its most adequate embodiment in the so-called arts of decoration, those that depend for their effect upon beauty of pattern and expressive design. In these Iran attained a mastery that scarcely faltered through the unequaled duration of her cultural history .... There is no term in Western languages that is quite satisfactory for such an art as that of Iran. Words like 'ornamental' or decorative' suggest something derivative and of secondary importance. The arts of many lands are partly unintelligible, without reference to Persian contributions. Europe is the heir of a medieval culture on which Persian influences, direct and indirect, had a profound effect; and even earlier the Iranian contributions to classical culture, though as yet imperfectly determined, were definite and perhaps fundamental. Iran is one of the central facts in the artistic life of Asia and the fountain source of much that was finest and most enduring in Eslamic (sic) culture, which disseminated Iran's influence across both Asia and Africa. (Badiozamani & Badiozamani, 2005, p. 12)

In late 1940s American William O. Douglas travelled to Iran and Kurdistan. He recorded many aspects of life in Iran including a section on characteristics of Iranians:

> In great measure Persians and Americans have a close spiritual affinity. The Persian is Aryan the stock that gave most Europeans their culture and ethnic characteristics. The Aryans of Persia have a darker skin than we; but they are more Nordic than Mediterranean. Their heads are long, their foreheads high, their noses narrow. They have a tendency to sparseness. They are a quick-witted, friendly people with a yen for tall tales and dry humor. They know the art of hospitality; they thirst for discourse and argumentation. They love the outdoors streams and mountains and the hunt. In the social sense they are as democratic as any people I have known. They have a reserve we associate with our New Englanders; but underneath they are close kin to our Westerners. These characteristics, most conspicuous among the tribes, tend to become diluted and modified in the cities. (Douglas, 1951, p. 53)

In 1958 American professor Raymond Gastil published an article to present his study based on observation and interviews which were carried out during his stay in Shiraz a year before. About traits of Iranians he wrote:

> There is the emphasis on personal manipulation of people within an established system, rather than a more creative handling of human and material resources to enlarge and alter the system. The attitudes necessary for cooperation, which is demanded by modern social systems, are relatively absent in Iranian culture. The Iranian historically distrusts any government, but he has no other organized institutions to work through. He distrusts those around him, and seems often to live in a state of psychological isolation and generalized fearfulness. Yet, in this state he frequently considers himself far superior to his fellows both intellectually and morally. His communication with others is by convention clouded with unreality, with elaborate praise and exaggeration. Moreover, the acceptance of untruth and pretense as legitimate in many types of communication inevitably adds to a gnawing distrust and disappointment with other persons and society. . . The cumulative pessimism thus engendered, aggravated by the failures of recent Iranian history, serves to jeopardize the constructive programs which the modernizing Iranian "wants" for his country. (Gastil, 1958, p. 329)

American scholar Richard W. Gable (1959) wrote an article about Iranians and their culture in collective and individual issues. He wrote:

> The people are widely known for their friendliness and hospitality, but a vicious competition exists in many interpersonal relationships and is especially noticeable in the public service. A highly centralized, complex government bureaucracy serves a loose, individualistic society. (p. 408)
>
> A person in the upper class would never engage in any kind of manual labor. Even a lowly clerk would not lift and move his typewriter to another desk; he would call a janitor. Consequently, especially when this trait is combined with a high degree of individualism which makes it difficult for persons to cooperate, work may go undone until a person of the appropriate status arrives or is hired to do the task. (p. 409)

The only equality in Iranian society is before Allah. Men are acutely aware of the differences that separate them (p. 409).

The family and religion are the most significant elements of Iranian society and culture. The focus of all Iranian life is the family. It is the most stable and fundamental social unit. . . Outside the safety of the family, life is unstable and often dangerous. Success, possibly survival, depend upon effective manipulation of other persons. Cooperation is further discouraged, and a viciousness in interpersonal relations ensues. (p. 410)

. . . the average Iranian is people-oriented. People, rather than things and the physical world tend to motivate him. . . Moreover, he views life around himself in a highly subjective fashion. . . Logic and rationality are frequently not employed to solve current problems. Instead, solutions are sought in traditions, quotations and anecdotes. . . Iranian reverence for tradition and a glorification of the past are easily discernible traits. The past weighs heavily on the present. (p. 415)

The Iranian's aesthetic and artistic inclinations cause him to hold himself aloof from the practical, work-a-day world. He may feel no particular devotion to his job or any reason to be particularly industrious. Loyalty to an employer, a company, factory or office is not a common trait in Iran. (p. 418)

A trait which can be found among most Iranians and which has serious consequences for every aspect of social and political life is a deep seated and pervasive pessimism. (p. 420)

In 1965 American professor Andrew F. Westwood wrote an article about political distrust in Iran and described the distrust culture of Iranians this way:

Iranians have found it exceptionally difficult to trust one another or to work together over time in any significant numbers. . . Where Americans tend to err on the side of idealism, Iranians tend to err on the side of cynicism. But it is not a consequence of ignorance, misunderstanding, or some special national psychological quirk, to be altered by various forms of education or exhortation. It is rooted in reality, confirmed by reality, and, of course, shapes the reality of politics in Iran. (p. 124)

In 1975 American scholar William G. Millward wrote an article about Iranology. He admired the westerner's endeavor to study Iran and denounced those Iranians who had recently criticized Iranology as westernized view. On Iranian people's attitudes, he wrote:

> It is an unalterable fact of the historical record that many Iranians subsequently could not easily accept domination and control by a people to whom they felt culturally superior. Anti-Arab sentiment has been a recurrent feature of Iranian national and cultural resurgence from the time of Ferdowsi to the twentieth century. The works of several early modernist Iranian writers, such as Akhundzadeh and Agha Khan Kermani, are redolent with unabashed anti-Arab bias. (p. 53)
>
> Like all peoples of Indo-European origin, the Iranians have a long and strong tradition of cultural superiority. (p. 59)

American cultural anthropologist Mary Catherine Bateson who is the daughter of Margaret Mead wrote a monograph on the Iranian culture and people in 1979:

> Iranians care deeply about sincerity. The ideal is someone in whom the exterior expresses the interior, who is not dowru, 'two-faced, hypocritical.' At the same time, Iranians believe that much that is good and precious is concealed . . . Iranians tend to look at others from the point of view referred to in Persian as badbini, literally 'seeing evil, suspicion, pessimism,'. . . Obsequious flattery, ostentatious virtue, and insincerity are the source of undeserved and unearned wealth and influence. Iranians will condemn whole categories of fellow Iranians on all of these counts, so that they combine to form a standardized critique or stereotype. . . Iranian culture explicitly accepts certain types of deception and dissimulation. To begin with, the values of kindness, courtesy, and hospitality stand higher in many contexts than the values of frankness and honesty. Why tell the truth when feelings will be hurt? Why, indeed, linger on painful truths? Even deaths in the family may be concealed when circumstances are not conducive to informing the bereaved tactfully and supportively. . . Further, Shiite Islam stands alone, among major religious traditions that emphasize the truth or falsehood of beliefs (most

notably Christianity and Islam), in allowing the believer to conceal his belief for his own self-protection. (Bateson, 1979, p. 126)

Relationships with non-intimates are governed by conventions of courtesy. The stylized patterns of thanking and deprecating, greeting and offering, and the elegant phrases that accompany them have an aesthetic value that gives to their performance a certain pleasure. Ritual courtesy (ta'arof) affirms basic values and represents a visible claim to virtues such as generosity and humility, and yet there is a certain ambivalence that surrounds it. For one thing, the courtesies are used too publicly and in relation to too many people for the underlying feelings to be always there, and yet they must be used, for social pressures dictate that the courtesies be preserved for the sake of ab-e ru. (Bateson, 1979, p. 128)

Frye (2003, p. 403) puts the U.S. in its European legacy and reviews and "traces the stereotyping of Persia in the popular imagination of the 'West' from ancient Europe until the America of the twentieth century. For him, in ancient times, both Greeks and Romans had a healthy respect for their enemies, such as the Acheamenids, Parthians, and Sasanians, even though they were considered barbarians. In the age of the Mongols, when Persians were rediscovered by European travelers such as Marco Polo, memories of ancient history also were revived. Persians were then considered in a friendly manner, in some measure because of the more tolerant Mongol Ilkhans, and then the Safavid Shiite dynasty, opposed to a common enemy, the Ottomans. Frye shows how Iran (Persia) has changed from being seen in ancient times as a "respected enemy," to an "envied enemy," a "respected friend," a "despised friend," and currently a "despised enemy" (p. 403). He recognizes that the present day embodies the lowest opinion that both sides have held of each other. He hopes that the mutual characterization of fanaticism may change once again, but for the better, into a common belief in globalization and the future.

Dallalfar and Movahed (1977-1979) conducted a research on a sample of 1109 expatriate managers of international corporations and organizations living in five major industrialized cities of Iran: Tehran, Esfahan, Ahwaz, Shiraz, and Kermanshah. In this sample, 972 respondents were American and the other 137 respondents were from various European nationalities plus a few Australians, Canadians and New Zealanders. This sample was consisted of 272 women and 817 men. Fifty percent of the men and 49 percent of the women had college degrees. Results of this study with high statistical significance indicated that (1) women were generally much happier than men; (2) women were more satisfied with life in Iran; (3) women were even more satisfied with life in Iran than with life in their native country; (4) More women than men had acquired a knowledge of the host country, Iran, prior to their arrival; (5) More women than men were fluent in Farsi, the native language, or had at least a basic knowledge of it; (6) More women than men had read books and articles about Iran; (7) More women than men had enjoyed their none-working activities in Iran; (8) More women than men liked the Iranian city where they were living; (9) In comparison with expatriate men, expatriate women were less xenophobic and prejudiced toward Iranians; (10) In characterizing Iranians, women were much more likely than men to use terms with positive emotional loadings (Dallalfar & Movahedi, 1996). They also found that the most frequent negative features that were attributed to Iranians were: arrogant, argumentative, egoistic, sensitive to criticism, reluctance to admit mistakes or ignorance, a tendency to blame others for one's error, intolerant, rigid, authoritarian, dogmatic, aggressive, rude, inconsiderate of others in public, lack of proper work ethic, no sense of urgency, poor motivation, a tendency to delay and to put off a task for a later time, dishonest, cheating, unreliable, Machiavellian, manipulative, opportunistic, tells you what you want to hear, and male chauvinistic. A relatively positive side of Iranians which emerged alongside the above portrait included such traits as: friendly, warm, generous, hospitable, kind, gentle, pleasant in informal person-to-person situations, helpful and eager to assist, outgoing, fun-loving, cheerful, and witty (Movahedi, 1985, p. 5).

In a Gallup poll conducted in June 1976, two years prior to the beginning of the Iranian revolution, only 37 percent of Americans gave Iran low ratings. In a poll taken about one year after the Iranian revolution, 60 percent of Americans viewed Iran as an enemy of the United States, and another 34 percent as an unfriendly country. In a poll conducted in 1989, a decade after the Iranian revolution, the number of Americans who held a negative opinion toward Iran had increased to 91 percent. Seven years after American hostages were released, still a majority of Americans thought that Iran was the only "enemy" country, compared to 39 percent who saw the Soviet Union as an enemy. In another poll, more than half of the respondents cited hostages, Khomeini, oil, the shah, anger, hatred, trouble, and troublesome nation as coming to mind when they heard about Iran. Moreover, about half of the participants described "all" or "most" Muslims as "warlike," "bloodthirsty," "treacherous," "cunning," "barbaric," and "cruel." Edward Said indicates that after the hostage crisis, TV programs such as *America Held Hostage* and *Nightline* represented the Iranian people, culture, and religion as "militant, dangerous, and anti-American" (Mobasher, 2012). The negative attitudes of Americans were not limited to the Iranian government and people; they were applied as well to Iranian people who were living in the United States. Between 1985 and 1993 the percentages of Americans who thought that the presence of Iranians in the United States was the source of problems for the U.S. increased from 40 to 60 percent. Only 20 percent of American citizens interviewed in 1993 held a positive view of Iranians and perceived their presence to be beneficial to the country (Mobasher, 2012).

Through analysis of public opinion in the United States shortly after the onset of the Iranian hostage crisis in late 1979, Johnston Conover, Mingst, & Sigelman (1980) studied the 'mirror image' which is the tendency for citizens to attribute the opposite qualities to their own and a competitive nation. The questions addressed in their study were (1) how quickly mirror image thinking can be activated, (2) whether mirror images apply to the leaders of nations as well as the nations themselves, (3) what types of traits play the most prominent role in mirror imagery, and (4) what factors predispose people to think in mirror image terms. Their study revealed that mirror images were very common just one month after the seizure of the American hostages in 1979, that they were more commonly focused on the nations (Iran and the U.S.) than on the leaders of the nations (President Carter and Ayotullah Khomeini), that they were most often evaluative rather than simply descriptive, and, perhaps most interestingly, that they were expressed most frequently by more highly educated and more knowledgeable people.

In its January 27, 1981 issue, the *New York Times* printed excerpts from a confidential cable sent by Bruce Laingen, chargé d'affaires at the United States Embassy in Tehran, to Secretary of State Vance on August 3, 1981. In this cable, Bruce Laingen had tried to analyze the dominant aspects of the "Persian Psyche" by listing a number of personality traits which supposedly portrayed the "Persian National Character." This curious U.S. diplomatic document was sent to the State Department with the specific suggestion that it "be used to brief both USG [United States Government] personnel and private sector representatives who are required to do business with and in this country." The United States' chargé d'affaires, in his "analysis" of the "Persian Psyche" or "Persian Proclivity," characterizes Iranians as egotistical; insecure; opportunistic; incapable of comprehending causality, with a distorted perception of reality; and aversion to accepting responsibility; and a mindset that often ignores longer-term interests in favor of immediately obtainable advantages (Movahedi, 1985, p. 1).

Slade (1981) presented a report on a survey of opinions American people had of Islam and Muslims in the beginning of 1980s. Hundreds of Americans were systematically chosen to participate in a telephone survey of 60 questions. Slade came to the conclusion that perhaps aggravating the perception that the Arab stance was hostile towards the West was the confusion of Iranians with Arabs. For her, no other group in recent history, with the exception perhaps of the Japanese during World War II, had had as bad an image in the United States as had the Iranians. This poll showed 86 percent to have a low opinion of Iran, and 61 percent a "very low" opinion. It was consequently to the detriment of the Arabs' image that an incredible 70 percent believed that Iran is an Arab country. Indeed, only Saudi Arabia and Iraq were more widely understood to be Arab. College graduates were even more certain that Iran was an Arab country. The influence of the hostage situation on Iran's unpopularity was evidenced by the 56 percent who cited "hostages" or "prisoners" as coming to mind when Iran was mentioned. Also cited, coming after "Khumayni," "oil" and the "Shah" in frequency, were "anger," "hatred" or "militant"(5%), "confusion," "turmoil" or "trouble"(5%), "troublesome country"(4%) and "cruel" or "rude" (1%). (pp. 148-149).

Tadayon (1982) conducted a meta-analysis. He compared open-ended and closed-ended studies regarding the view of Americans toward Iran. He mentioned differences between qualitative and quantitative research toward the subject, but these two methods both proved that the reputation of Iran in the U.S. was damaged after the hostage crisis. Tadayon also believed that hostage crisis "created an unprecedented American obsession with Iranian affairs, and thus Iran came from relative obscurity in the U.S. media and among the American public in the early and mid-1970s" (Tadayon, 1982, p. 89).

Beattie et al. (1982) studied how level of education and degree of contact with target groups affect stereotypes held by different occupational groups in post-revolutionary Iran. Male university lecturers, taxi drivers and factory workers from Isfahan rated target groups (Americans, English, Arabs, and Iranians) on 22 seven-point trait scales. University lecturers perceived Americans firstly as 'progressive' and then 'practical,' 'industrious,' 'materialistic' and 'musical,' in that order. In fact, 'progressive' and 'industrious' appeared among the five strongest stereotypes for all three subject groups. Both the drivers and lecturers agreed that Americans were primarily 'progressive'. The stereotypes held of Americans by all three groups tended to be favorable (10 out of 15 were favorable). In fact the only unfavorable stereotype mentioned by more than one group was 'materialistic' mentioned by both lecturers and drivers. 'Aggressive,' 'pleasure-loving' and 'ambitious' each appeared among the top five stereotypes in the case of only one group. 'Practical', 'materialistic' and 'musical' were traits assigned by at least two of the subject groups. The stereotype 'musical' presumably derives from the influence of American pop music before the revolution. Their overall conclusion was that Americans were more favorable to Iranians while their subjects showed lower opinions for the British and particularly Arabs.

Campbell (1995) analyzed six mainstream feature films portraying Iranians released between 1978 and 1991 to demonstrate pervasiveness and destructiveness of media stereotyping. These films were *Silver Bears* (1978); *Into the Night* (1985); *Down and Out in Beverly Hills* (1986); *Madhouse* (1990); *Not Without My Daughter* (1990); and, *The Hitman* (1991). She concluded that these films represent sheer entertainment, but because the images duplicate those presented on television and in newspapers, they underscore "factual" portrayals. Even a seemingly innocuous stereotype, such as extreme wealth, can affect the viewer negatively as a rival who may overpower the working class and so he or she could be constructed as an enemy. Therefore, Campbell believes that in the dichotomous American culture in which the world is divided into "us" and "them," films such as these, particularly in the context of a political climate, not only celebrate hostility towards Iranians, they foster enmity and promote military aggression.

Keshishian (2000) employed interpretive theory to conduct her autobiographical study. Her qualitative research showed how media news coverage shaped perceptions of American people and affected her own life and those of other Iranians living in the United States after the Iranian hostage crisis which started in November 4, 1979. She revealed that it became difficult for Iranians to function in the American society during and after the crisis. According to Keshishian, her colleagues made racial comments at the office and threatened to take violent actions against Iranians if the American hostages were not released. She notes that only after years and thanks to her Christian-Armenian identity, "friends, colleagues, and neighbors had accepted" her into the American society (Keshishian, 2000, p. 237).

Results of a public opinion poll taken after the 9/11 attack indicated that 27 percent of Americans considered Iran as the country that posed the greatest danger to the United States, and 47 percent thought Iran was a greater threat to the world than Iraq was before the removal of Saddam Hussein. This poll puts Iran as a greater threat to the United States than China (20 percent), Iraq (17 percent), North Korea (11 percent), or even al-Qaeda terrorists (4 percent). The number of Americans who consider Iran as the single biggest threat to the United States has quadrupled since 1993 (Mobasher, 2012).

By conducting an email survey, Ahmad-Zadeh et al. (2005) showed that their American participants did not believe in common stereotypes about Iranians in the Western media. This study also showed that Iranians have "positive stereotypes" about American people. However, they delimited their respondents to Iranian and American university students and professors. They interviewed their Iranian respondents while American respondents were reached to by email. A similar study by Mirani et al. (2006) showed that Iranian respondents had favorable attitudes towards Americans. However, their project failed because they couldn't convince American potential respondents to answer their questionnaire.

In 2007, World Public Opinion Organization ran a survey on Iranian's and American's opinion on different issues concerning both countries. Through questionnaire, interview and web survey, they asked Iranians and Americans about key international issues. Results showed that forty-nine percent of Iranians had an unfavorable opinion of the American people (33% very, 16% somewhat). Forty-five percent had a favorable opinion (9% very, 36% somewhat). These results also showed that a clear majority of Americans had a negative view of the Iranian people. Fifty-nine percent said they had an unfavorable opinion of the Iranian people (20% very), while only 29 percent said they had a favorable opinion (Kull, 2007).

Terror Free Tomorrow organization (2007) studied opinions Iranians hold for multiple issues, including the relations with the U.S. The survey was conducted by telephone from June 5th to June 18th, 2007, with 1,000 interviews proportionally distributed according to the population covering all 30 provinces of Iran. 68% of Iranians who participated in this study favored normal relations and trade with the United States.

Heisey (2008) examined the perceptions students at Hiram College in the U.S. had for Iranians and found an average of 40 percent of the responses to be negative. In his report titled "The Great Satan Versus an Axis of Evil," he concluded that where the media were the sources of the information for students, there was high degree of negativity in perceptions of Iranian people.

After participating in a conference in Iran in 2005, American professor Lynn Schofield Clark (2008) criticized some aspects of life in Iran, while appreciated the sense of seriousness Iranian youth have for better life. She specially concentrated on women issues and appreciated Iranian women who now represent more than 60 percent of Iranian university students. Stewart Hoover (2008) who had also participated in the same conference expressed his surprises in Tehran: "Once four scholarly colleagues and I (as well as my wife, Karen) arrived in Tehran and began listening to the discourse there, my view shifted 180 degrees." He continued "Iranians are wonderful, warm, cosmopolitan, hospitable people. They have a powerful sense of their own historic place as one of the great civilizations of history. These conversations were thus not just about today and the material prospects for tomorrow. They were about how Iran might find its place among the influential cultures and nations of the world. Its youth culture will play a major role in shaping that place, if our experiences in Tehran are any indication" (pp. 101-102).

Ahmad-Zadeh-Namvar (2008) conducted an email survey in which Americans expressed more negative perceptions of Iranians than Iranians did for Americans. Through open-ended questionnaires, Ahmad-Zadeh-Namvar found that in general, her 50 American respondents in the American academia were particularly suspicious about Iranian nuclear activities and the Iranian role in the region, and, by generalization the same negative traits were attributed to all Iranians. Analyzing 70 open-ended questionnaires completed by Iranian academics and students, Ahmad-Zadeh-Namvar concluded that more than a half of them were positive about Americans.

In August of 2008, the Public Affairs Alliance of Iranian Americans (PAAIA) commissioned Zogby International to conduct a national public opinion survey of American perceptions of Iranian Americans, Iranians, and Iran. The results of this PAAIA/Zogby survey indicated that about half of all Americans had a favorable impression of Iranian Americans, as well as the Iranian people. On the other hand, about one-eighth of all Americans had an unfavorable impression of Iranian Americans and the Iranian people. Significantly, however, about one-third of Americans were not familiar with either Iranian Americans or the Iranian people. The similarity of the American public's overall impressions of Iranian Americans and the

Iranian people perhaps indicates that such impressions are in large part formed by media reports on Iran (Public Affairs Alliance of Iranian Americans, 2008).

Shahghasemi and Heisey (2009) explored cross cultural schemata of the citizens of the two countries. Two groups of students (209 from the Faculty of Social Sciences at the University of Tehran and 255 from the School of Communication Studies at Kent State University) participated in their qualitative study. Respondents were asked to express their impression of the people of the other country and after that they were asked how they got that image. Their results showed that Iranian respondents had more positive cross cultural schemata towards American people than Americans had of their Iranian counterparts. "The 'Negativity,' 'Positivity' or 'Neutrality' of these cross-cultural schemata was evaluated according to the language of the responses comparing to the cultural context of the respondents" (p. 147). Examples of negative cross-cultural schemata Americans in this study had of Iranians were "Poor, Need Help, Oppressed, Evil, Bad Government, and Wear Turbans" (page 148). Examples of negative cross-cultural schemata Iranians in this study had were "Bully, Immoral, Drone, Ignorant, and Selfish" (p. 152). For both groups, the mass media were the primary sources of schemata. Researchers also found that both for their 209 Iranian respondents and 255 American respondents, personal contacts proved to be the source of positive perceptions about the other people. They also concluded that Iranian media cover more positively the American people (and not government) than do the American media of the Iranians. The Americans' own thoughts and beliefs accounted for almost one quarter of their source of a positive influence.

Shahghasemi (2009) distinguished 11 cross-cultural schemata of American people in the Iranian Persian weblogs. The qualitative analysis of 1500 Persian weblogs in four main blog providers revealed that the election of Obama as U.S president had positively affected Iranian bloggers more than any other thing. The distinguished schemata in his work were: (1) "Americans as Fair and Aware Voters" 24%; (2) "Americans as Unaware Public" 18%; (3) "Americans as Nationalist

People" 14%; (4) "Americans as Nice People" 11%; (5) "Americans as People Who Are in Control of Their Country and Government" 8%; (6) "Americans as Bully People" 7%; (7) "Americans as Highly Educated People" 6%; (8) "Americans as Joyous People" 4%; (9) "Americans as People Who Are Fair to Women" 3%; (10) "Americans as People Who Love Iranian Culture and People" 3%; and (11) "Americans as People Who Have no Clear Image of Middle East and Muslims" 2%. A review of comments by Iranian bloggers in this study showed how politics efficiently affects Iranian views on American people as the majority of these schemata have at least one political element. Both negative and positive comments were expressed on Americans as political actors and even sometimes as soldiers.

In summer 2009, World Public Opinion organization conducted a poll on 1,003 Iranians across Iran. Interviewing was conducted by a professional survey organization located outside Iran which used native Farsi speaker interviewers who telephoned Iranians (8 in 10 Iranian households had a telephone line by this date). Many issues were sought in this poll among them was Iranian's attitudes towards Americans. Iranians showed largely positive attitudes toward the American people with 51 percent of those polled expressing favorable feelings toward Americans (13 percent very favorable) (World Public Opinion, 2009).

Yekta Steininger (2010) conducted a qualitative study on a group of Americans to reveal their attitudes towards Iranians. She interviewed American specialists who had worked, lived and conducted research on Iran or were familiar with Persian language. The first question in her survey was "what comes first to your mind when you think of Iran?" Her respondents mostly praised Iran for its long history of art, philosophy and scientific endeavor. A majority of the respondents revered Iranians not only for their historical civilization, but also because they have been able to combine into one unique culture. While emphasizing the pride that Iranians took in their culture, many of participants also pointed out that in relation to Western powers, Iranians felt culturally raped and politically repressed. In line with this feeling of cultural insecurity that the American interviewees sensed in Iranians, there existed suspicion of outsiders. All of interviewees in her research stressed the importance of Shi'i Islam in shaping of Iranian culture and of the Iranian identity and the way Iranians think. However, when asked whether they believed Iranians were very religious or fanatical about religion, most of them also stated that Iranians were not fanatical about religion. Rather, educated Iranians viewed religion as a private matter which served as a guideline for the good and the ethical. Some of the American scholars held that Iranian's ambiguity about their collective identity, or their senses of cultural superiority which coexisted with those of cultural inferiority, were beneath the additional ambiguity and complexity that Americans perceived in the Iranian mode of communication. And, Many of them said Iranians are extremely proud of their past.

Heisey and Sharifzadeh (2011) explored the role of political representation of Americans and Iranians in the media content and how it affect perceptions of their teenage participants. These teenage students were chosen from two schools in Ohio, USA and Tehran, Iran. They asked their teenage participants to draw an individual from the other country. Their study revealed that almost all of the drawings of Iranians and of Americans showed the influence of the political images portrayed in the media. The Americans' drawings depicted Iranians to be people who harbor terrorist inclinations and the Iranians' drawings showed Americans as people who use force to dominate the world as illustrated in the bombing of Iraq. Examples of these drawings follow.

Heisey and Sahrifzadeh came to the conclusion that perceptions Iranian participants have of American people could be attributed to what they read in their school textbooks about America's history and role in the world and to what they saw in their media. However, American participants were more likely to adopt the image of Iranian people as it is represented in the mainstream media.

Mobasher (2012) reported on two studies he had carried out in 1990s and 2000s in Texas. The first project was conducted between 1993 and 1995 in Dallas, and the second project was completed over a two-year period from 2003 to 2005 in Dallas, Houston, and Austin. Participant observation was the primary method employed for both research projects.

The first survey was completed in mid-1990a during Mobasher's fieldwork in Dallas and included 485 first-generation Iranian men and women. The remaining two more recent surveys were conducted between September 2003 and May 2004 mostly in cities with the largest Iranian populations in Texas (Houston, Dallas, and Austin). The first of the two more recent surveys included a non-random sample of 105 young Iranians who were either born and raised in the United States or were born in Iran and migrated to U.S. when they were very young. The participants from the second survey, however, included 507 adult Iranians, most of whom left Iran during or after the Iranian revolution.

An American teenager views an Iranian.

An Iranian teenager views an American.

He came to the conclusion that there were three distinct images (positive, very negative, and mixed) of the United States and its people in the minds of Iranian immigrants. With the exception of a minority of *optimist* Iranians who harbored a positive perception of the United States and viewed Americans as kind, warm, sociable, informal, honest, hardworking, and patriotic citizens, most Iranians were either deeply *ambivalent* and conflicted or bitterly hostile and *cynical* toward the United States and its people. While the ambivalent Iranians perceived Americans as "honest but simple-minded, kind but misinformed, hard-working but wasteful, and resourceful but irresponsible," the cynical Iranians generally viewed American people as "stupid, ignorant, naive, selfish, hollow, unaffectionate, superficial, credulous, gullible, callous, ethnocentric, overconsumptive, and materialistic." These negative, often racist and ethnocentric views, however, were politically motivated. The Iranians who harbored such negative feelings toward Americans found them politically immature and unsophisticated, ignorant about global political issues, and continuously manipulated and misinformed by their government. It is noteworthy that most of these Iranian immigrants were themselves easy prey for conspiracy theories concerning the "invisible hands of the powerful elites" that were responsible for controlling and "brainwashing" Americans (Mobasher, 2012, pp. 70-71).

American chef, author, and television personality Anthony Bourdain travelled to Iran in 2014 and said in a TV show "We got in on a window that seems to have closed since then. But the people were incredibly gracious and welcoming. In fact, I was surprised: Tehran was the most pro-American place I've ever been . . . The difference between the political Iran we live with on the news, and the Iran that everyday Iranians live in" (Haynes-Peterson, 2014).

In a comparative qualitative study, Sharifi, Shahghasemi and Emamzadeh (2017) explored cross cultural schemata two group of Iranian women had of American people. 50 women from middle class families from cities other than Tehran, and 50 women of upper class socio-economic status living in Tehran participated in this study. All of them were over 50. They were asked about their first impression when they hear the phrase "an American citizen," and then they explained how they came to have this image. Researchers first analyzed the answers and categorized them based on their language. Then, they gave each category a code, so they were able to do further analyzes of association using SPSS. Results showed that personal contact and communication with Americans was a strong predictor for positive cross cultural schemata, while consuming state media content was the main source for negative perceptions for Americans. These results, moreover, showed that both groups of women had generally positive attitudes towards American people, although the level of positivity was much higher for Tehrani participants.

ANALYSIS

A review on the literature on how American people view Iranians reveal some interesting issues. First, in spite of general positive opinion of American missionaries, travelers and educators living in 19th or 20th century in Iran, perceptions American people have of Iranians are now generally negative. Almost all reviewed studies after 1979 show how American public view Iranians with suspicion and pessimism. Secondly, in each study whenever American participants tend to be more educated, the reported cross cultural schemata of Iranians will be more positive. Thirdly, where there is a personal contact and communication, Americans express more positive impressions of Iranians. And fourth, American people's cross cultural schemata towards Iranians are highly media driven and we know that media are everything but impartial.

There is already a wealth of literature on how the media further the interests of a small group of elites. The *media* serve *dominant* definitions, that is, those that *serve the interest* of the capitalist *class*. The *media* take their cue from the elite (Goode & Ben-Yehuda, 2009, p. 65). It is their function to amuse, entertain, and inform, and to inculcate individuals with the values, thoughts, and codes of conduct that will integrate them into the institutional structures of the wider society. In a world of concentrated wealth and major struggles of class interest, to fulfil this task requires systematic propaganda. In contexts where the levers of power are in the hands of a state system, the monopolistic control over the media, often pinpointed by official censorship, makes it clear that the media serve the objectives of a dominant elite. It is much more difficult to see a propaganda system at work where the media are private there is no formal censorship (Herman & Chomsky, 2002, p. 1).

Very identical to the Herman-Chomsky thesis is the Michael Parenti's work. The media, in Parenti's argument, are owned by large corporate conglomerates which are operating in a capitalist system which is looking profit above all else. Government adopts as national interests the goals of main capitalists (profit, growth, secure markets at home and abroad) and it conducts reforms only if they are compatible with the primary interests of big business. The media are extensively interconnected through boards of directors with those main capitalists (multinational corporations and banks) and the banks are major stockholders in the major media. Both government policy and the media serve the interests of the dominant class, which is variously described by Parenti as "corporate leaders," the "business class," "moneyed interests," or the "corporate financial class" (Gibson, 2004, p. 134).

Though I subscribe partially to critical stance towards media in capitalist economies, I should emphasize that I am not this pessimistic. I don't believe that there are some villains in media headquarters who create clandestine strategies to defame Iranians or any other people. I think profit-seeking is the main drive of most of the media in the West and this is why they simply misrepresent other people and cultures. More stories and depictions about exotic people and cultures entails more audience and more audience means availability of more eyeballs to sell to the advertisers. And this is a fact that misrepresentations have always elements of reality. After about four decade of enmity, there has been many incidents that made Americans susceptible of acquiring negative perceptions of Iranians.

For example, the hostage crisis of 1979 marked a radical negative shift in American public perception of Iranians (Mobasher, 2012). What was a relatively positive, though still stereotypical and oversimplified, pre-revolution and pre-hostage image of Iran—hospitality, Persian carpets, oil, caviar—vanished. Iran suddenly was depicted as the United States' first enemy and a new source of instability in the Near East, replacing the defunct "Soviet threat." In addition to being "religious fanatics" and "backward," Iranians were also referred to as "crazy," "stubborn," and "terrorists" (Keshishian, 2000, p. 100). Few non-Iranians try to understand Iran in all of its complexities since the media have made every further effort redundant. Since the Islamic Revolution of 1979, only a small number of European and North American scholars and political and social scientists have visited Iran, and even fewer have spent significant amounts of time living in Iran (Van Gorder, 2010, p. 2). The attribution of unity and conformity to another nation or people seems to be a widespread, if not universal, trait. Stereotypes can be both good and bad, but it seems they are ubiquitous, at least among most ethnic or religious groups. for many people it almost falls naturally to place all inhabitants of a land, such as 'the French,' 'the Persians,' or 'the Americans,' or everyone in a religious group such as 'the Catholics,' or 'the Muslims,' in a single category, even though upon reflection this is found to be absurd. On the other hand, certain cultural or social features, which are accepted as natural or proper by the majority of a people, do separate them from others (Frye, 2003).

It is my idea that no single fieldwork can properly explain the image of Iranian people in the mind of U.S. Americans without digging well into cultural, historical, social and political context in which this image (or images) take shape. Therefore, the next two chapters try to sketch the historical and political background that have largely shaped what Americans think of Iranians.

Chapter 2

AMERICAN MISSIONARY LIFE AND WORK IN IRAN

INTRODUCTION

Cross cultural schemata do not develop in void. They are complicated and are affected by complicated factors. In order to study cross cultural schemata that Americans have of Iranians, I decided to put them in their contexts. This will help us to have an idea of what factors are contributing to the current state of perceptions regarding Iranians. One important issue in this respect is politics. Politics has been, and is, important in shaping cross cultural schemata. But, after a preliminary study on Iran-US political relations, I found that this history is deeply intertwined with history of American missionary life and service in Iran. The American missionary work of 19th century is an important part of the Iranian history, which has been largely overlooked because of many reasons. For our purpose, their work and writings were the first sources for shaping Americans' perceptions of Iranian people.

American evangelical bodies were acquainted with Persia and had preliminary programs for evangelizing this country as early as 1800s. A document from 1806 said that the doctrine of Trinity was well known in some remote parts of the world in other names and for example the

Persians "pay worship to Mithra, whom they call . . . threefold Mithras. This shows that the doctrine [of trinity] is known in Persia" (Frends to Evangelical Truth, 1806, p. 490). On May 24, 1815, an American missionary in India named Samuel Newell wrote a letter back to American Board of Commissioners for Foreign Missions (ABCFM) and recommended they thought of establishing mission stations in other parts of the world including Persia (Woods, 1833). American Board of Commissioners for Foreign Missions had been founded in 1810. Nine years later two missionaries were sent to the Middle East. Levi Parsons was the first American missionary who prepared the ground for thinking of the possibility of sending American missionaries to Persia. As of 1817, for two years he served as an effective mission's promoter, soliciting contributions and organizing Palestine Societies, particularly among the youth, for the support of a mission to be based in Jerusalem. Some accepted his proposal and endorsed him: a group of New York Indians gave Parsons $5.87 and sent a message "to their forefathers in Jerusalem." In a farewell service at Park Street Church, Boston, Parsons and his colleague Pliny Fisk were given a generous mandate: Two great questions were to be ever in their minds, "What good can be done, and by what means?" for Jews, pagans, Muslims, and people in Egypt, Syria, Persia, Armenia, or other territories which they might investigate. Fisk and Parsons sailed in November 1819, arrived at Smyrna in January 1820, and went to the island of Scio, where they tried to study Modern Greek. Then they travelled Asia Minor, visiting the "seven churches of Asia" noted in the Book of Revelation, and distributed tracts and Testaments. At the end of 1820 Parsons went on to Jerusalem, the first Protestant missionary to enter with the intention of making that city his permanent base. His reports received much attention in America (Anderson, 1998). Parsons on May 5, 1821 wrote in his journal that he had sold Persian testaments to people in Jerusalem (Morton, 1832, p. 211). On May 26, 1824 four American missionaries in Beirut wrote a letter to the American Board of Commissioners for Foreign Missions and proposed establishment of new missions in other regions including Persia: "The difficult, arduous, and perilous work of journeying must likewise be continued, in order to ascertain more precisely . . . to survey and select new missionary stations. There are several fields where it is desirable that extensive journies (sic) should be taken without delay, such as the Barbary states, Abyssina, and Persia" (ABCFM, 1825, p. 26).

Because the Ottoman government did not permit American missionaries to proselytize Muslims, and the Catholics objected to any form of interference, the work of first American missionaries to Middle East and Ottoman Empire was principally with the Greek Orthodox, Armenians, and Nestorians (Dodge, 1972). Nestorians are Syrians; they speak a modern dialect of the Ancient Syriac which is the language Jesus spoke when on earth, and ecclesiastically goes back to the ancient Syrian Church (Laurie, 1887). By the end of 1820s, there was enough information about Iran (then Persia) to consider a possible mission in this country. The first American missionaries to visit Iran were Eli Smith and Harrison Dwight, who arrived in Tabriz during December 1830 (Heravi, 1999). But they were not the first Americans who set foot on the Iranian soil. For example in 1807 Edward Scott Waring who was a British traveler reported that American's had sent one or two ships to Iranian port of Bushehr some years earlier for trade but they were not successful in buying a cargo of drugs because the Britons did not let local merchant to deal with them (Waring, 1807). He also reveals that Iranians he met were curious about the U.S. as they called it "Yungi Dooneeya" (Waring, 1807, p. 254). They generally asked questions about the people and terrain, rivers and mountains in the U.S. Also, James Justinian Morier who was a British diplomat and author met Prince Mohammad Ali Mirza, eldest son of Fathalishah in 1809 in Persian court and reported "the conversation turned upon Yengee Duniah, or America, a subject upon which all Persians are very curious and inquisitive. On this topic, we were surprised (sic) to find the Prince, as the French would say, *ferré à glace*. He appeared to have just been reading the history of America. He talked not only with historical but geographical knowledge, which of all other, is the rarest amongst Orientals. He told us the distinction between North and South America with great accuracy and entered into the details of the history of Mexico in a manner that greatly astonished us" (Morier, 1812, pp. 196-197).

Therefore, Smith and Dwight were not coming to a territory in which people had no idea of US Americans at all.

Anyhow, they wrote more than 500 pages about Iran and in consequence of the favorable report of Smith and Dwight, under the patronage of American Board of Commissioners for Foreign Missions, that body soon resolved upon the formation of a mission among that branch of primitive Church. In 1831, the ABCFM decided to extend its mission to Persia and sent the first *American missionary* to Iran to found the Persia Mission. Justin Perkins arrived in Tabriz in 1834, and subsequently moved to Urmia to work among the Nestorian Christians there (Lorentz, 2010). He and his family endured many hardships and perils en route to Persia and after the arrival, he immediately started working. He also started sending reports and letters back to America.

James Lyman Merrick was an American Presbyterian missionary in Iran from 1834 to 1845. He studied at the Princeton and Columbia theological seminaries. In 1834 he was ordained as a Presbyterian evangelist at Charleston and was immediately sent on a mission to Iran. He stayed in the cities of Tabriz, Shiraz and Urmia until 1845. Upon his return to the United States he was assigned Congregationalist church in South Amherst (1849-1864) and taught "oriental" literature at Amherst College (1852-1857). Today, we know that Merrick was the first American missionary who was ordained to especially research the possibility of establishing a mission particularly for the Muslims in Persia. In its 1834 issue, American Board of Commissioners for Foreign Mission's Prudential Committee provided a detailed account of Persian cities and regions, the languages and level of religiosity and general traits of the people to Merrick and asked him to spend the first years studying the possibility of establishing the mission to the Muslims of Persia. His main objective, the Committee emphasized, was:

> [. . .] to ascertain where it is expedient for the Board to form Missionary stations. Nor will the Committee expect merely the results of your investigations; but all the more important reasons, upon which your opinions are founded; -such as relate to the situation of the place; its

distances from other well-known places of easy access; the nature and comparative safety of the roads; the population of the place, and the various sects and classes into which the inhabitants are divided, with their character, intelligence, manners, and means of improvement; the number of souls within the neighboring country, upon whom the station might exert an influence; whether these are shepherds, farmers, or traders; whether peaceable, or addicted to war and plunder; whether they are Sheah or Soofie Mohammedans; whether that philosophical infidelity prevails, which is denominated Soofeism; whether there are followers of Zoroaster, or Jews, or nominal Christians; what impression the Mohamedans appear to have acquired concerning Christianity; the degree of security which might be expected for the persons and property of a Christian mission; whether the press, which is now unknown in Persia, could be introduced, and operate without obstruction from the jealousy of the government. Or danger from the superstitious bigotry of the people; what would be the expense of transporting paper and books from the nearest or most frequented sea-ports; whether the Bible and other books could be freely introduced and dispersed among the people; whether schools could be established for Mohammedan children; whether the king' who has severely persecuted the Soofies at the call of the moolahs, would not raise the sword of the persecution against the mission, in case its influence should be felt and create alarm; the nature of the climate and the disease of the country; the course of trade, as indicated by the routes of caravans; the stability and character of the government; and, in a word, whatever is necessary to give the Committee a complete view [. . .]. (ABCFM, 1834, p. 405)

At their annual meeting held at Utica, N. Y., October, 1834, the Board of Missions presented a convincing and urgent plea for a suitable physician to engage in the emerging labours of that mission. They believed that reducing the body ailments would have made their ideas more convincing. This is how Doctor Grant were sent to Persian:

> In view of these considerations, I abandoned an increasing and delightful circle of practice in Utica, and, with Mrs. Grant, was on my way to Persia the following spring. . . We arrived at Tabreez (sic), one of the chief commercial cities of Persia, on the 15th of October, 1835, and

met with a cordial reception from the few English residents in the place, and from our respected associates, the Rev. Justin Perkins and lady, who had preceded us to this place. (Grant, 1841, pp. 4-5)

In 1842 Thomas Laurie was ordained to mission to the Nestorian communities. He became sick and returned to the U.S. in 1846. He spent the rest of his life writing on mission and its outstanding figures.

Fidelia Fiske (1816-1864) was the first single missionary woman in Persia and founder of Nestorian Female Seminary. As a precocious and devout child in rural Massachusetts, Fiske read Timothy Dwight's *Theology* when she was only eight. In 1843 Justin Perkins visited Seminary of Mount Holyoke in which Fiske was teaching and requested two single women to pursue educational work among Nestorian girls. Fiske was chosen from volunteers and she embarked that year to be the first of many unmarried women missionaries educated at Mount Holyoke. Fisk opened a boarding school for girls at Urmia that she south to manage along "Mount Holyoke principles." The purpose of the seminary was to make Nestorian girls better wives and mothers and to revive their Christian faith. During her 15 years of service in Urmia, Fiske converted approximately two-third of her students (Anderson, 1998).

On June 9th, 1847 Joseph Gallup Cochran and Deborah Plumb Cochran were married and left the same month for Boston to sail for Persia. Cochran was a missionary under the American Board of Commissioners for Foreign Missions to the Nestorians from 1847 to 1871 (Shavit, 1988). Their son Joseph Plumb Cochran was born in the little village of Seir in Persia, overlooking the plain of Urmia, on January 14th, 1855. By natural inheritance he entered into the missionary character and the missionary service (Speer, 1911).

John H. Shedd and Sarah Jane Dawes were married on July 28, 1859, and shortly afterwards sailed for Persia under appointment by the American Board of Commissioners for Foreign Missions to the Nestorian Mission at Urmia. Their son William was born six years later (Shedd M. L., 1922). William become a missionary himself and later in this chapter we will read about his fate.

There is no clear profile of all American missionaries in Iran's 19th century. Yet, some of them have been mentioned in third sources. For example, Professor Edward G. Browne who was a British scholar reported in late 1880s that he had patrolled the labyrinth of Tabriz Bazaars along with Mr. Whipple who was an American missionary (Browne, 1893). Samuel Graham Wilson who was born in 1858 in Indiana, Pennsylvania was an American Presbyterian missionary in Persia. He was ordained in July 1880 and left for Persia soon after. While on furlough in 1886, he married Annie Dwight Rhea, the daughter of Samuel Audley Rhea, who was himself pioneer missionary in Persia (Anderson, 1998).

Isaac Grout Bliss was an American missionary and agent of the American Bible Society in the Near East. He and his wife mainly stationed in Turkey but he toured in Turkey, Syria, Egypt and Persia, studied the needs and opportunities of many nationalities and tribes consulted with missionaries and recruited large numbers of colporteurs (Anderson, 1998).

Although the American missionaries claimed their cause was only to serve Christianity, they kept their eyes on their Christian rivals. Missionary work was divided between the American Presbyterian mission, which was based in the northern half of the Country, and the Anglican Christian Missionary Society, which was based in the southern half of Persia (Spellman, 2004). As we will see in this chapter, Russian missionaries and French Lazarist missionaries were also active in 19th century Persia. L'Alliance Israelite, the French Jewish organization, opened schools in Hamadan, Isfahan, and Tehran. Similarly, the Zoroastrian community in India financed a school for their coreligionists in Yazd (Abrahamian, 2008). In such a competitive sphere, new and more effective strategies for American missionaries were necessary.

By 1870, the ABCFM had turned over all of its mission tasks in Persia to the Reformed Nestorian Churches which were under the direct management and financing of the United Presbyterian Church in the USA (UPC/USA) Mission Board. This was an inevitable shift but one that was strongly opposed by Reverend Perkins. When the ABCFM closed in 1870, they, probably optimistically, claimed that since Reverend and Mrs. Perkins had come to Persia, there had been over three thousand conversions to Christ among the Assyrian Nestorians of Urmia. As many as fifty different villages surrounding Urmia had churches at this time, and 960 local children were being educated in their many schools. One of these schools, the American School in Seir, was active for almost forty years (Van Gorder, 2010, p. 139).The Presbyterian Board also expanded the Mission throughout northern Iran: stations opened at Tehran in 1872, Tabriz in 1873, Hamadan in 1880, Rasht and Qazvin in 1906, Kermanshah in 1910, and Mashad in 1911. In 1883 the Presbyterian Board reorganized the Iranian field into two separate missions. Urmia and Tabriz constituted the "West Persia Mission" and the remaining Iranian stations were called the "East Persia Mission." The two jurisdictions were not reunited until 1931 (Heuser, 1988). In the Western Mission, at Urmia, were Rev. Messrs. John H. Shedd, D. D., J. E. Rogers and their wives ; Joseph P. Cochran, M. D. and his wife; Mrs. D. P. Cochran, Miss N. J. Dean, Miss M. Morgan, Miss E. Cochran, Miss M. K. Van Duzee. At Tabriz were Rev. Messrs. J. M. Oldfather and S. G. Wilson and their wives; Dr. G. W. Holmes and wife; Miss M. Jewett, Miss G. Y. Holliday, Mrs. L. C. Van Hook. At Salmas were Rev. F. G. Coan and his wife, Miss C. O. Van Duzee and Rev. J. N. Wright. In the Eastern Mission, at Tehran, were Rev. Messrs. J. L. Potter, S. L. Ward and their wives ; W. W. Torrence, M. D., and his wife ; Misses S. J. Bassett, Cora Bartlett and Annie G. Dale. At Hamadan were Rev. J. W. Hawkes, Mrs. Hawkes and Miss Annie Montgomery (Perkins H. M., 1887).

In 1870 an Assyrian protestant mission was sent to Tehran to distribute bible. Two years later, James Basset was sent to Tehran and Hamedan to study the possibility of establishing a mission in these two cities. Basset reported back that the ground was much better in Tehran in comparison to Hamedan. By that time, Tehran had only 60000 residents (Elder, 1960), almost 200 times smaller than now it is. In 1878 James Basset travelled to Mashhad to study possibility of establishing a mission. Although Mashhad was a highly religious city, he could come in contact with Jews and Muslims and invited them to Christianity (Elder, 1960).

There is no study particularly obsessed with the number of American missionaries in 19th century Persia. Other related statistics regarding their local colleagues, number of converts from Assyrian and Muslim communities and etc. are missing. Yet, one can find useful statistics in different resources. For example in 1855, the church in Urmia listed 158 members, and in 1862 an indigenous presbytery was organized (Van Gorder, 2010, p. 138). By 1871 there were, in addition to the mission station at Urmia, forty-eight out-stations in the various villages where natives served as teachers and preachers (Yeselson, 1956). By 1879, there were at least fifty-two Presbyterian missionaries throughout Persia (Van Gorder, 2010, p. 138). By 1880 number of missionaries in Urmia was about 14 (Saleh, 1976). In the year 1884, twenty four American missionaries conducted stations in Urmia, Tehran, Hamedan, and Tabriz. 230 native assistants, most of them Nestorians, taught and preached; there were twenty-five churches with 1,796 communicants; 4578 attended services; 208 pupils lived in boarding schools, 2,452 attended day schools; and 1,680,890 printed pages were distributed (Yeselson, 1956). At the end of the 19th century, besides the missionaries, there were about fifty families of naturalized American citizens and a large amount of property under Dr. Shedd's care. The extensive work being done by the Relief Committee, of which he was the head, made it necessary for him to use every possible means for protecting supplies and the recipients of American charity (Shedd M. L., 1922, p. 228). In 1886, Winston who was the second American ambassador to Tehran reported that there were no more 20 Americans in Persia (Yeselson, 1956). John G. Wishard who was an American Physician in Tehran in late 19th and early 20th centuries has said that "we have no way of knowing exactly the number of citizens of the Great Republic who have visited Iran, but, exclusive of children born in Persia of American parentage, the number is under rather than above three hundred" (Wishard, 1908, p. 9). As I mentioned earlier, it is difficult to determine exact number of American missionaries in Iran's 19th century and research has to be done on this subject.

HARDSHIPS AND DEATHS

By the mid-19th century, the United States was a modern country. Telegraph and photography had already been invented and introduced to the society, railroads along with telegraph had let American politicians to control distant corners of the country, and most prestigious universities of today had been established which some of them trained physicians to take care of citizens health. For people who lived in such an advanced society, it must had been very hard to live in among people who were not even acquainted with advancements of the new world. Travelling to reach the place of their assignment took some months and was accompanied by many threats and perils. This shows that they were so determined about their goals. Just comparing some examples of these travels with today's travel with the help of tourist agencies gives us a sense of how hard their work was.

Asahel Grant left Oneida County, New York, in 1835 with his young bride. He had to climb passes, ford rivers, and somehow avoid bandits to get from village to village. It is a harrowing story of disease, misfortune, and sometimes death and Grant's wife and twin baby girls died in Iran in 1840 (Taylor, 2005).

Sixty-two days after leaving Boston, Mr. And Mrs. Cochran reached Smyrna. Two weeks more brought them to Constantinople. The Atlantic passage had been hard for Mrs. Cochran, and when they reached Erzroom, where the cholera killed people in thousands, she was taken sick with it, and as winter had set in, they decided to spend the winter here instead of going on to Urmia. The mission house overlooked the cemetery, and Mrs. Cochran used to say that the fighting of the dogs and wolves at night over the bodies of the dead which they easily dug out of the shallow graves did more than anything else to make her determined to stay alive to get to Urmia. Mr. Cochran spent the winter studying Syriac with a Nestorian preacher who had been sent by fellow missionaries to meet him. In March their first child was born, and late in the summer of 1848 they reached Urmia (Speer, 1911, p. 25).

Furthermore, American missionaries had to deal with different epidemics while they had no effective medical means to confront sickness. Plague and Cholera was very widespread during 1830s in Persia and neighboring countries and killed many including some American missionaries (Newcomb, 1854). Cholera has been one of the deadliest diseases of human history. It is estimated that Cholera alone killed tens of millions of people in the 19th century (Lee, 2003). In my own region in the south western part of Iran, old people still remember from their previous generations' memories of the *maraz* [sickness] that killed many of the people and sometimes annihilated whole tribes.

The living condition of American missionaries was also very terrible. In 1851 a group of American missionaries were working in Gawar seventy miles west of Urmia. Mr. Coan wrote how their lives were miserable like local people and as a result Mrs. Ray and Mrs. Crane wives of two American missionaries fell ill and died (Elder, 1960). Fidelia Fiske wrote in her journal in 1959 "Perhaps bereaved missionary mothers In Persia do not realize how much their patient suffering has done for their poor Nestorian sisters. The short lives of those twenty missionary children, who lie in Persian graves, were a precious offering to Christ. They were all missionaries, and did not go home till their work was done. Each one had a place to fill among the instrumentalities employed by the Master to promote his kingdom in Persia" (Laurie, 1863, p. 278). Justin Perkins himself lost his child Judith, whom he later called "the Persian Flower" as she was a great lover of flowers (Perkins J., 1853).

But, sickness and horrible living condition of Americans in Iran's 19th century was not the only cause of death. Speer (1911, p. 24) was cheerful that no American missionary was killed en route to Persia: ". . . we see the mercy of God shown to the missionaries in the fact that thousands upon thousands of miles have been travelled by them through deserts, over the roughest mountains, amid perils of robbers, and perils of avalanches, and perils of rivers, yes, and even perils of wild Nestorians, and yet in no such journey has any one lost his life by accident or violence;" yet, it should be noted that that does not mean no American missionary in Persia lost his or her life as a result of violence.

In late 1890s Mrs. Wright a school teacher was killed by another former Iranian colleague because of personal reasons (Elder, 1960). The murderer was an Armenian who was convicted to life imprisonment. Rumors spread that he would not stay in jail and he eventually escaped more than a year later. As Mrs. Wright was an Iranian citizen, American government did not bother itself putting pressure on the Iranian government (Yeselson, 1956). On March 8, 1904, Benjamin W. Labaree who was an American missionary, was murdered by Kurdish tribesmen (Malick, 2008). The Murderer escaped to Turkey and then came back to Persia without being trialed. On April 21, 1909, Howard C. Baskerville a Presbyterian Mission to Tabriz School took up arm to defend against the royalist forces who wanted to abrogate the Iranian constitution. He was killed in the first day of the battle (Kinzer, 2011).

During the mid-1910s, Turkish government was so hostile to Christians, and Iranian Christians were in fear of being massacred by nearby Government who had already massacred hundreds of thousands of Armenians. Some estimations say one and a half million Armenians lost their lives. American missionary William Ambrose Shedd and his wife were forced to evacuate Urmia on July 31, 1918, along with thousands of other Assyrian Christians. They retreated for six days, at which point Mr. Shedd became ill with cholera and died shortly thereafter. Mrs. Shedd's group escaped further from the warzone with the aid of the British towards Iraq, and she buried her husband along the way, about seven miles east of Sain Kala. Mary Lewis Shedd reached Hamadan on August 24. On October 2, she wrote that probably seven or eight thousand died, were killed, or were taken prisoner on the journey she had recently completed (Shedd M. L., 1922).

These are only some examples of hardships American missionaries endured in Persia. They were in continuous state of fear and they were threatened by religious people (Muslims or Nestories), politicians, landlords, the British, the Russians etc. The more I read about them, the more I saw how faith can give man strength and power. They remained faithful to their cause, something we do not see much in our time.

HEALTH CARE AND RELIEF SERVICE

Christian missions have traditionally been linked to the provision of medical facilities (Hellot, 2005). Instances of relief efforts grew along with the nation, almost all of it on a voluntary basis. Famine was the most common disaster that brought forth American resources, although concern for victims of war or political violence also stimulated American relief efforts. Missionaries and diplomats often brought word of the need for help in places like Crete, Persia, China, and Turkey (Rivas, 2002, p. 153). James Basset who was an American Presbyterian missionary described his unbelievable encounter with famine in 1972: "Four miles beyond TurkmanTchai (sic), we passed the ruins of a village which a few months previous contained one hundred families. It was now reduced by the famine to fifteen households. Men, women and children were met in the way slowly travelling westward. Many sat by the way eating herbs and roots which they had dug up" (Bassett, 1886, p. 71). Elsewhere he wrote:

> "The famine had been very severe during the winter. At first only refugees from other places died from this cause, but later many of the citizens died. In the nine months preceding, five thousand six hundred and thirty dead bodies were carried out of one gate for burial, and one thousand one hundred in the last forty-six days. In the same period of nine months there had been borne through another city gate five thousand dead bodies. It was thought that the water had become polluted, since some of the water courses passed near or under the cemeteries." (Bassett, 1886, pp. 76-77)

This horrible famine along with other similar events was a great opportunity for missionaries. They could collect more than 40000 $ from American people and spent for feeding people. Sometimes people were asked to work in exchange of money but they were so hungry that they couldn't even work (Elder, 1960).

In previous section we saw that Asahel Grant was the first American physician who was dispatched to treat the Iranian patients. Although Iran already had a brilliant history in medical sciences, by the time Dr. Grant entered Iran, the country was in turbulence and according to Laurie (1853) the medical science was nothing more than −sometimes dangerous- superstitions. Asahel Grant in Urmia gave native doctors samples of medicine and lent instruments that they could use in their own practice (Daniel, 1964). Moreover, he himself was moving from place to place trying to visit patients for free (Laurie, 1853). By this, he was in hope that before starting to invite people to Christianity, people would become interested in the philosophy behind his benevolence (Elder, 1960). Also, occasionally a missionary wrote a pamphlet on public health. Americans excelled in setting fractures and removing external tumors and cataracts (Daniel, 1964); these diseases were rampant among Persians in the 19th century.

In 1839 the mission was reinforced by the arrival of Mr. and Mrs. Jones. In 1840 Dr. Wright and Mr. Breath were welcomed to the broadening field of usefulness in Urmia. Dr. Wright was for many years the "beloved physician," and Mr. Breath rendered valuable service as mission printer. He had stood near Lovejoy, the abolitionist, when he was shot at Alton, Ill, and was wont to regard this circumstance as giving him a fresh impulse in the cause of Christ and of humanity (Perkins H. M., 1887, p. 25).

Joseph Plumb Cochran, an American Presbyterian missionary, was involved in the construction of the first modern medical school in Iran. In addition, an American Memorial School was established in Tabriz in 1881 (Kambin, 2011). Cochran trained a dozen helpers to become physicians, and went on numerous medical trips throughout the area (Anderson, 1999). In the summer of 1879 he sent to the Board the following appeal:

> Since arriving here last December I here seen and treated over 3,000 patients in the dispensary and at my house. Persians, Kurds, Jews, Nestorians, and Armenians all come together, listen to the religious service, and receive treatment. Some come a distance of three or four days' journey, a few even further. There is no skilled physician within 120 miles in any direction; the native surgery is terribly rough or barbarous, and the medical practice is little better. A Christian physician and surgeon has a vast field and a remarkable influence. But here arises a

difficulty. Many cases I see but once. Many do not follow directions. In some cases powders have been given to be taken, one daily. The patients, instead, have bolted them all at a swallow, saying the medicine might as well cure at once as to take several days. One man received a powder for an eye wash. He poured the powder all into his eye at once, and came back, saying it had burned out his eye. The cost of a hospital building need not be large, $1,500 or $2,000 would answer the present need. The running expense will be comparatively small. Some will be charity patients, but the majority who come to us can either provide for themselves or get their friends to defray their actual expenses. So far we have received enough from the patients treated to pay their board and nursing. (Speer, 1911, p. 61)

Cochran was popular among local people and when he died at the age of 50 in Urmia, tens of thousands of people joined his funeral and mourned him. Dr. Packard, who was heading the hospital before and during World War I, continued Cochran's work, turning the hospital into a training centre and a medical research centre (Hellot, 2005). Young brilliant Iranian boys and girls were taught here by Dr. Wright, Dr. Van Norden, Dr. Holmes, Dr. Miller and Cochran himself (Speer, 1911, p. 186). His hospital gradually developed into an educational center and eventually became University of Urmia. Cochran is still much revered in Urmia.

A new mission was founded in Tehran in 1872, but it was not until ten years later in 1881 that the medical work of the mission was started by Dr. W. W. Torrence. These medical missionaries did not delimit themselves only to mission work but engaged in other activities, as the cases of Dr. Torrence and Dr. George Holmes illustrate. Dr. Torrence soon became well-known in Tehran both medically and socially with an entrée into the court. He obtained the Shah's permission to try to raise funds and secure a piece of property to build a hospital (Mahdavi, 2005). James H. W. Hawkes opened a medical facility in Hamedan and led the program for fifty two years. James Bassett founded the first Presbyterian Church in Tehran in 1872, and this work was followed by building a hospital. An initiative to make a medical training center in Tehran was furthered with the arrival of Dr. J. G. Wishard who established a Presbyterian hospital in Tehran (in 1893) (Van Gorder, 2010). Other American mission hospitals were founded in Hamedan (by Dr. Funk in 1903; expanded in 1916), in Tabriz (by Dr. Lamme in 1913), and in Mashhad (by Dr. Cook in 1916). Dr. B. W. Stead initiated medical services in Kermanshah in 1905; he established a regular clinic there in 1912 and a small hospital in 1922 (Sajjādī, 1989). These programs were widely praised by the Persians because as we said earlier, at the time a number of serious epidemics, such as cholera and the black plague, were sweeping across the country (Van Gorder, 2010). We can imagine what a hospital could mean for Persians by that time.

It was the extension of health care system in the last decades of the nineteenth century, including a significant increase in female doctors and nurses that became of great importance for Muslim women in the more remote regions of the Middle East. The missions in Persia (both in the cities and in the countryside) made good use of these female agents, who could get in touch with women who until that time had had no contact with Westerners at all (Murre-van den Berg H., 2005). Before that, cultural barriers strictly hindered American male doctors visiting Persian women. Dr Georg W. Holmes was the first American missionary doctor who started working in Tabriz in 1881 and seeing cultural problems got him convinced that missionary headquarters in the U.S. should sent a female physician to this city and as a result, Mary Bradford was sent to Tabriz and arrived by 1888 (Elder, 1960). She was the first female physician in Persia (Mansoori, 1986). In 1889 Dr. Mary Smith was the first American female physician who was sent to Tehran. As a result of efforts of Dr. Blanch Wilson in late 19th century the first hospital was established in Hamedan. The hospital was located in estates named Whipple Memorial Hospital (Elder, 1960). Dr. Mary Smith established a medical training center in Tehran in 1890 (Van Gorder, 2010). By 1905 Dr. J. D. Frame was sent to Rasht hospital to serve the mission in Guilan (Elder, 1960).

EDUCATION

In January 1835 Perkins opened the first modern school in Iran. He started with 7 students at first day but by the next day 17 other students enrolled. Without any facilities and even blackboards and chalks, they filled a box with sand and wrote on sand (Elder, 1960). The place of class was the basement of Mr. Perkins house (Perkins H. M., 1887). As there were no books, the lessons were written on cards and hung on the walls. The scholars were a selected group of Nestorian boys or young ecclesiastics. In 1845 Mr. Stoddard took charge of this school and the site was transferred to Mount Seir. Mr. Stoddard, after 14 years of service, left the charge to his associate and successor Mr. Cochran, who, from 1847 to 1871, made this school eminently his life work. Under these two teachers, about 120 young Nestorians were educating for four or more years and others for a shorter time. After the death of Mr. Cochran, the school was suspended for three years and then reopened under supervision of Mr. Oldfather in the city of Urmia. One problem was that this school had no suitable building. A new site near the city of Urmia was bought and new buildings erected in 1879 through the gifts of Christian women from the Women's Missionary Societies of Philadelphia and Chicago in America (Hellot, 2005).

The first modern girl school in Iran was established by Mrs. Grant in March 1938 with only 4 Nestorian girls (Elder, 1960). Judith Campbell Grant had received a thorough classical and mathematical education and could speak several languages. Despite losing an eye because of sickness, she could successfully establish this school (Anderson, 1998). Mrs. Grant died one year later and American missionaries managed her school for 4 years before delivering it to Fidelia Fisk (Elder, 1960). Stoddard and Stocking were two teachers at boy Schools who also worked with Fisk (Elder, 1960). Through the efforts of zealous Fidelia Fiske, the girl school was turned into a boarding school in 1844. Fiske was a determined woman who "combined in a remarkable way, deep spirituality with great practical ability" (Van Gorder, 2010, p. 137). For fifteen years Fiske was principal of the Girls' Seminary at Urmia. Rufus Anderson who was an American minister and secretary of the Board for many years said that of more than a thousand missionaries whom he had known, none left a brighter record than hers. He added, "It seemed as though she spoke and acted just as I would have expected the Saviour to speak and act in the same situation" (Laurie, 1887, p. 5).

At the time of Perkins's arrival in Urmia, there were only about forty Nestorian men able to read and write and among the women only one, the sister of the patriarch (Macuch, 1987). After a half century of their mission in Iran, American missionaries held a ceremony near Urmia. It was estimated that more than 600 women who were among the attendants were literate (Elder, 1960). According to Afary (1996) from the 1870s Muslim girls attended the American Presbyterian School in Tehran, but it did not attract girls from the community at large because of the religious implications. The missionary schools afforded the first opportunity for the education of women in Persia by creating a school system that included Sage College for women in Tehran (Mansoori, 1986). Other female missionaries were active in other cities, mainly in north western part of the country. Mrs. Schuler established the first American missionary school in Rasht during early 1900s (Elder, 1960).

In 1870 the village schools (outstations) had more pupils than the "urban" schools in Urmia or in Khosrowa. This difference is not surprising, and is not unexpected in a country where the population was predominantly rural. However, the period for which the rural schools were open was short, and did not exceed the time interval of the stoppage of agricultural work in the winter (namely four or five months). It was deemed necessary to deal with the "most urgent" matter in the schools, and the main aim was to provide the basis for religion. "The mere evangelistic work can be done by native evangelists better than by us," Shedd, the Presbyterian missionary, wrote in 1871 (Hellot, 2005, pp. 273-274).

Presbyterians were engaged in establishing schools beyond Urmia in 1880s and 1890s while also expanding their evangelistic work. In 1887, Reverend Samuel Ward opened a boarding school for boys. In 1896, the American Presbyterian missionaries Dr. Samuel Martin and Mrs. Mary Jordan helped to open Alborz College, which became very popular among the elite (Van Gorder, 2010, p. 142) and many of them became great men. This school is still important in Iran and many of its graduates are now statesmen. It was located in the Armenian quarter of Tehran. Beginning as a grade school in 1873, the school soon attracted many Muslim students and adopted Persian as its language of instruction. In 1898, Rev. Samuel Jordan arrived to assume leadership of the school, and championed the school's growth into a junior college (1924) and finally into an US-accredited liberal arts college in 1928 (Asgard, 2010). Samuel Martin Jordan was one of the most devoted American instructors in Iran. He taught for more than 41 years. He said to students to learn not only to know, but also to move away from "Lootiabad" where louts and clowns abide in a den, to settle in "Adamabad" (the abode of man) (Saleh, 1976, p. 17).

By the end of the 19th century, more than 8000 students had been graduated from about 120 American missionary schools (Elder, 1960). Speer (1911, p. 22) wrote "Today the scholars in our own schools number nearly 3,000, but the example and influence of our educational work has not been limited to our own community, for in all the villages of Urmia schools are the common thing now. Many adults have learned to read, chiefly in the Sabbath schools." In 1909, the Persian-American Educational Society was formed among the American Baha'is with the overt intention of assisting the Baha'i schools in Iran. In 1911, Qudsiyyih Ashraf became the first Iranian woman to travel to the West under the auspices of that society in order to complete her education (Momen, 2005, p. 360). All foreign schools were closed in Iran in the year 1940 (Saleh, 1976) as by this time, Reza Shah was seeking a modern educational system which was not dependent on foreigners.

American missionaries knew exactly that single dimensional approach to education was less effective and their whole efforts could be nulled as soon as someone or some condition put an end to it. So they started to work on other issues like modifying Assyrian language or introducing printing press. The national language of the Assyrians is divided into two branches; the first one is called Classical Syriac, it is literary, clerical, and classical language, popularly called "the old language." This language never become vernacular among the public, but was limited to the church, and was taught in few churches and monasteries. The second language is called modern, spoken or vernacular language, known popularly as Surethor "the new language." It was well understood by all eastern Assyrians, although in the forms of several different dialects. By reducing the new language to writing, just like the Classical language, the American missionaries helped to create the concept of holy language outside the Church walls (Shmuel, 2011). The person second in literary matters only to Perkins was David Tappan Stoddard. He died in Urmia at the age of 41, after having labored there from 1843 till 1857. In this relatively short period he made an important contribution with regard to the language. He was the first to write a grammar of the modem language, which was published in 1855. This grammar was widely distributed in America and Europe, and gave Western linguists an ability to learn about this hitherto unknown language (Murre-van den Berg H., 1996). Stoddard compiled a dictionary, which, although never published, formed the basis of the *Dictionary of the Dialects of Vernacular Syriac* by Arthur John Maclean which appeared in 1901. It is likely that he also contributed to the grammar and spelling book that appeared in Urmia for use in the schools, aside from several publications under his own name, of which the *Outline of Theology (Ktaba d-Te'ologia),* which appeared posthumously in 1857, is most impressive. He was further occupied with the care for the Male Seminary, first in Urmia, later in Seir, and as such played an important part in the training of the Assyrian assistants (Murre-van den Berg H., 1996).

After inventing this new writing, Justin Perkins started negotiation with American Board of Mission on sending a printing press to Urmia. The first printing press was sent in 1937 from Boston, but it was heavy and therefore carriers could not pass it through rouged mountains of Trabzon. Therefore they sent it back to Istanbul and sold it (Nategh, 1996). In 1940 a small printing press along with a print expert named Breath arrived at Urmia after a long and dangerous travel (Elder, 1960). Apart from his work in supervising the work of the press, Breath devoted much time to the cutting of the Syriac type fonts. He died in Urmia in 1861 (Murre-van den Berg H., 1996). William R. Stocking, who was mainly occupied with the supervision of the Female Seminary, also contributed to the press, just as Albert L. Holladay and Dr. Austin H. Wright, the latter being a physician, who alongside his regular work did much in helping Perkins in later revisions of the Bible translations (Murre-van den Berg H., 1996). Austin H. Wright (1811-1865) served as a missionary in Urmia between 1840 and 1865 (Malick, 2008).

In 1876, the number of pages which had been printed in Syriac since 1835 with the one press of the American mission was 21 million. In an 1877 report, it was claimed that the "press has been running continually. Aside from the monthly paper *The Rays of Light* (the circulation of which has been about 450 copies) there have been printed lesson papers for the schools" (Hellot, 2005, p. 280).

Zahrire d-Bahra "Rays of Light" emerged in 1849 for the first time in the new history of Assyrians (Shmuel, 2011). In the early years of *Zahrire d-Bahra*, most articles were written by the missionaries, although probably translated and corrected by their Assyrian assistants. As literacy rose among the Assyrians, more and more of them contributed to the magazine and wrote articles for that. Towards the end of the century this volume became an important forum for discussions within the Assyrian community (Murre-van den Berg H., 1996).

Talk of printing in other languages began to appear around 1870 with the consideration of a project to translate and print the Bible in Azeri Turkish. This was consistent with the mission's new focus on reaching all sections of Persia (Malick, 2008). In 1880 a Persian type font was added. Patriots and authors in nearby Tabriz were excited by this event and soon arranged to have their newly established newspaper printed in printing press in Urmia (Saleh, 1976). In 1892 a pamphlet on cholera was printed in Persian; that was also printed in Assyrian. A Persian hymnal for the Tehran station was also printed (Malick, 2008). As a rival to the Protestant *Zahrire d-Bahra*, the Catholic Lazarist mission in Urmia produced another periodical, *Qala d-shrara*, which first came out in 1896. This included a considerable number of news items which today are of some historical importance (Brock & Witakowski, 2001). In 1904 *Ūrmīārtādoksētā* ("orthodox Urmia") was introduced, edited by the Russian Orthodox mission; and in 1906 the periodical of the national movement, *Kokba* came into the being (Macuch, 1987).

Rev. Benjamin W. Labaree worked in Urmia from 1860 to 1906. Under his supervision, the Biblical translation of the early period was thoroughly revised. The work was started somewhere in the eighties, and resulted in the edition of 1893. It was printed by the American Bible Society in New York and it is this version which is reprinted until the present day. Another influential missionary of these later days was William Ambrose Shedd. He taught at the College in Urmia, was editor of the magazine *Zahrire d-Bahra,* and was actively involved in endeavors to regulate further the spelling of the modem language (Murre-van den Berg H., 1996). Shedd knew exactly the power of propaganda when he wrote "the history of Christianity in the Sassanian Empire shows that there had been a very active and successful propaganda among the Iranians" (Shedd W. A., 1904, p. 292). He opposed narratives about Islam as a religion which was forced to non-Arab people by violence and terror and saw its power in convincing people of other faiths to convert. Also, a collection of publications was introduced by the Rev. James E. Rogers, who served in the mission between 1882 and 1885 (Malick, 2008).

The freedom of expression that came along with the Iranian Constitutional Revolution of 1905-1911 and the need for printed religious and educational materials in languages other than Assyrian, accompanied with the ever increasing focus of the missionaries on work among Turks, Persians and Kurds, allowed them in Urmia to consider a greatly expanded role for their press. In 1907 the missionaries stated that "With the coming great awakening in Persia our Press must serve not only the Syrian people, but also the great Mohammedan population. We must step in and supply the needs of this new mental hunger, otherwise it will find food in other quarters. Clerks, Government employees, and all others who know French are reading French books, and thus are coming under the influence of its license and infidelity. Our Press can and must be the means to give them the truth in religion, in history and science in their own tongue" (Malick, 2008, pp. 13-14).

There were four missionary printing-houses in Urmia before the end of World War I, the Iranian Assyrian writers and poets were producing much more than they were able to publish (Macuch, 1987). The introduction of these facilities in Iran left a very deep and enduring effect on Iran. For decades to come, people in these region were pioneers in furthering modernization and progress and without the resistance of Tabriz – a city in which a vivid public sphere was formed as a result of missionary activities and other factors- the Iranian constitutional revolution would fail.

EVANGELIZATION

When planning for the new mission in Urmia, the secretary of the Board, Rufus Anderson, together with Smith and Dwight, carefully considered what the objective of the new mission should be. They came to the conclusion that the goal of the missionaries should be to contribute to a renewal of the Church of the East and to the restoration of its former glory, as it existed in the time of the great missions to Mongolia and China (Murre-van den Berg H., 1996, p. 5). Almost all of any early missionary endeavors were, in fact, confined to working among Armenian and Assyrian Christian communities, and all Christians were officially discouraged from openly proselytizing Muslims. The missionaries' hope of gaining a foothold and moving from foreign efforts to an indigenous church primarily revolved around launching hospitals, schools, universities, and orphanages before establishing local churches (Van Gorder, 2010, p. 125).

Nevertheless, American missionaries were always obsessed with finding ways to prepare the ground for conversions among Muslim populations. They did not accept Islam as a genuine religion. In one of the articles in year book of ABCFM, the writer calls the prophet of Islam, "False prophet" (ABCFM, 1819, p. 273). Justin Perkins said in his diary "Any false religious system corrupts most fully those who have most to do with it and are the most devoted to its support. Probably no class of men in the world now more fully personate the Pharisees of old than Persian

Mollahs. As lying is one of the most common vices of the Persians, the proverb is perfectly natural and true that such and such a one, noted for this vice, will lie like a Mollah, if such be the priests, what must be the people?" (Perkins H. M., 1887, p. 63). This view was shared by other missionaries. One day in the autumn 1845, Mr. Stocking, Miss Fiske and Deacon John were riding together when the Deacon asked in English: "If we ever have a revival here, what shall we call it?" Mr. Stocking replied, "First get it, then we will find a name." And when it came the Nestorians at once called it "an awakening" (Laurie, 1887, p. 84).

James Lyman Merrick never gave up the calling to evangelize the Persians that he experienced as a student at Amherst College, but his career ended up one of deep frustration. After years of preparing himself for his chosen mission, the American Board charged him to acquire an intimate understanding of the languages and doctrines of Muslims, and to travel extensively through the cities of Persia and, if possible, beyond to cities in Central Asia where the mysterious "kings of the east" may be awaiting the stimulus of the Gospel to play their prophetic parts (Marr, 2006, p. 142). His method was to preach publicly on the streets against Islam and to distribute copies of Christian texts which attacked Islam among Muslims. Not surprisingly, these enterprises prompted frequent death threats (Van Gorder, 2010). When Merrick and two German missionaries started their work in Isfahan, some people plotted to kill them. Therefore, the authorities assigned 30 guards to ensure their safety. Merrick in his report says that though there was some hopes for evangelization of people in Tehran, this hope was totally vain as far as Isfahan was concerned (Elder, 1960). This inspired Merrick to write to his overseers, "I am at length convinced that public preaching to the Persians is at present, not only inexpedient but impracticable" (Van Gorder, 2010, pp. 138-139).

In 1836, "thoroughly convinced that the time has come for a successful attack on the religion of the false prophet," Horatio Southgate was funded by the Protestant Episcopal Church to travel to Turkey and Persia (Marr, 2006, p. 141). Southgate was generally positive on Persians and their culture, but his method of denouncing Islam was not appealing to Muslims of Persia. After debating with Persians in Turkey, he finally showed his exasperation by describing the Persian as a "wily antagonist" who "likes nothing better than to display his subtlety in disputing about essences, substances, and spirits [. . .] a metaphysical chaos, where there is neither shore nor bottom (Marr, 2006, p. 141).

The printing press, which began its mission in 1844, was active in the dissemination of Christian literature: "the Old and New Testaments in the spoken language, text-books, commentaries, periodicals, and pamphlets. A glance at the results of the evangelistic labours speaks for itself. Probably about 5,000 souls have joined our Church since the first communicants were recorded, twenty years after the establishment of the Mission" (Speer, 1911, p. 22). The renaissance of the Syriac language was a double-edged sword. One of the American missionaries emphasized this in 1872: "The Nestorians of Persia speak Turkish. The mission has created a new language [neo-Syriac] for them. It would have been better if it had been Persian" (Hellot, 2005, p. 282). Ironically, the Persian authorities themselves encouraged the printing of works in Syriac, so as to avoid potential evangelism among Persians. A report in the Presbyterian archive from 1872 states: "The serparast asked the mission for a bond that books and tracts are not to be made or circulated in languages other than Syriac." Hence Christian writings were tolerated in Persia as long as they were written in Armenian or in Syriac, but not in Persian (Hellot, 2005).

On the last Sabbath of Justin Perkins in Persia, in June 1869, he was asked "Looking back over these thirty-six years, have you seen as great results as you expected?" He replied: "Far more. I expected to see a congregation or two gathered, but God has given revivals, and has raised up preachers, and gathered in harvests of souls. He has been better than my faith" (Speer, 1911, p. 24). After Justin Perkins's death in 1869, American Board of Mission decided to extend its mission to other Iranian ethnicities and religions (Elder, 1960). By 1876, Spellman reports, there were "enough converts to warrant the founding of a church, whose services were sometimes attended by Muslims." This led the government (in 1880), under pressure from furious Muslim clergy, to issue an order forbidding all Muslims to attend any Christian service or to visit any chapel inside a hospital or church. Regular public services were resumed only two years later when this law was overturned by British colonial pressure on the Qajar government. The back and forth of this decision-making process reveals many things about the situation in Persia (Van Gorder, 2010, p. 125). In 1842, a Royal *Farman* was issued, prohibiting Christian proselytism, but in 1881 and 1882 orders were issued to put an end to the missionaries' work among the Muslims (Hellot, 2005, p. 282). By 1880s, in Gook Tapeh near Urmia more than half of the 1500 residents had converted to Protestantism and hundreds were considering converting to Protestantism (Elder, 1960).

When Asahel Grant started visiting patients in Iran, his ability procured him a great name among people. "Especially did the sight restored to many by removal of cataract give him an immense influence to employ for Christ" (Laurie, 1853, p. 65). Apart from benefiting from Western medical knowledge in regions where little medical expertise existed, these visits also provided missionaries with ample opportunities to spread the Gospel (Murre-van den Berg H., 2005). By and large, the mission doctors were inhibited by instructions which bade them to regard their medical skill and practice "only as a means of furthering the spiritual objects of the mission" (Daniel, 1964, p. 82).

In 1843, an Ottoman chieftain named Badir Khan Beig sacked and burned the villages of Tiary, and people were left homeless and hungry. Some of them came to Fidelia Fiske's seminary and asked for help. She said they had nothing to help but they could accept their girls in the school and people accepted out of despair. They even said "thank you." This was the first movement of the school towards the evangelization of Kurdistan (Laurie, 1863). Not only were the women organized for church work in some of the larger villages, going from house to house and visiting systematically neighboring hamlets on the Sabbath, but Miss Van Duzee had a class of from five to fifteen Muslim women, and taught a young Mullah, who asked for baptism. She also gave home visits to Muslim women, one of whom took her book with her to the vineyard that her son might teach her to read. As many as two Muslim women gave evidence of conversion and remained steadfast under persecution (Laurie, 1887).

The raising of local children in missionary families, although not often described as a separate activity, formed an important part of the missionary work all over the world. Initially, kids were frequently brought to missionaries as a sign of trust, and soon the missionaries encouraged such temporary adoptions as good opportunity to communicate to these children the evangelical teachings in all its aspects. A new generation of protestant wives and mothers who would transmit the new faith to the coming generation (Murre-van den Berg H., 2005).

Before the missionaries' arrival, the Christians of Azerbaijan were divided among four churches. In 1900, two churches were added to these four: an Evangelical Church (resulting from a new scission in the Eastern Syrian Church), and an Orthodox Church (affiliated with the Russian Orthodox Church). This diversity of Christian sects, at the start of the twentieth century, might appear to be a measure of the missionaries' success, or it might be seen as something that shows the religious tolerance of the Persian authorities. However, the division was a sign of the serious divisions within the Syriac-speaking population. The churches built at that time clearly display these disparities and divisions (Hellot, 2005).

The most obvious places to look for Protestant missionary influence are the communities of the converted. The Protestant communities were rather small, probably consisting of no more than about 30,000 members in all of the Middle East in 1908 (Richter, 1970) and most converts originally belonged to the Eastern Churches rather than Islam or Judaism (Murre-van den Berg H., 2005, p. 111). Also, a number of Jews were affected by the preaching of the American missionaries and converted to Christianity (Hellot, 2005, p. 301). There were also other processes which were not appealing to American missionaries. By the end of 19th century thousands of American nationals had converted to Bahaism (Cole, 2005) and 'Abdu'l Baha himself personally visited the United States in 1912 (Van Gorder, 2010, p. 91). Also, there are signs that some of the descendants of American missionaries in Iran converted to Islam in the coming decades.

In this sense, we can say the main objective of the American missionaries to evangelize Iranians was not met. At the beginning they thought if they presented their ideas to Persians, they would massively convert to Christianity. British and North American missionaries were inspired with the triumphalist mindset of their times which made them convinced that they shared the "white man's burden" to civilize and educate Orientals who were invariably considered to be more primitive. This was obviously not a mindset which was going to be very well-received among the proud people of Persia (Van Gorder, 2010, p. 127).

As we saw in this section, there were some Persians who converted to Christianity, but now, there is no trace of them. I tried to ask experts and some Iranian Christians about their fate in suspicion that they might had been victimized in much more traditional Iranian society of early 20th century. I got the best answer from Heleen Murre-van den Berg:

> Although these groups never were very big, I would say that from all of these groups considerable numbers have migrated to the west - starting in the late nineteenth century and going on till today. Christians in general migrated in greater percentages than Muslims, and Protestant Christians migrated in higher percentages than other Christians.
>
> I haven't heard of specific cases of forced back-conversion to Islam, though it is likely that this happened sometimes, perhaps mostly under pressure by family. In addition, women might have converted back to Islam (or at least, withdrawing from Christianity) in cases of marriage with a Muslim.
>
> Answering your question, I would say in addition to those Protestants and Evangelicals that still live in Iran, openly or hidden, the majority of these converts left the country over the years. Unfortunately, this is based mostly on talks to such Christians over the years, not on hard evidence. All in all, their numbers were never very big. (Murre-van den Berg, 2014, Personal Communication)

The complaints made by certain missionaries make it possible to detect the first manifestations of a "brain drain," particularly among the Syriac Christians competent in English, and part of the English or American missions. In the 1870s, a disillusioned missionary indicated: "The more enlightened and evangelised they become, the stronger will their propensity grows to migrate" (Hellot, 2005, p. 281). In 1882, J. H. Shedd expresses his concern over the emigration of Nestorians:

> Ishaak and Yohanan, two young Nestorians who have worked with us during several years, left for America: they are proficient in English and Oriental languages. It is a mistake that these men go to America to prepare for the work in Persia . . . It is a disease which will soon run its course and work its own cure.

Some of these "Christian emigrants" would come back to Urmia as doctors (like Dr Youanan or Dr Jessie M. Yonan), lawyers or teachers (like Kasha Yosif Benjamin or Y. M. Neesan). Even the bishop, Mar Yohana, who died in 1874, had gone to the United States after he met Smith and Dwight in 1930 in Iran (Nategh, 1996, p. 157). By the late 19th century in America, George Malech founded the Persian Christian Benevolent Society of Chicago. He was also the Persian representative for ten years of the Berlin-based Evangelical Association for the Advancement of the Nestorian Church, which financed an orphanage outside of Urmia (Van Gorder, 2010). These instances prove claims of Murre-van den Berg that American missionaries' endeavors were much more undermined by migration, rather than persecution.

At the end of World War I the mission had to be closed. In 1922 some missionaries were able to return, but the mission was closed for good at the order of Reza Shah (Murre-van den Berg H., 1996, p. 5). This marked the end of evangelization by American missionaries, though, they stayed in Iran and engaged in clandestine endeavor under the guise of education until 1979. Even after that, they continued their work outside Iran and as we see at the end of this chapter, they have gained some success.

INTERCULTURAL COMMUNICATION STRATEGY

In the past centuries, Iranians have proven to be much more tolerant to Christians, in comparison with major neighboring countries (Nategh,

1996). American missionaries knew that in order to make any changes, they had to have direct and effective interaction with local people, authorities, social leaders and particularly, Assyrians. If Assyrians had not sent their children to their schools, if they had not bought and read the productions of the printing press, and if they had not opened their houses and churches for the preaching of the missionaries, the latter probably would soon have left (Murre-van den Berg H., 1996). American missionaries from the first contacts tried to look like local people. Justin Perkins dressed like ordinary Nestorians and frequently called them "my nation." They lived in the small, poor and dark tents which were not in any sense comparable to their houses back in the U.S. (Elder, 1960). Mrs. Rhea widow of an American missionary in Iran whose acquaintance with Justin Perkins began during his last years in Persia wrote "God made him for the place and he fitted in exactly. He suited Persia and the Persians. They are a people fastidious, formal and polite in the extreme. Dr. Perkins calls them the Frenchmen of the East. A person with rough and boorish manners could have no influence over them whatever, or gain their respect, if lacking in good manners" (Perkins H. M., 1887, p. 66). On occasion, American missionaries did not lose any chance to interact with members of the Iranian nobility. Perkins's journal is full of narratives that indicate the extent to which royal princes were emulating the West: attempting to learn English, establishing schools to spread the Western education, adopting western customs, wearing European clothes (Spellman, 2004, p. 158).

Dr. Asahel Grant did his medical job so prudently that, though his services were entirely gratuitous, he gave no offence to the native doctors who were much less expert. There was no show to attract customers, and he was ready to aid the native practitioners with both medicine and instructions (Laurie, 1853).

Joseph Cochran took part in church and evangelistic work, and became the friend and counselor to provincial governors, Kurdish leaders and members of royal family. He was a wise conciliator and diplomat as well as proficient doctor. He spoke flawlessly from childhood the two languages of the common people, Turkish and Syriac; he knew the cultural climate and ways of thought of the people (Anderson, 1999). Mrs. Cochran wrote about her husband in 1878:

> I really think it is remarkable with what dignity Joe conducts himself here. People knew him as a boy; Peracarried him when a baby, but never does he or anyone else treat him with the slightest disrespect. He is such a proper youth, Joe is. I have to laugh at him sometimes, while I secretly admire him for it. I know I worry him sometimes with my democratic ways, but it is very trying at times to conform to the code of etiquette of this country. (Speer, 1911, p. 55)

He was extremely careful from the outset to conform to all proper social and cultural manners of the local people. He was recognized accordingly as a Persian gentleman, and he had access as a welcome visitor to the homes of the nobility, while he came, in time, to be almost idolized by the poor, to whom he was as polite and attentive as to the Governor or the Crown Prince (Speer, 1911).

As I said earlier in this chapter, American missionaries soon recognized the importance of language and started to learn and talk in the language of local people. Justin Perkins not only knew the language of Nestorians, but he is also known as a notable linguist of Nestorian language. Dr. Wright had an extraordinary talent in learning native languages (Elder, 1960). Basset started learning Farsi to become able to directly communicate with Tehran people (Elder, 1960). And, as a result of their success and reports, selective language training in the foreign service began in 1895 through the assignment of officers as "student interpreters" to the American legations in Persia, Korea, and Siam (Israel & Anderson, 2002, p. 454).

The foreign missionaries set out to gather information regarding the living conditions of Muslims in Iran, and to disperse Western beliefs and ideas. It is through these types of channels that Iranians in the nineteenth century heard stories about the standard of living and social and political reforms in Europe and America (Spellman, 2004). This new stream of information was one of the main causes of the future upheavals and developments in the history of Iran and jeopardized not only the existing political and social establishment, but also life of missionaries themselves.

As the Qajar Dynasty became weaker, xenophobic and anti-Christian sentiments became more prevalent. Negative views of foreigners were easily transferred onto the vulnerable missionaries in their midst so that many missionaries resorted to protection in European and North American embassies (Van Gorder, 2010). The ulama opposed the limited steps the *Qajars* took toward Western education and particularly missionary education. The ulama were also against the steps toward reform and to concessions granted to Westerners (Kedie, 1988). Muslim clerics were not the only major groups against missionary influence. While the local Christian clerics began losing influence, a new "horizontal" solidarity appeared between Muslim, Christian and Jewish notables (Hellot, 2005). In general, different group of Christian missionaries spent much energy competing and undermining each other and at the same time all of them had to fight local Christian leaders as well (Nategh, 1996). This was a fertile environment for generating stories about misconducts by American missionaries and surviving this dangerous environment was not possible only by adopting an effective intercultural strategy.

POLITICAL STRATEGY

We saw in the previous sections that American missionaries came to Iran in a historical epoch in which Iran was in the most vulnerable situation. Iran had already fought and lost wars and even worse, great pieces of lands had been separated from this country by imperial British and Russian forces in a humiliating way. Cholera and plague had afflicted the nation and economically the country was bankrupt. Qajar rulers were incompetent and corruption was very rampant. Politically, this made a great opportunity to American missionaries to make a huge success. The rulers of the Qajar government were open to accommodating foreign interests and made few prohibitions against the arrival of Christian missionaries. Some rulers even believed that the missionaries might provide a positive impetus for modernization of the country. The shah's officials were eager to maintain good relations with the imperial powers by helping the *English Mullahs*. The royal family members may have also hoped to gain certain other advantages, or insights about the West, from their visiting foreign missionaries (Van Gorder, 2010). A report on Persia's approach to Christianity in 1818 admits: "it is said that the present Prince Royal of Persia has greatly exerted himself to correct the excesses of the religious zeal in the Mussulmauns (sic) employed in his service and to protect the Christians who might suffer from their violence" (ABCFM, 1819, p. 133). Elsewhere in the same document we read:

> Though not yet prepared to receive Christians in the capacity of teachers of religion, Persia gives many encouraging indications, that the delusions of the False Prophet are losing their hold on the minds of the acute and intelligent . . . If these statements should prove correct, we may anticipate at no remote period, a free entrance for Christianity into that Kingdom. (ABCFM, 1819, p. 273)

Moreover, the Iranian officials could hope that this newly emerged power that was the U.S. might save Iran from the treacherous dominance of the Russians and the British, as Naser-ed-din Shah naively wrote to American President Cleveland and implicitly asked him to exploit Persia and dispel Britain and Russia (Yeselson, 1956).

In 1835 Ghahraman Mirza, a favorite brother of the king and prince of Azerbijan, sent his uncle to visit the missionaries and inspect the seminary. As a result of this favorable visit there was sent, though unsolicited, a Farman, of which the following is a translation:

> "The command of His Highness is: Whereas, the very honorable and respected gentlemen, Messrs. Perkins and Grant, at Oroomiah (sic), are attending to the education of the people, and render the people useful by teaching them European science, the grace of our Excellency and Highness having become favorably disposed toward them, we order and command three soldiers for their safety at this harvest season and onward; and in accordance with this grace, we command that they shall be

honored and have occasion to praise our beneficence. It is our command that the exalted and noble lord, Nedjelf Kooly Khan, governor of Oroomiah (sic), shall take care to protect them in every respect, and he shall give to each of the three soldiers, the guard of their safety, three dollars per month, and never shall he neglect it. It is ordered that the trusty secretaries arrange and execute the sum of this blessed command." (Perkins J., 1843, p. 287)

In 1838 the governor of Urmia wrote to the missionaries, "Hitherto, I have regarded you as my brothers; now that the English embassador (sic) leaves the country, I assume the place of father to you" (Perkins H. M., 1887, pp. 24-25).

Naser-ed-din Shah, the Iranian king permitted the construction of schools, chapels, and hospitals, and he allowed the missionaries to distribute their religious books (Yeselson, 1956). But, in 1851 the Shah repealed an 1842 Farman that had outlawed proselytizing among Christians, and in 1878 it was made legal for Jews to become Christians (Yeselson, 1956). A Farman in 1880 forbade Muslims from receiving instruction from Christians or attending their churches (Yeselson, 1956). But, in the same year Christians got some privileges. A noteworthy interreligious development took place in 1880 when the Protestant groups were allowed to elect a representative to deal with cases in their interest before the government. About the same time, American missionaries were allowed to establish committees to address the legal affairs of their community, free of the shariah law courts based on Islamic standards. Even the Qajar crown established that Muslims who converted to Christianity were allowed to retain their rights to property and inheritance. In 1881, the law which stated that the testimony of a Christian could not be used against a Muslim was overturned by the direct intervention of the British Foreign Ministry in Tehran. This meant that, from now on, "Christians would be placed on a footing of equality with Muslims in giving of [legal] evidence" (Van Gorder, 2010, pp. 125-126). Moreover, John G. Wishard who was Director of the American Presbytery Hospital in Tehran in late 19th and early 20th centuries has stated that Qajar kings themselves were highly intended to have American physicians in their courts and the American physicians had a high place in the Iranian court (Wishard, 1908). These successes were great but not enough for the American missionaries who aspired to proselytize the whole Middle East.

Missionaries were reluctant to engage in internal political struggles and for example when Howard Baskerville was killed during the Iranian Constitutional Revolution, he acted against the instructions of American authorities. And, as I said, after the Qajar dynasty, when Reza Shah came to power, he saw missionary activities against his strategy to build an independent country and banned all missionary activities.

DISCUSSION

American missionaries started the first contacts between Iranians and Americans. They were very important in shaping Iran-U.S. relations, even today. Yet, they failed in their number one priority which was evangelizing Persia and the Middle East. In fact, they under-estimated the power of the Islamic episteme in the lives and minds of Iranians; also, related to this was the fact that Islam has been better localized to the social, cultural and even geographical environment of this region. They just thought that if they simply present their ideas and beliefs, Persians would convert to Christianity. Yet, they finally found it was hard; moreover, in this era 'Islam' also controlled social life of people and conversion to Christianity would culminate in immediate bankruptcy in social capital. Only few Muslims accepted to convert to Christianity and nowadays we do not know any protestant Church in Iran except for those whose ancestors were Christians of other sects. It is hard now to estimate how many Nestorians, Armenians and Persians are descendants of those converts of 19th century to Protestantism; but, a rough assessment is something five to ten thousand. It was only in the modern day with vast lifestyle change that Christian missionaries could succeed in proselytizing Iranians. There can be no doubt at all that nowadays considerable number of Iranians, both inside and outside Iran, have come to Christian faith (Chapman, 2011; Kim, 2013). In Iran more Muslims have turned to Christianity in the last twenty years since the Iranian revolution than in the last one thousand years combined (Bartlotti, 2001); though I personally believe a group of these people only do this to get asylum in a prosperous country. This is an existential threat to a political system which is based on Islamic –Shi'ite- values and therefore, it is not surprising that measures have been taken against this trend. In terms of organizational encounters, as a reaction to the presence of Christian missionary societies and publications "Shi'i clergy circles tried from the 1960s onward to train some sort of Muslim missionaries. At the same time, efforts were made to provide their coreligionists and notably the Muslim youth with fundamental knowledge of the 'enemy's' religion and ideology, in order to immunize them from Christian propaganda" (Tavassoli, 2011, p. 188). We cannot say that Muslim missionaries in the West were not less successful than those who want to proselytize Muslims. This struggle will go on.

Although American missionaries of 19th century were very successful in gaining respect of the Iranian people and even found faithful friends among the Muslims clergy, in the second half of the 20th century their efforts and good name was wiped out by cultural repulsion the traditional Iranian society started to develop again Westerners. Their schools, colleges and hospitals had contributed to the diffusion of western ideals (Mansoori, 1986) and not all the Iranian people of that time liked it. Brian Street (1975) provides a complementary perspective in his study of the impact of the introduction of modern education on a village in Iran in the early 1970s. The Shah's government used education as an instrument for the 'modernization' of the entire country, and trained and sent out teachers and instructors into rural areas. "Those being educated in rural areas are thus the recipients of a philosophy which belongs to an alien social group and is being channelled through external institutions consciously devised to alter local life patterns" (Bartlotti, 2001, pp. 107-108). These contradictions finally contributed the Islamic Revolution of 1979.

Despite all these failures, one great success of the American missionaries has always been underestimated. We saw in the previous sections that American missionaries were very prudent not to intervene in political issues. Yet, they left great impact on two Iranian revolutions, namely, the Constitutional Revolution (1906) and the Islamic Revolution (1979) by diffusing education. For about 70 years, they provided education to the Iranian children and let them knew about more effective political systems of the West, before the Constitutional Revolution of 1906 became inevitable. Also, by renewing the educational system of Iran, they helped development of a generation of young students who in 1979, to the surprise of the world, chose Islamic values, instead of a Western system.

Chapter 3

IRAN AND UNITED STATES IN HISTORICAL CONTEXT

INTRODUCTION

Understanding how American people perceive Iranians or vice versa would not be possible without knowing the broader context in which these perceptions have shaped. As we will see later in this book, in order to know other people, we have to make categorizations. These categorizations are governed by highly complicated mixture of geographical, psychological, cultural, social, economic and last but not least, historical information. History is important, particularly in our time in which history is recorded, circulated, and constructed by texts and images. Historical enmities descend down centuries through written accounts and sometimes through myths and fables. Eventually, they may culminate in wars and massacres, right in our 21th century at the dawn of the new millennium. One prominent example in this respect is what we see in Syria. Deducing the conflict into a mere wars of factions, and neglecting the historical roots of the conflict which goes to thousands years ago will culminate into roadmaps which are unable to put an end to 6 years of bloodshed, and unfortunately, we will see the worse in the future.

Anyway, I want to dedicate a whole chapter to the history of Iran-U.S. relations to provide a context for current state of affairs. This history has been very tense in the last four decades; but, it would be surprising for most of the people to know how these two nations used to be friends, especially when compare their relations with that of Iran-Britain or Iran-Russia, two colonialist countries who milked Iran to its starvation and detached or annexed vast territories from it.

It was the 1953 CIA coup against popular Mosaddegh and following struggles after the Islamic revolution which first wiped out good image of the U.S. in the mind of Iranian people and then made it the most hated enemy of Iranian politicians. Despite these enmities, however, I will discuss how these two countries are still helping each other unwittingly, or sometimes deliberately.

EARLIEST CONTACTS

It is very hard and perhaps impossible to determine how first Iranians and Americans started the first contacts. But, in the previous chapter we saw that in the 1800s or perhaps earlier, Americans embarked in Bushehr, in south Iran to buy drug cargos but the British did not let them to do business there. Also, in the same period, American religious publications speculated possibility of establishing a mission to Iran (then Persia). In 1810 the American Board of Commissioners for Foreign Affairs was founded and this institute sent two missionaries were sent to the Middle East. They were followed by many men and women who devoted themselves to missionary work in the Ottoman Empire and soon afterwards in Iran. Because the Ottoman government did not permit them to proselytize Muslims, and the Catholics objected to any form of interference, their work was principally with the Greek Orthodox, Armenians, and Nestorians (Dodge, 1972). An important part of the relationships between Iran and the U.S. remained religious for the next 100 years and religion is still one of the main factors that influence political relations between these two countries. From 1830s to 1870s Presbyterian missionaries labored to establish the foundations for a new Christian church in Iran. Their evangelical work was done mainly in the northern part of Persia. The missionaries had some success and between 1870 and 1934 the scope of their activity was expanded. Mission stations were opened in Tehran, Tabriz, Hamedan, Kermanshah, Qazvin, Rasht, and Mashhad. One of the most significant results of the missionary labor was the establishment of an effective modern educational system from primary to college level in a nation that had no secular education (Mansoori, 1986).

The first groups of American missionaries came to Iran in a particular period of history. By that time, Iran was in turbulence and Fat'h Ali Shah Qajar was passing his last years of kingship (he died in 1834). During the reign of the Qajars, pressures were being exerted upon the country from three directions: in north from Russia; in the east from British India and the new buffer state of Afghanistan; and in the west from the Ottomans and the British in the Persian Gulf. For the Qajars, the focus of both their internal and foreign relations, therefore, was on resistance to external pressure and intervention (Farmanfarmaian, 2008). At that time Iranians were well acquainted with Europeans. In 1815, Abbas Mirza, governor of Azerbaijan, had sent five Iranian students to London to study modern sciences (Fazeli, 2006). Abbas Mirza, possibly the only popular Qajar royal family member today, was desperate to do something; he even naively proposed that "a village" in Azerbaijan of Iran be given to "Germans and British" to come there and live beside Iranians (Nategh, 1996, p. 19). He was in hope that these people will take with them science and technology.

The Treaty of Turkmanchai (signed 1828), drawn in sixteen clauses, had forced Iran to give up all lands and territories north to Aras to Imperial Russia. The immediate aftermath of the war with Russia and Iran's humiliating defeat was the assassination of the Russian envoy Alexander Griboedov, who arrived a few months later (Daryaee, 2012). This assassination did nothing but increasing pressure on all Iranians. Economically, the country was ravaged by increase in population, diseases, security problems, corruption, and foreign interventions who took advantage of this situation. As early as the 1830s bazaaris complained to the government about the large-scale import of foreign manufactures

(Kedie, 1988). In this turbulence, American missionaries could work more free and their useful and effective activities along with other humiliating defeats of Iranians in wars convinced Qajar rulers to think of new allies.

In 1851, George P. Marsh, American Minister Resident at Constantinople, negotiated a treaty with Persia. After amending the treaty to include a "most favored nation" clause, the United States Senate gave its advice and consent to ratification. The Persian government took no further action, however, and the treaty died (Yeselson, 1956). The Treaty of Commerce and Navigations (signed in 1856) was the first diplomatic covenant the United States and Persia made. The treaty lasted until 1928 (Alexander & Nanes, 1980). The treaty was signed by Iranian Ambassador Farrokh Khan Ghaffari (Amin-ol-Molk, later Amin-ol-Dowleh) and American Minister Carroll Spence (Saleh, 1976). A ratification was needed in both capitals. Persian approval came along with a royal decree and a second-degree Order of the Lion and Sun issued in Spence's honor. Yet, in spite of apparent ratification of the treaty by the U.S. Congress, the shah's willingness to receive a high-level U.S. representative in Tehran was not fulfilled, possibly because of British pressure on the United States (Amanat, 1997, p. 288).

Among many abortive attempts aimed at improving Iran's southern defense, in 1859, two years after Iran's defeat in the war with England, Naser el-din shah was hoping to seek U.S. support in order to build up a naval presence in the Persian Gulf. In what appears to be Iran's first endeavor to purchase arms from the United States, shah instructed his minister for foreign affairs, Mirza Sa'id Khan, to negotiate through the Persian envoy to Istanbul, Mirza Husayn Khan (later Mushiral-Dawla), the possibility of purchasing from the United States a fleet of warships and merchant ships to be employed in the Persian Gulf. In his letter Sa'id Khan, acknowledging "the perfect skill of the government of the United States in this area," asked Husayn Khan to ascertain, preferably in secret, from his U.S. counterpart in Istanbul the cost of such a fleet, as well as the necessary human resources, training, and maintenance. On the margin of Sa'id Khan's official letter the shah added in his own hand: "God willing, I wish to gradually purchase warships and launch them in the Persian Gulf. I regard purchase of ships from the United States a necessity" (Amanat, 1997, p. 417).

Shah was willing to offer the United States some military and commercial bases in the Persian Gulf "to remain permanently in the hands of the agents of that state on lease or license in order to build residences and offices for their representatives and harbor for their Ships." Given Iran's uncompromising circumstances, such a generous invitation to the Persian Gulf was not altogether unwarranted. Article 15 of the draft of the treaty with the United States, which the British envoy obtained through his spies in the Persian court, went on to demand that because the Persian government did not have "vessels of war," the U.S. government was thus committed "not to neglect the protection of the Persian merchants carrying the flag of that country, nor allow any violence or irregularity toward them." Article 16 went even further, necessitating engagement of the United States in protection of "all the Persian islands and ports in the Persian Gulf against the violence and attack of the enemies, weak or strong, Christian or non-Christian." In exchange for the Persian court's help and "full honor" to U.S. vessels of war, the United States, in the event Iran wanted to establish territorial claims over its islands (including Bahrain) in the Persian Gulf, would provide vessels for Iran "on the rate of the day." It is no wonder that Murray [then British ambassador to Persia] viewed the Persian initiative as a move "aimed so directly at the destruction of our maritime influence in the Persian Gulf" and asked London to block the agreement (Amanat, 1997, p. 288). This was the beginning of Iranian interest in American weapons and military advisers which continued to the present day. The Iranian military got generally negative comments from visiting U.S. Army brevet Major General Emory Upton, who had arranged with then U.S. Army General in Chief William T. Sherman in 1875 to take a two-year evaluation tour of foreign armies. Upton, whose writings would later influence military reforms in the United States, may have let his own unhappiness with the hostility of Congress to America's small and much deteriorated post-Civil War peacetime army shape his attitudes on Iran. He concluded his remarks by noting that "the capital of Persia, like that of all countries where military institutions are neglected, lies at the mercy of a few disciplined battalions" (Ward, 2009, p. 81).

AMERICAN LEGATION IN TEHRAN

The growing surge of American missionaries was one of the main reasons that American diplomatic relations with Iran during Qajar Dynasty were elevated to a more active level. We saw that the first serious contacts between Iranians and Americans initiated by American Presbyterian missionaries. Therefore, it is not surprising that Samuel Greene Wheeler Benjamin who was the first American diplomat, (1837–1914), was himself the son of a former Presbyterian missionary to Turkey. He presented himself in Teheran on June 11, 1883. His first act as ambassador of the United States was to erect a one-hundred-foot flagpole so that "residents throughout the city could see the Stars and Stripes." Thus, he began America's highly visible presence in Iran (Van Gorder, 2010, p. 139).

The reason for establishing this legation was not merely political. Rather, it was more religious or even personal. In 1880-1881 a Kurdish tribal leader named Shaikh Obaidullah attempted to create an independent state of Kurdistan. The effort eventually failed but during the turbulences some Christians were killed. The dangerous position of American missionaries during the rebellion which made them vulnerable to threats, culminated in establishment of this legation in Iran. Senator Dawes who happened to had some relatives among missionaries in Iran, in 1880 repeatedly urged for immediate action to protect American citizens in Urmia. He could not find considerable support among the public because by that time American people knew nothing about Persia or Iran. About a quarter of century later, Doctor John G. Wishard wrote "The description of any land visited by less than four out of a million of our citizens cannot be said to be very well known, and ought to present some interesting phases of life from many standpoints" (Wishard, 1908, p. 9).

Nevertheless, Dawes did not give up. On February 6, 1882, he called for the files of difficulties confronting American citizens and stressed the need to establish diplomatic relations between one of the youngest and one of the oldest nations of the time. On August 3, 1882 the Foreign Relations Committee submitted a bill to the House asked an appropriation of 5000$ to cover the salary of a Chargé d'affaires and Consul General in Iran. The bill was approved (Saleh, 1976). Upon arrival, Benjamin found that many Iranian officials had even never heard name of United States (Yeselson, 1956). When America established diplomatic relations with Iran, the population of the country could barely reach 9 million. There were dozen medium sized cities of which only Tehran, the capital and Tabriz, the trading center in Azerbaijan, had a population of more than two hundred thousand (Yeselson, 1956).

In 1888, Naser el-din Shah sent Haj Husayn Quli Khan Sadr al-Saltana (later called "Haji Washington") to be the first Iranian envoy to United States (Mahdavi, 2005). On October 5, 1888, he presented a letter by Naser el-din Shah to President Cleveland. In this letter, the Shah made an impassioned request for American help to save Persia from Britain and Russia. The shah even pleaded to have his country's resources exploited by America and hoped for a treaty of alliance:

> The government of Persia, which is an old established and independent kingdom of the world, have special message to her young and prosperous and powerful sister. . . But we have two great neighbors which instead of assisting us . . . always internally endeavoring to prevent us . . . you help us with your sicences (sic) and industries and send your companies and merchand (sic) and manufactures (sic) to our country . . . Hoping that our reqist (sic) for the present will be strictly secret from any person besides your highness . . . (Yeselson, 1956, p. 40)

This letter shows that Tehran regarded the U.S. as a potential third power leverage in countering British and Russian influence and intervention in Iran. Given the absence of American imperialism in the Middle East at that time, despite heightened U.S. imperial aggression in Latin America and East Asia in the closing years of the nineteenth century, Iranian nationalists considered the U.S. as a benign imperial power, disinclined to breach Iran's sovereignty (Bonakdarian, 2007).

On March 8, 1904, Reverend Benjamin W. Labaree was murdered by Kurdish tribesmen near Mont Ararat in northwestern Persia. The ringleader, Mir Ghaffar, was a sayed (this title means he was from the descendants of the prophet Mohammad) which made it difficult for the Persian Government to arrest him. The Labaree's affair was the first important event in diplomatic relations between two countries up to that time. Many approaches to retaliation were discussed and eventually his widow received a compensation and perpetrators escaped to Turkey (Yeselson, 1956); it was not surprising that he later came back without prosecution.

THE CONSTITUTIONAL REVOLUTION

Contact with the West contributed in developing modernist thinkers and a primary middle class in Iran; it also helped to create widespread social incommodity. The intellectuals, anxious for rapid progress, expressed increasing discontent with the slow pace of modernization and the high degree of corruption in the Qajar court. The traditional middle class, left defenseless against foreign forces who competed for raw resources in Iran, gradually came to the conclusion that the Qajars were interested more in empowering the state against society than in protecting the society against the imperial powers. Meanwhile, the general population, especially the urban artisans and the people from rural areas, suffered a slight decline in their standard of living, partly because of Western competition, partly because of greater taxes, and partly because the gross national product failed to keep up with the gradual growth in population (Abrahamian, 1982). By the end of the year 1905, protesters had started challenging the policies of Qajars and widespread corruption in governmental bodies. A series of demonstrations, clashes and events convinced Mozafar el-din Shah to sign the constitution in August 1906. He died shortly afterwards.

When Muhammad Ali Shah (r. 1907–9) ascended to the Qajar throne, he determined to reverse the constitution but lacked the military power to act decisively. The young shah was described by an American adviser to the court as "perhaps the most perverted, cowardly, and vice-ridden monster that had disgraced the throne of Persia in many generations" (Ward, 2009, p. 94). The members of the first Majles were compelled to fight for their very existence from the day that the Parliament was established. Their unequal struggle against "Muhammad Ali Shah and the foreign powers who largely aided him terminated when their Chamber was bombarded by Colonel Liakhoff and his Cossacks" (Shuster, 1912, p. 241). The country fell into turbulence and a popular uprising ensued in Iranian major cities. Mohammad Ali Shah was supported by the Russian forces and they jointly started suppressing the uprising. On April 21, 1909, Howard C. Baskerville, a Princetonian teacher who, having been employed by Presbyterian Mission to teach in their Tabriz School, took up arms with his students despite admonitions by the Mission and Consular authorities, and gave his life on the battlefield the first day of combat (Saleh, 1976). He was revered as a martyr and called "the American Lafayette." Many took his sacrifice as proof of how much more admirable Americans were than other foreigners (Kinzer, 2011). An unknown Persian poet wrote a famous poem on him and other victims of that battle: *"Bloody flowers are scattered everywhere; among them, I see a Christian flower."* In July 1909, the revolutionary forces marched into Tehran and Mohammad Ali Shah escaped to Russia.

In 1911, Iran was in a difficult situation. The country was in turmoil, the British and the Russians had divided Iran into two regions of influence through Anglo-Russian Entente of 1907, and corruption had paralyzed the country. In this situation, the Iranian Majles appointed American William Morgan Shuster to manage the financial and bureaucratic system of the country. Shuster, was appointed treasurer-general by a large majority in the Majles, and asserted his authority with a strong willpower. He investigated the Belgian customs officials who enjoyed Russian support; organized a special enforcement team to collect taxes throughout the country, even in the north; and confiscated the property of a prince whom the government announced to be a traitor to the country but who claimed Russian citizenship. This confiscation, in the words of the British minister, overfilled the tsar's "cup of indignation" (Abrahamian, 1982, pp. 108-109).

In 1911, the British started to occupy some southern Iranian territories. The Russians also threatened Iran partly to secure their markets, partly to enforce the 1907 Agreement, and partly to hinder the Shuster mission. The Russians, occupying Anzeli and Rasht in November 1911, gave a three point ultimatum to Iran: the firing of the Shuster mission; the promise not to employ foreign advisers in future without the consent of Britain and Russia; and the payment of an indemnity for the expeditionary force in Anzeli and Rasht. They threatened to occupy Tehran without further notice unless these demands were met within forty-eight hours (Abrahamian, 1982).

The humiliating invasion of two hated enemies made a public sentiment among Iranians. There was a strong public support for Shuster in Iran and the MPs were under heavy pressure to reject the ultimatum. Aref Qazvini, the famous revolutionary poet of the constitution era wrote "shame on the house from which the guest is ousted; give your life, but don't let your guest go; if Shuster goes from Iran, Iran will be ruined, Ah, young men, don't let our country be ruined, . . . we will be [symbol of] historical dishonor, if we let Shuster go." Three hundred women hid guns under their veils and marched towards Majles to talk to president. In the main hall they confronted him, and lest he and his associates should doubt their meaning, these cloistered Persian mothers, wives and daughters exhibited threateningly their guns, tore aside their veils, and confessed their decision to shoot their own husbands and sons, and leave behind their own dead bodies, if the deputies failed in their duty to uphold the liberty and dignity of the Persian people and nation (Shuster, 1912).

Nevertheless, scared from the angry ultimatum of Russians, the Iranian authorities expelled Shuster in December 2011. He left among tears of Iranians. Mohammad Ali Shah, the deposed king took the opportunity and gathered forces and attacked Iran to reclaim his thrown but failed and fled again and never returned. He, and all Iranian kings after him died in exile.

WORLD WAR I

Before and during World War I, Iran and United States both declared neutrality, and both were drawn into the war. Despite Iran's declaration of non-alignment, Russians from north and the British from the south started marching towards Tehran with a pretext that a German coup was about to occur. Although they came to gates of Tehran, they decided not to abolish the Qajar reign. They were only challenged by tribal or independent forces. Between late 1915 and mid- 1916, German influence among the southern tribes of Iran was at its height, but it soon ebbed with just a small pressure from the British. By encouraging rebellion among the Bakhtiari, Qashqai, and Tangistani tribes, German agent Wassmuss and his men briefly eliminated British control in all but a few territories in the south. The tribes diverted British troops from Iraq to Khuzestan and blocked British lines of communication between Tehran and the Persian Gulf ports (Ward, 2009). Before World War I, imperial Germany sought influence in Iran because Germany considered it, along with the crumbling Ottoman Empire, fertile ground for German trade. To Persia, Germany represented a source of top-quality Western technology and, since the Germans had no colonial record in the Middle East, a benign foreign power that could counter the British and the Russians (Lane, 1995).

On the other side of the globe, United States declared neutrality when World War I started. But, Germans made a mistake in 1915 and sank *Lusitania*, which was a British liner on her way to U.S. with 128 American citizens onboard. Therefore, United States was forced to enter the war in April 1917. Although America suffered 110000 casualties (43000 of them died of influenza) in World War I, the political, hegemonic and technologic achievements gained through this war made United States a superpower.

Col. J. N. Merrill, an American officer who had helped establish the Treasury Gendarmerie for Shuster and then advised the Government Gendarmerie, was recruited by the Iranian authorities to help build the South Persia Rifles and later served with the Kerman brigade (Ward, 2009). Hostility to the South Persia Rifles, including from its Iranian members, was so intense in late 1917 that the British approached the United States to take over the unit and substitute American officers for British ones to indulge the Iranians. Lacking officers with the language skills and territory knowledge to take on the task, Washington declined the request (Ward, 2009, p. 121). Also, hastening the departure of the British troops from Iran, Reza Khan (soon to be Reza Shah after successfully abolishing Qajar Dynasty with his own) sought aid from U.S. by both offering a northern concession to the Standard Oil Company of New York and appointing Dr. Arthur Millspaugh of the State Department as treasurer-general of Iran (Abrahamian, 1982). Upon arrival, Millspaugh found the Persian treasury empty and the fiscal administration a chaos, but with the assistance of the Persian authorities and the military, he solved some of the problems. A budget was established, taxes were collected, and brigandage greatly diminished (Colby & Williams, 1925). Yet, Millspaugh's endeavor to reduce the military budget in favor of economic reformations was not appealing to Reza shah and he dismissed Millspaugh in 1927.

Tehran had sent a delegation to the Paris Peace Conference of 1919 with exorbitant or superfluous demands. These included the abrogation of the 1907 Anglo- Russian Treaty; the abolition of the existing capitulations; the restoration of Iran's former imperial boundaries to the Oxus River in the northeast and to Baku, Yerevan, and Mosul in the northwest; and millions of dollars in war reparations. Ignoring the warring nations' violations of the Iranians' declared neutrality, the victors considered Iran a neutral power and deemed its representatives ineligible to sit at the negotiating table (Ward, 2009, p. 124). American Secretary of State Robert Lansing backed Iranians to abrogate 1919 Anglo-Persian Agreement which put Iran an economically and militarily dependent to England (Sicker, 2001) but the agreement was only abolished two years later by Iranian Majles. One of the reasons Americans denounced this agreement was that they needed Iranian oil while this agreement made Britain an unchallenged client or even owner of the Iranian oil reservoirs. In 1920-21, the giant Standard Oil Company of New Jersey (today's Exxon) began to negotiate for an oil concession in northern Iran, as did Sinclair Oil two years later. Further endeavors were made by Amiranian Oil, a subsidiary of the

Seaboard Oil Company, in 1937 and by Standard Vacuum Oil (today's Mobil) in 1940. Although these endeavors failed, they demonstrated the deep American interest in Iranian oilfields (Bill, 1988).

Drug abuse and production also affected Iran-U.S. relations. Opium had been produced in small quantities in Iran for centuries, but with the expansion of the Far Eastern market in the nineteenth century it took on a new importance (see books on Opium Wars for further details). By 1889 opium exports were estimated to be worth about 1.9 million *krans*, making it Iran's top export. Expansion in cultivation of opium increased domestic consumption of it. In 1904 it was estimated that of approximately 7,000 chests of opium produced that year in Iran, 2,000 were consumed domestically. Opium production was reputed to yield a profit for landowners about three times that of grain, and allegedly laborers who worked on opium fields received higher wages—or, in cases of sharecropping, a better division (Hansen, 2001). Persia depended deeply on opium-based revenue and had a deeply established opium culture of its own, one that transcended class lines. As a result, implementation of international accords by either country was not feasible in the 1920s and early 1930s. Diplomatic efforts to force compliance would almost certainly have failed (Walker, 2002, p. 459).

Prior to the second Geneva Opium Conference in 1925, Moshar-ol-Molk, Persian minister for foreign affairs, announced that it would be difficult to establish an international anti-opium movement. The foremost obstacle was that some countries would collapse if they stopped producing opium, even for those states fundamentally in agreement with the strict U.S. objectives. It was "impracticable suddenly to place a prohibition on [the opium business] without ... the substitution of other products for the production of opium, and the adoption of an appropriate decision whereby the domestic consumption of opium could be gradually stopped." Persia's request for a program of crop substitution was not appealing enough to U.S. officials. Elizabeth Washburn Wright, the widow of Dr. Hamilton Wright, had examined firsthand the opium situation there and became an advocate of increased silk production as a replacement for opium. She made the case for economic diversification in informal talks with the

Department of State and in her capacity as a consult to the Opium Advisory Committee. Arthur C. Millspaugh also made the connection between Persia's economic stability and the status of the opium business (Walker, 2002, pp. 460-461). He decided that opium cultivation should be prohibited but only during a period of some years and the process should be fairly gradual.

During 1920s, United States and Germany were trying to get involved in Iran and compete Soviet and Britain (Khatib-Shahidi, 2013). By the late 1920s Germany's advisers were in charge of Iran's arsenal, its pilots flew the German built planes of Iran's air force, and its technocrats assisted establish the Iranian National Bank. After the Nazis came to power in Germany, Reza Shah turned to Berlin as a source of technology and again as a counterweight to Russia. The Nazis, for their part, saw Iran as a key element in their strategy to isolate the Soviet Union and Britain's Indian Empire (Lane, 1995). In 1934 the shah, prompted by his Berlin legation, decreed that from now on, the name "Iran" would replace "Persia." A government pamphlet explained that while the latter name was associated with recent Qajar decadence and referred to the province of Fars only, the former invoked ancient glory and signified the birthplace of the Aryan race (Abrahamian, 1982). By the end of 1930s, 2000 German technicians, military advisors and agents were living and working in Iran. In 1939, Germany donated 7,500 German books to Iran, most on natural sciences and technology (Schayegh, 2009). Not only there were Germans, their pan Aryanist ideology was appealing to many Iranians. This ideology continued to have supporters in Iran for decades to come. For example, Tehran Asian Games of 1968 provided Iranians with the perfect opportunity to promote their agenda, especially as it coincided with the prevalence of television coverage. Having defeated Hong Kong, Taiwan and Burma in the early rounds, Iran's football team was pitted against Israel in the finals in front of an estimated 30,000 crowd at Amjadi'yeh stadium. Perhaps for the first time in Iranian history, cries of 'Death to Israel' were to echo around a football ground during what proved to be a narrow 2-1 victory for Iran's team. Anti-Jewish chants were reinforced by balloons thrown in the air which carried the Nazi swastika (Fozooni,

2004). Even in 2004, during a friendly match between Iran and Germany football teams in Azadi Stadium in Tehran, thousands of Iranians in the stadium shocked German football team members by performing Nazi salute. I still see many people in Iran who overtly or covertly express appreciation of "master race."

WORLD WAR II

Just like World War I, both Iran and United States announced their neutrality when the war broke out in 1939, and, just like the World War I, both were drawn in the war. We saw in the previous section that when the war broke out in 1939, Germans had strong influence in Iran. They were very successful at first months of war and many, including Reza Shah thought they would take the world soon. But, soon it was discovered that this would be far from easy. Reza Shah for once found himself on the wrong side of history, and the consequences of the unprovoked Allied invasion in World War II were disastrous for Iran. Its army was crushed, its monarch left the country, and the Red Army, saved from defeat by supply lines running across Iran, undermined Iran's sovereignty and territorial integrity. Perhaps most important for the future of Iran's armed forces, the United States was drawn inexorably into Iranian affairs. The Americans provided another opportunity for Iran's military leaders to embrace reform and address their long- standing problems with professionalism, training, and other aspects of military effectiveness (Ward, 2009).

By the end of World War II, America came to represent nearly half of world product and held a monopoly over nuclear weapons (Nye, 2013). This meant, America no longer could be equal with other countries. New policies had to be adopted and not all of them were appealing to other nations. One of them was privileges and protections American citizens enjoyed in other countries. Between 1855 and 1900, fifteen countries including United States obtained capitulation rights in Persia. Russia had already had its right as she had imposed it on Iran in Turkamanchai treaty

(Yeselson, 1956). For Americans, such immunities may be limited, that is, they were restricted to a specific territory or area. Or they may be unlimited or non-specific, that is, universal in their application. Guaranteeing such immunity, especially in Islamic and Asian countries, resulted in the eventual development of a system of extraterritoriality which the United States established through negotiation or unilateral imposition in fifteen countries: Algeria (Algiers), Borneo, China, Egypt, Iran (Persia), Japan, Korea, Libya (Tripoli), Madagascar, Morocco, Samoa, Tanzania (Zanzibari Muscat), Thailand (Siam), Tunisia (Tunis), and Turkey (Ottoman Porte) (Davids & Nielson, 2002, p. 81). Throughout the war, the American soldiers in Iran enjoyed de facto extraterritorial rights and were immune from prosecution under Iranian law (Bill, 1988).

In 1942 Millspaugh was recalled to Iran as a virtual economic manager. He brought the same competence and energy he had shown in his earlier mission; but after twenty years, both Millspaugh and Iran had changed. Millspaugh had lost most of his flexibility and Iran had gained a technical bureaucracy that, expectedly, regarded itself at least as competent as Millspaugh and his assistants (Cottam, 1979). Prime Minister Soheili, encouraged by Millspaugh, proposed to balance the budget by dramatically reducing the army from 65,000 men to 30,000. The shah objected and came up with the demand that the army should be increased to 108,000. Eventually, General Ridley who was the head of the American military mission set the figure at 86,000. The American minister commented, "the shah is averse to Millspaugh's curtailment of the military budget because this threatens his control of the army on which he hopes to maintain himself in power" (Abrahamian, 1982, p. 185). Disappointed from Iranian media, officials and even American embassy in Iran, Millspaugh went back to U.S. in 1945.

Americans believed Iran should be empowered militarily and philosophically against Soviet Union and hence, initiated some plans. The Gendarmerie's American advisory team, led by Col. H. Norman Schwarzkopf, was the first to arrive in August 1942. Schwarzkopf, a 1917 West Point graduate, had assisted to create and then led the New Jersey State Police, which gave him an excellent background for restoring the

Gendarmerie (Schwarzkopf had become famous for leading the investigation into the Lindbergh baby kidnapping and was the father of Gen. H. Norman Schwarzkopf Jr., the commander of U.S. and coalition forces in the Persian Gulf War of 1991) (Ward, 2009). Another mission to the Iranian army was headed between 1942 and 1947 by Gen. Clarence Ridley as intendant general to the Iranian Armed Forces. Ridley who had replaced Gen. John Greely, tried to empower the organization and forces of the badly weakened Iranian army (Bill, 1988).

In 1945, politically and militarily backed by Soviet Union, Azerbaijan Democratic Party declared autonomy from central government. Iran sent forces to reclaim vast north western territories but they were stopped by Russian army in Qazvin. America on this situation supported Iran and finally, the lost territories came back to Iran.

In 1946 American policy in avoiding intervention in Iran ended dramatically with the forceful support by Ambassador George Allen of the anti-Soviet policy of Ahmad Qavam and his successors (Cottam, 1979). Ahmad Qavam was born in 1878 into the most powerful aristocratic family in modern Iranian history. Eight individuals from this extended family served as prime ministers in nineteenth and twentieth century Iran including Qavam's brother Hassan Vosuq (Vosuq al-Dawlah) and his second cousin Muhammad Mosaddegh (Bill, 1988).

Tehran could not convince Washington that the 1947 Truman Doctrine, which provided substantial military aid to Greece and Turkey, should be extended to Iran. Similarly, Tehran's repeated requests inclusion among the recipients of the Marshall aid plan of 1948 or join the North Atlantic Treaty or some other similar defensive treaty with the U.S. also failed. Iran would only receive modest U.S. economic and military assistance (Bonakdarian, 2007).

Mutual Defense Assistance Act (MDAA) of 1949 gave an important opportunity to Iran. Signed into law by President Truman on 6 October of that year, the MDAA (later incorporated into the Mutual Security Act of 1950) gave the president broad power to conclude mutual defense assistance agreements with friendly nations and to provide these countries with a wide range of military items and services. In its initial authorization

Congress awarded $I billion to members of the newly formed North Atlantic Treaty Organization (NATO); $21 million to Greece and Turkey; $28 million to Iran, the Philippines, and South Korea; and $75 million for the "general area" of China. These appropriations were increased in subsequent years, reaching a peak of $5.2 billion after the outbreak of the Korean War (Klare, 2002, p. 109).

On December 2, 1944 Iranian popular MP Mosaddegh suddenly proposed an oil bill in the Majles that forbid the government from granting any oil concessions without Majles's approval. Masterfully presented, this proposal caught the leftist Tudeh party members off guard and passed overwhelmingly (Bill, 1988). And finally, forced by the Iranian nationalists and religious leaders, the Iranian oil industry was declared national on 20th March 1951. Worse than that for the British, on 28 April 1951, the Majles nominated Mosaddegh as new Prime Minister.

THE COUP

The post-WWII era witnessed a dramatic growth in leftism throughout the World. In some cases like Cuba, China and North Korea, there established a communist government and these governments are still there, though with different content. In the same era, Iran also witnessed a growth in communist activities and Tudeh party which was loyal to communism gained much popularity. The United States had concluded in late 1952 that Mosaddegh's government would not be able to solve the oil dispute with Britain and further worried that Iran was "at risk of falling behind the Iron Curtain." America became more open to the idea of a coup against Mosaddegh following Dwight D. Eisenhower's replacement of Harry S. Truman as President in 1952. Eisenhower was convinced, unlike Truman, that Mosaddegh would be incapable to resist a communist coup, should it be attempted by the Tudeh Party in Iran. With these Cold War motivations in mind, Eisenhower endorsed Operation Ajax (the American code name for the coup against Mosaddegh) in June 1953 (Garret-Rempel, 2008). During 1950s and 1960s, although Americans claimed to prefer liberal democracies as allies, they did not become involved in the domestic affairs of their clients unless there was communist subversion or invasion. The only criterion for an alliance with the United States became anticommunism (Kimball, 2002, p. 24). Therefore, overthrowing Mosaddegh did not spark serious objections in the international arena. In August 1953, the 37 year old Kermit Roosevelt, Jr. who was grandson of U.S. president Theodore Roosevelt, took charge in CIA's operation to return Mohammad Reza Pahlavi, the former Shah of Iran, back to power and overthrow Mosaddegh's government. Nobody was sure about the success of the operation but it eventually succeeded. United States handed the Government to General Fazlollah Zahedi and assisted it by 2 million dollar. Dr. Hossein Fatemi who was Minister of Foreign Affairs in Mosaddegh government was eventually arrested and executed. Mosaddegh lived his last years of life under house arrest. Mosaddegh still enjoys wide range of popularity among Iranians as much as United States is blamed for Operation Ajax. Even today after more than 6 decades, there are still debates in both countries if Operation Ajax was a mistake. In February 2016 for example, when Bernie Sanders was criticizing American foreign policy with Hillary Clinton in a debate, he brought up the issue of overthrowing Mosaddegh in Iran to show how Americans did mistakes in different parts of the world.

The containment ring around Russia and China was nearly completed with the Baghdad Pact of 1955, which grouped Iran, Iraq, Pakistan, Turkey, and Great Britain into an alliance. The United States never formally joined the alliance (renamed the Central Treaty Organization, or CENTO, after Iraq dropped out in 1959 following a coup against the pro-British Hashimite monarchy) (Kimball, 2002, p. 24). On 5 March 1959 bilateral defense pacts were signed with Iran, Pakistan, and Turkey (DeConde, Burns, & Logevall, 2002).

Well into the 1960s, the Americans came to conclusion that the solution to Iran's security problems was economic development and political reform, but the shah of Iran proved more persistent in empowering and expanding Iran's army. The U.S. military mission was reorganized in 1950 as the U.S. Military Assistance Advisory Group (MAAG) to train and help the Iranian army in using the increased military aid and equipment from United States. The Joint Chiefs of Staff reported that keeping the natural defensive barrier provided by the Zagros Mountains under Allied control was very important to regional defense plans (Ward, 2009, p. 191).

When John F. Kennedy came to power in 1961, Iran was on the verge of a revolution against the Shah's reforms. In fact, at this time several forces which pursued a revolution, joined by feudals who saw the land reforms of Shah against their interests, started an unsuccessful uprising. To stabilize the situation, Shah's Administration attempted to promote democracy through a development plan based on the tenets of modernization theory (Collier, 2013). Nevertheless, Washington instead decided to bolster the Shah's regime to carry out social and economic reforms that coalesced as the Shah's White Revolution in 1963. Policy-makers relied in part on a psychological profile of Iran to shape their decisions, believing that the Iranian people were psychologically unprepared to rule, and that the Shah was psychologically unprepared to give up power (Warne, 2013). John F. Kennedy, had an articulated ideological approach to foreign policy based on economic rather than military aid, and he stated that he did not like authoritarian regimes, such as that of the Shah of Iran. It is thus understandable why some historians have described the Kennedy years as the nadir in relations between Iran and United States, after which the transformation of relations between the two nations began to gradually develop (McGlinchey, 2013). This development was very important in providing the most sophisticate American weapons for Iran in the next years.

Iran progressed from a low-priority military assistance recipient in the 1950s to a military credit purchase partner in 1964. The change was characterized by frequent difficulties and disagreements as the Shah's demands and Washington's ability and/or desire to fulfill those demands rarely coalesced until the end of the Johnson Administration. In 1971, Iran was the biggest customer for America's arms. One year later, in May 1972, the Shah agreed to a deal with Richard Nixon that gave him a blank check to purchase whatever arms he wanted, except nuclear weapons, and to make those purchases without any interference or oversight from united states; in this sense, it was a highly unique agreement. What followed was an annual multi-billion dollar arms purchase pattern that made Iran within a few short years from a relatively underdeveloped country militarily into one that wielded one of the most technologically advanced military forces in the world (McGlinchey, 2013). Although U.S. arms exports to Iran were motivated primarily by national security considerations, the Nixon administration was not unmindful of the economic dimensions of exporting arms to Iran. Facing a significant balance-of-payments crisis as a result of Vietnam War costs and the OPEC oil price increase of 1973, United States came to conclusion that military sales were practical means for recouping some of the massive dollar outflows. Accordingly, Nixon gave a green light to U.S. arms firms to provide the Shah of Iran with some of America's most advanced and sophisticated weapons, including F-4, F-5, and F-14 warplanes (Klare, 2002, p. 112).

Along with military development, the socioeconomic development was also hastened largely by the increasing oil prices. Hitting a new record of $555 million in 1963-1964, the oil revenue continued to climb reaching $958 million in 1968-1969, $1.2 billion in 1970-1971, $5 billion in 1973-1974, and, after the quadrupling of oil prices, near $20 billion in 1975-1976. Between 1964 and 1974, the cumulative oil income came to $13 billion. Between 1974 and 1977, it reached $38 billion (Abrahamian, 1982). Thins money could help the country becoming one of the most technologically sophisticated countries but what is called "oil curse" started to turn shah's aspirations into the most terrible nightmare. Incompetence and corruptions started to spread down the bureaucratic pyramid. In the words of a publication associated with the Pentagon, "by 1977 the sheer scale of corruption had reached a boiling point . . . Even conservative estimates indicate that such [bureaucratic] corruption involved at least a billion dollars between 1973 and 1976" (Abrahamian, 1982, p. 449). This situation created a great class struggle and made leftism even more appealing to young educated Iranians.

Shah also increased the annual military budget from $293 million in 1963 to $1.8 billion in 1973, and, after the quadrupling of oil prices, to $7.3 billion in 1977 (at 1973 prices and exchange rates). Buying more than

$12 billion worth of Western-manufactured weapons between 1970 and 1977 alone, the shah built up a great ultra-sophisticated arsenal that included, among other arms, 20 F14 Tomcat warplanes with long-range Phoenix missiles, 190 F4 Phantom fighter planes, 166 F5 fighter aircraft, 10 Boeing 707 transport planes, 800 helicopters, 28 hovercrafts, 760 Chieftain tanks, 250 Scorpion tanks, 400 M47 tanks, 460 M60 tanks, and 1 Spruance naval destroyer. By 1977, Iran had the biggest navy in the Persian Gulf, the most sophisticated air force in the Middle East, and the fifth largest army in the world. As if this were not enough, the shah placed orders for another $12 billion worth of weapons to be delivered between 1978 and 1980. These included 202 helicopter gunships, 326 helicopters special in troop carrying, 160 F16s, 209 F4s, 7 Boeing planes, 3 Spruance destroyers, and 10 nuclear submarines. Arms dealers started to jest that the shah read their manuals in much the same way as other men read *Playboy* (Abrahamian, 1982).

This massive U.S. arms transfers to Iran at this time alarmed many members of Congress at the scale of the sales program and its potential for abuse. These concerns were increased by reports that U.S. arms firms had used bribery to solicit major orders from Iran. After investigating these accusations, the Senate Foreign Relations Committee concluded in 1976 that U.S. weapons sales to Iran were "out of control" (Klare, 2002, p. 112). Carter, despite strong congressional criticism, sold the shah of Iran sophisticated AWACS radar systems (McCrisken, 2002, p. 102). In December 1977, President Carter visited Iran and lauded it as "an island of stability in one of the most troubled areas of the world." He declared that the Shah of Iran was a great leader who had won "the respect and the admiration and love" of his nation. What both the Shah and President Carter had failed to understand was the underlying dissident culture and how little time the Shah had to enact his policy agenda (Cook & Rawshandil, 2009, p. 19). Widespread criticism of Iran's human rights record in the West convinced Jimmy Carter to raise the subject during his election campaign. Among the most serious assertions were those from US Congressional committees which raised doubts about the stability of the

Shah's regime, and argued that he should not be sold the sophisticated American arms he had asked for (Shahidi, 2007).

In May 1977, Secretary of State Vance visited Iran, where he held important meetings with the Shah. on May 13, during two and a half hour meeting at Niavaran Palace, Vance invited the Shah to Washington in November, told him that the United States had decided to finalize the pending sale of 160 F-16 aircraft, promised that the president would try to convince congress to approve the Shah's request for the sophisticated airborne warning and control system (AWACS). He also said that the U.S. appreciates the liberalization and open door policy of the Shah (Bill, 1988). During one of his regular military parades in Tehran in October 1978, the shah of Iran hosted a delegation of American military officials that included American Army colonel Colin Powell. As the colonel sat in the reviewing stand, an elite troop named the "Immortals" in conscious imitation of fabled Persian warriors of Achamenids marched in front of them. Powell, a future chairman of the Joint Chiefs of Staff and secretary of state, noted favorably their tailored uniforms and martial élan (Ward, 2009, p. 1).

Powell and Vance were high rank American officials who visited Tehran during the 1970s, but in fact, the number of ordinary Americans in Iran's 1970s was astonishing. Michael Axworthy writes: "There were Americans everywhere in Teheran (sic) in the 1970s. Author and professor James A. Bill has estimated that between 800,000 and 950,000 Americans lived in or visited Iran between 1944 and 1979 and that the number resident there increased from fewer than 8,000 in 1970 to nearly fifty thousand in 1979. Ten thousand were employed in defense industries around Isfahan alone" (Van Gorder, 2010, p. 14). Also, at the end of the shah's regime, all of those American personnel employed to work in the Iranian military, with exception of six senior officers were paid for and maintained by Iran. Their salaries, allowances, transportation, the schooling of their children, and all other incidentals were financed and facilitated by the Iranian government. They wore arm patches indicating that they were members of the Iranian armed forces (Sullivan, 1981). This, along with unprecedented dependence of the shah's regime on the United

States, the memoirs of 1953 coup, and cultural pessimism embedded in the Iranian-Islamic culture about American and Western culture in general, and a global leftist movement which blamed America for all vices in the world contributed to the development of a widespread anti-American sentiment in Iran. And, this anti-American sentiments along with inequality, corruption, uneven development, the global climate of rebellion in the 1960s and 1970s in the modern world, influence of leftist ideas in youth subcultures and last but not least, the policy of open doors imposed by President Carter contributed to one of the greatest American loses in the contemporary history.

THE ISLAMIC REVOLUTION

In February 1979, a popular uprising in Iran toppled down one of the most powerful men in the world. This revolution also turned politics upside down. In one swift blow, it wiped out Americans' "island of stability" in the region, their main "policemen" in the Persian Gulf, their major customer of high-tech military products, their main recycler of petrodollars, their second-largest reservoir of reliable and relatively cheap oil, and last, but not least, Israel's valuable friend in the hostile Arab and Muslim world. In other words, the revolution, in one swift blow, annihilated the famous Nixon doctrine that had appointed the shah to be the guardian of America's strategic interests and provider of oil in the Persian Gulf. In Kissinger's words, the shah supported the United States on virtually every major foreign policy issue. In return, the United States gave the shah "everything he wanted"- including help in starting a nuclear program (Abrahamian, 2004, p. 98). The shah had one of the most effective and sophisticated armies in the world, but, a widespread internal unpopularity took him down.

Yet, Anti-American sentiments was one important driving force for the Iranian revolutionists. On February 10, 1979, a notable American journalist was killed while trying to cover clashes in Dushan Tapeh, Tehran. Four days later, Iranian revolutionary forces attacked the U.S. embassy in

Tehran and took Ambassador William H. Sullivan along with other employees and diplomats. They soon released the hostages (Sullivan, 1981). After the revolution, Iranians urged that the United States must extradite the shah, who was there for medical treatment (or at least it was claimed that he was there to do so). When they did not get their favorite response, they stormed in the U.S. embassy and took diplomats and employees. They later released women and black hostages but took others for 444 days. Now, it was Americans time to develop anti-Iranian sentiments.

The uprising of the Iranian people, the collapse and exile and subsequent death of the shah of Iran, the establishment of an Islamic government in Tehran and the political and ideological transformation of Iran –symbolized most painfully for Americans by the attack on the U.S. embassy in Tehran and the holding of U.S. citizens hostage for 444 days- represented nothing less than a political explosion in one of the most sensitive regions of the world (Sick, 1985, p. VII). All through the Revolution, U.S. perception of Iran was based on inexact and perhaps inaccurate evaluation of the situation in Iran. This is sometimes blamed on the U.S. withdrawal of many of its intelligence assets from Iran out of respect for the Shah. The misunderstandings and lack of information factored into the Revolution and subsequent hostage crisis (Cook & Rawshandil, 2009). American and international media broadly covered the hostage crisis. As Saied (1980) said, these negative perceptions were further intensified by references to Iranian leaders as "anti-modern, "fundamentalist," and "irrational;" and referred to the people in Iran as "religious fanatics," "leftist-backed," and "backward." Thus, as Said has commented: "for however much the Iranian had gained his or her freedom from the shah and the U.S., he or she still appeared on American TV screens as part of a large anonymous mob, deindividualized, dehumanized—and *ruled again* as a result" (Keshishian, 2000, pp. 99-100).

Americans felt very humiliated. Under the pressure from public, Carter completed his series of mistakes and approved a rescue mission. By April 1980, Delta Force and other units taking part in the rescue operation were ready, and on April 11, 1980, President Carter authorized Operation Eagle Claw, which began and ended tragically on April 24, 1980, on the desert sands of Iran. The U.S. forces had sent eight helicopters but problems caused only six to get to the destination. At site, one other helicopter broke up and hence, Carter aborted the operation but when helicopters wanted to take off, one of them crushed into a transport airplane which contained both servicemen and jet fuel and 8 American servicemen and soldiers were killed at once (Celmer, 1987). This was a debacle and someone had to be found to help. Saddam Hussein, took the opportunity and attacked Iran in September 1980 with green light from United States. The war started very good for Saddam, but after 8 years, he got nothing.

Though during 1980s United States helped Iraq and Iran according to situation, by 1988 Reagan administration put heavy pressure on Iran to accept the cease fire terms. Saddam's frequent chemical raids were overlooked, some Iranian navy ships were shot and sank and even United States' USS Vincennes shot down an Iranian civilian airplane with 290 people onboard. United States also had started to fight in other fronts. Problems resulting from the Iranian Revolution led to establishment at The Hague of the Iran-United States Claims Tribunal in 1981. It was reported in April 2000 that the tribunal had settled 3,700 claims cases involving hundreds of billions of dollars (Davis, 2002, p. 70).

Although the end of the Cold War alleviated some of the urgency once associated with decisions regarding arms transfers, such transactions remained a significant factor in U.S. foreign policy. In the mid-1990s, for example, the United States arranged major new weapons deliveries to Saudi Arabia, Kuwait, and the United Arab Emirates in order to enhance their capacity to resist a possible attack by Iran or Iraq (Klare, 2002, p. 105).

When Khatami came to power in 1997, he said he wanted to solve Iran's problem in the U.S. When September 11 attacks happened, Iran accused "terrorist Taliban" responsible and allowed some citizens to hold night street vigils to express sympathy with America. Jack straw, the

British foreign minister, visited Tehran for what he termed a "historic visit." He thanked Iran for its help over Afghanistan and announced that "Iran stood together with Britain in opposing terrorism of any kind." Colin Powell, the U.S. secretary of State, shook hand with the Iranian foreign minister and told media that Tehran would be included in the coalition against terrorism (Abrahamian, 2004, p. 95).

When the United States invaded Afghanistan, Iran offered to rescue stranded pilots, opened up its ports for the transit of humanitarian aid, and asked the anti-Taliban Northern Alliance whom it had armed to fully cooperate with the coalition forces. What is more, Iran was crucial in Geneva in putting forward a deal by which Hamid Karzai, the American favorite, was nominate a president of Afghanistan. American diplomats acknowledged in Congress that Iranians had been "extremely helpful in getting Karzai in as the president. They had been even walked arm-in-arm with American negotiators in Geneva" (Abrahamian, 2004, p. 96).

Everything went on as it seemed the two countries were going to befriend again, but, to the surprise of Iranians, in his State of the Union Address to Congress on January 29, 2002, President Bush used the expression, the Axis of Evil, to include Iraq, Iran, and North Korea: "States like these, and their terrorist allies, constitute an Axis of Evil, arming to threaten the peace of the world. By seeking weapons of mass destruction, these regimes pose a grave and growing danger" (Heradstveit & Bonham, 2007, p. 422).

In 2005, when Mahmoud Ahmadinejad came to power in Iran, all doors were closed and Iran and the U.S. again became determined enemies. It was only by 2013 presidential election of Iran that both countries again found themselves on the negotiation table. And, it was in the same year that Iran and U.S. presidents talked over phone after more than three decades of fierce enmity. Rouhani administration proved to be willing in sorting out things with the U.S., but, Iran and U.S.'s enmity is something both countries are benefiting from it and hence the friendship will not take place in the near future.

DISCUSSION

Although "Iran" and "U.S." are associated with enmity, distrust and hatred, the two countries have had a history of friendly relations. In fact, if we accept that these two countries have about two centuries of contacts, it could be said that a majority of this time was passed in friendship and mutual respect.

America came as a third power, a savior from treacherous exploitation of Iran by British and Russian empires. During World War I, America was still benevolent to Iran but, the rise of Nazi Germany made the previous deal impossible. During early 1940s, United States enjoyed a very positive image throughout Iranian society. As the Iranian-American interaction increased through the decade, however, that image was somewhat darkened. By 1950, Iranians had a partly positive, partly negative view of America and Americans. This change resulted partly from the sudden influx of Americans into Iran and the increasing intervention of U.S. policy on the Iranian affairs (Bill, 1988). Washington was highly reluctant to assume extensive responsibility in Iran until the months leading up to the 1953 coup, while periodically endorsing Iranian nationalist and democratic aspirations (Bonakdarian, 2007, p. 10). The American coup of 1953 ruined decades of endeavors by American missionaries and advisers to build trust among Iranian people.

At this epoch, foreign professionals and technocrats were employed or invited by the Iranian government. Following them came the culture of the consumer society: films, Coca Cola and hotdogs, yielding alienation for the elder Iranian generation and seduction for the Iranian youth (Stümpel-Hatami, 1999). The whole cultural pillars of the Iranian society was about to be replaced by values which was even against the Christian missionaries' cause. In 1979, Iranian people surprised the world and chose Islam as their way of life. As we said, these changes along with other factors contributed to an uprising which culminated into an Islamic Revolution.

In a short period of time, two countries started to fight each other and this hate was augmented by the coming years. Iran and United States will not be friends, at least in the near future. Yet, that does not mean that cultural ties between two countries were cut. Notable American scholars like Williams Jackson, A. Olmstead, Eric Schmidt, Harold Lamb, Arthur Upham Pope, George Cameron, Will Durant, Richard Fry, T. Cuyler Young, Donald Wilber, Myron Bement Smith, Richard Ettinghausen, Joseph Upton and many others devoted their lives to the cause of Persian and Iranian studies (Saleh, 1976). Many are still living through pages and pixels. Also, there are Iranians in the U.S. who are bridging both societies wittingly or unwittingly.

On another front, intercultural communication has been on the rise. From the 1830 century to the beginning of the 20th century, only 130 Iranians are known to have gone to the U.S. According to the 1995 Statistical Yearbook of the U.S. Immigration and Naturalization Service (INS), data were not reported separately for Iran in the first quarter of the 20th century. But it has been said that since 1925, a total of 215,325 Iranians have been allowed to permanently reside in the U.S. From 1925 until 1950, only 1,816 Iranians had been admitted as permanent residents. By 1960, this number had risen to 3,388, and by 1990 it had reached 10,339 annually. Although these figures include both immigrants accepted and those who adjusted their status after arrival, they show that the bulk of Iranian permanent migration to the U.S. has occurred since the 1960s (Bozorgmehr, 1998). Today, half a million Iranian-American citizens are living in the U.S., mainly in California. These people have to interact with other citizens and later in this book we will see how this has been important in shaping cross cultural schemata about Iranians.

Chapter 4

STUDYING AMERICAN CROSS CULTURAL SCHEMATA

INTRODUCTION

As I said earlier in this book, this study is going to explore cross cultural schemata American people have of Iranians. I tried to give a historical-political context in which these schemata take shape. I also presented a short critical review on the role of the media in shaping these schemata, though most of the time, I made it clear, they do so unwittingly. Here, I want to present a framework in which mental images including cross cultural schemata are developed.

One of the main issues concerning all branches of the human sciences, is the question of how we know the world. Answering this crucial question is what distinguishes many philosophical schools of thought. Almost all philosophers have allocated part or all of their works and even lives exploring answers to this question. We know human mental abilities are ordered into a complex system, the overall function of which is said to be cognition. Cognition is the way Homo sapiens perceive and learn, how they think and reason, even how they remember and imagine. As this process is very routine to all of us, we take it as reasonable and simple but we must know that there may be many complications. It seems that the nature of cognition will continue to remain a realm of debate among philosophers, biologists, the clergy and recently, artificial intelligence experts. Of course we are aware that cognition is something that its very existence is depended on existence of an organ named "brain." But, this does not mean we know enough about it. After hundreds of years of studying the brain, the human science still cannot properly explain how this incredible organ inside our skulls could get beyond itself and reach out into the world. It could be said that everyone who has gone to college and taken some courses in physiology, neurology, or psychology would have the same difficulty (Sokolowski, 2000). Moreover, it seems that all human brains work similarly and there is no education that can thoroughly substitute the current system that is mainly based on categorization.

When we place some new data from our new experiences into an existing class of data in our brains, tagging this new experience as an instance of something we are familiar with, we are in fact categorizing the experience. Obviously, we categorize often without needing to consciously and intentionally run this process, but, it is still the case that categorization does not take place in one step. Before we can categorize something, it must first be perceived. Thus some preliminary cognitive activity has already fulfilled that allows people to focus attention on a specific thing once we start to categorize (Moskowitz, 2005). In this preliminary attempt to identify something, we search for closest match between the features of the perceived object and the features in potential categories to which this object might belong. Therefore, a category is called to surface in our mind whenever we encounter stimuli in the environment that possess features of the category. Category activation is the last stage of an interaction between some stimulus in the environment and the human perceptual system, in which we will give a heightened state of accessibility and readiness to a certain category. Human beings, therefore, do not directly activate or awaken a category from its shelf in memory. This responsibility is to some extent left to cues. Cues are information that exist exterior to the mind, such as the characteristics of the object encountered in the environment that have inherent or acquired associations with the category which we need to activate. A certain cue cannot immediately trigger or activate a category, even if its place is within that category. Rather, the activation level of the category will increase, like a battery accumulating a charge. Once the level of activation reaches a specified threshold, the category is activated. The lesson is that even if a certain stimulus does not sufficiently activate the category, a weak stimulus that comes along soon after may add just enough stimulus to push the accumulated charge above threshold and initiate activation of the category (Moskowitz, 2005). All the same process is used to know, remember or perceive other people.

SOCIAL COGNITION

One of the defining characteristics that sets Homo sapiens beings apart from other animals is not only our capacity to think, but also our ability to be aware of what we are thinking. A second characteristic, although shared with some other species, is our sociability and the crucial importance we place on relationships with others. These two characteristics together create what social cognition is about (Pennington, 2000). Social cognition, therefore, is not different from other kinds of cognition. But, the point is that, as other humans are, like us, very complicated, social cognition is known to be much more sophisticated as compared to other cognitions like for example, our cognition of objects.

Although making sense of the behavior of other people is central to our daily functioning and even survival, making sense of other minds poses one of the gravest challenges to human cognition. Compared to the causes of everyday physical events and objects, those factors influencing the behavior of people are far more changing and far less steady. Nevertheless, although we can never directly access another person's mind, we can make sense of others by accounting for the fact that each member of a society has unique intentions, motivations, beliefs, and desires guiding his or her behavior. To put it another way, despite scarce input about the contents of others' mental states, interactants are able to reconstruct the content of other minds with tremendous accuracy and complexity. Given the unique demands of considering other people's mental state, psychologists have become increasingly interested in whether social cognition can be fulfilled on the basis of the same mental processes we deploy for nonsocial purposes or whether we instead draw on a set of processes specifically responsible for meeting the unique cognitive demands of interpersonal interaction (Zaki & Ochsner, 2011). While some psychologists, such as Simon (1976), see no substantial difference between cognition and social cognitions, others like Zajonc (1989) believe there is a gap between the two. Anyway, as I said earlier, my view is closer to the former perspective and I take it that there is no fundamental difference between social cognition and other kinds of cognition.

One important issue in social cognition is "face." The human ability to understand faces is particularly impressive when we think of it in the context of the many different social inferences we perform, as well as the high level of accuracy and relatively low effort with which they are typically made. Even very short glimpses at a person's face may give us enough cue to gain information relevant to determining his or her age, race, health state, emotional state, and identity. Face perception has also been said to be something that is supporting insights about social category membership. All of these inferences are central to social perception, but it is the latter category of inferences that are of particular importance (Ito, 2011). Later in this book we see how American respondents refer to faces when they reported their cross cultural schemata of Iranians.

We can highlight three cognitive processes that we examine to our social world. First, information we receive about members of our group or people outside our own group or groups is *interpreted;* this means that insight is given meaning often by both the social context and our previous knowledge, cultural values, etc. Rarely do we interpret someone's behavior in a vacuum; what we know about someone all feed into the interpretation made. Second, social data is *analyzed,* this means that a preliminary interpretation may be adjusted, changed or even rejected. For instance, whilst the first impression we make of another person —mainly through his or her face, as I said- may be extraordinarily effective, further acquaintance and interaction with the same person may seriously change this impression. Third, social information is *stored in memory* and we may recall or retrieve it. Recalling information from memory may need considerable effort; effort that we sometimes do not like to make. And, we should add that the term "social world" refers *both* to other people and ourselves. Theory and research in social cognition may equally be about other people, ourselves, and, which is most probably, about ourselves in interaction with other people (Pennington, 2000).

SCHEMATA

In the previous section we saw how all cognitive activities necessarily involve some kind of classification. One type of such classifications that according to Pennington (2000) makes a less prejudiced image of other people is called "schema." The concept of the schema can be traced back to Plato and Aristotle, but Kant is generally known to be the first to talk about schemata as organizing structures that mediate how we see and interpret the world (McVee, Dunsmore, & Gavelek, 2005). In psychology, the term schema is typically first attributed to Bartlett (1932) who was a cognitive psychologist whose research on how stories are transmitted from person to person, especially stories from a culture different from that of the original people, inspired many researchers in the field of literature studies. When stories come from foreign cultures, there is always a possibility that the content and form of the story are unfamiliar to the perceiver. Bartlett specifically studied such unusually structured stories and found that the stories seemed to evolve as they were transmitted, gradually becoming more coherent to the perceivers, but losing some important details from the original version. He reasoned that people have prior knowledge about the form and structure of stories, and that the new information is interpreted and recollected in the context of their prior structures. These schemas were said to transform the way the information is codified and remembered, thus leading to the generation of stories that were more coherent with the perceivers' schemas and further removed from the original "foreign" form. The schema was said to be an abstracted set of prior information about a class of events that provides emergent meaning to understanding and memorize the events (Moskowitz, 2005). This, however, does not mean that every group has its own schemata. As McVee et al. (2005) argue, schemata emerge from the social interactions between an individual and his or her environment and therefore, it is not unlikely that through time, we see changing and even opposing schemata in every social group.

As the nature of schema is evasive and abstract, there has been different conceptual approaches to it. Alloy, Clements, & Koenig (1993, p. 57) defined schemata as "organized representations of prior knowledge in memory that guide information processing." According to Mandler (1979), a schema "is formed on the basis of past experience with objects, scenes, or events and consists of a set of (usually unconscious) expectation about what things look like and /or the order in which they occur" (Kellogg, 1997, p. 167). For Fiske and Linville (1980, p. 543) "the schema concept refers to cognitive structures of organized prior knowledge, abstracted from experience with specific instances; schemata guide the processing of new information and the retrieval of stored information.' Endicott and his colleagues (2003, p. 408) give a more compact definition of schema: "the term, schema, refers to a network of information that functions to organize an individual's knowledge and experiences." Werner et al. (1998) hold that the schema is a generic term for a variety of memory structures that lead people to expect to see or experience certain things in certain settings. For Foldy (2006, p. 351) "schemata are knowledge structures or mental templates that individuals impose on an information environment to give it form or meaning." Oller (Oller, 1995, p. 282) suggested that from Piaget (1947, 1952) forward, the term schema has come to describe the kind of organization that enables its user to handle certain kinds of tasks more efficiently than would otherwise be possible. Fiske and Taylor (1991, p. 139), define schemas, or schemata, as "people's cognitive structures that represent knowledge about a concept or type of stimulus, including its attributes and the relation among its attributes." These structures are organized as prior knowledge and shape what is perceived and remembered, but they involve people and situations. "In general, when a dimension is important to you in yourself, it is salient to you in others" (Fiske & Taylor, 1991, p. 168). Nishida (1999, p. 577), holds a similar stance: "Schemata are generalized collections of knowledge of past experiences which are organized into related knowledge groups and are used to guide our behaviors in familiar situations."

Schemata facilitate and may determine the way we encode new information. For example, schemata influence what to pay attention to and what not; usually information coherent with a schema is stored in memory and inconsistent information removed or forgotten. Schemata help us to process information effectively. Schemata also influence what we remember about everyday situations and may cause us to go beyond the information given when trying to recall details of an incident (Pennington, 2000). In fact, the complex system of mind uses schemata, sometimes to assess other or the same schemata.

What distinguishes schemata from stereotypes is that the schemata are more flexible while the stereotypes are mainly solid. As Holliday et al. (2004) argue, the hardening of schemata could be said to suggest a sloppiness of thought when this happens. A schema, therefore, may become a stereotype when this occurs. The media can encourage people in sloppiness of thought by frequently portraying issues in a reduced and inaccurate way. This may, of course, serve political purposes (Holliday, Kullman, & Hyde, 2004). Therefore, we can see that in the academic literature the implication of the word stereotype is generally negative, whereas schema is a more neutral term, simply referring to a template that helps people process information more efficiently (Foldy, 2006).

The special theoretical approach one takes towards schemata, will yield different classification of them. Pennington (2000) classifies schemata into five themes: social schemas, person schemas, self-schemas, role schemas and event schemas. Taylor and Crocker (1981) offer five types of schemata: person schema, self-schema, role schema, event schema, and context–free schema. Imamoğlu (2007) replaces context-free schema with "place" schema while Fiske and Taylor (1991) delete context-free schemata and reduce the subcategories into 4. Again Schrodt (2006) adds the "group schema" to classification of Fiske and Taylor and increases the number of the types of schemata into 5. Corte (2007) goes further and divides self-schemata into "positive" and "negative" self-schemata. Some scholars consider self-schemata in terms of appearance schemata (see for example Jung and Lee, 2006).

Werner et al. (1998) believe that there are three kinds of schemata: frames, prototypes and stereotypes (as we saw earlier, the present study does not perceive stereotypes as schemata), and scripts. Oller classified schemata into three kinds: content, formal and abstract schemata (Sasaki, 2000), while Mayer et al. (1993) present type schemata, significant other schemata, and "other" kinds of schemata. Sew Ming (1997) considered content schemata and placed them vis-à-vis linguistic schemata. Malcolm and Sharifian (2002) argue that each type of schemata can be universal, idiosyncratic, cultural, or societal. Meanwhile, Pazy (1994) recognized 11 types of schemata and categorized ten of them in three types: time, scope, and agent schemata. For Nishida (1999), there are 8 types of schemata: fact-and-concept, person, self, role, context, procedure, strategy, and emotion schemata. According to Stockwell (2003), schemata can be divided into situational types (such as the restaurant), personal schemata (that embody behavior and social roles) and instrumental schemata (that contain our knowledge of undertaking actions and practicing skills).

CROSS CULTURAL SCHEMATA

The kind of schemata which we consider in this study is cross cultural schemata. Cross cultural schemata which are sometimes simply called "cultural schemata" first used to refer to patterns of understanding texts and sagas from other cultures, but, gradually it was adopted in intercultural communication studies to study how people see others, particularly when their cultures are different. The present study also uses the term "cross cultural schemata" in this sense. In 2009 I published an article with Professor D. Ray Heisey from Kent State University. As I mentioned in chapter 1, that study included Iranian students at University of Tehran and American students at Kent State University. We simply asked them to express their impression of the word "an Iranian citizen" or "an American citizen." In that study we defined cross cultural schemata as "abstract mental structures that one makes according to his/her past experiences or shared knowledge about the members of other cultures and thus makes them more understandable" (Shahghasemi & Heisey, 2009, p. 146).

In the first chapter we saw how cross cultural schemata can produce negative and image of people; yet, people may sometimes not stop there and put these negative images in action. We reviewed the work of some scholars who seriously criticized the West for making categorizations of other people. Yet, we see most of these theorizations themselves use the same categorizations against "the West!" This is beside the fact that they largely see unnecessary to criticize the image media in other parts of the world show of the West and Western people. My stance to cross cultural schemata, therefore, is not negative. Cross cultural schemata are needed to understand other people. This is the only way to do so. Our mind has no other tool, except categorization. Moreover, not all cross cultural schemata are negative. Cross cultural schemata of Asian students' skill in math, Italians being great lovers, and English people being polite are not negative.

Therefore, this study takes cross cultural schemata as something neutral per se. Based on occasion, they might be negative, positive or stay neutral, though this negativity, positivity or neutrality is itself evaluative. They can be manipulated to serve political purposes as much as they can be employed to build friendship and harmony. If we look at the mediascape, we see that a great deal of what is portrayed in the media, is in fact a voluntary or involuntary endeavor to build a cross cultural schema which most of the time favors the media owners – and we know well that today media are mainly governed by financial mandate, which means they have to entertain more people to be able to sell more eyeballs to advertisers. Later in this book we see how media have affected cross cultural schemata Americans have of Iranians.

METHOD AND PROCEDURE

Before starting this project, I was thinking of telephone survey. I thought I could buy a VOIP service, collect a number of American landline telephones, and start sampling. Making phone calls to U.S. from Iran is expensive and VOIP services were not so much rampant in Iran. Moreover, Iran was under heavy international sanctions and it deemed uneasy to carry out such an international project. Another problem was the sensitivity of the issue in Iran. What could be the reaction of the Iranian authorities, had I revealed results that were not appealing to them? Some professors in the Department of Communication warned me that I should not be so ambitious because if I failed in my project, I would have lost two years. Finally, after my supervisor witnessed my conviction, approved my proposal and gave me a green light to start my work. As I said, Iran was (and is) under international sanction and there was no possibility of international payment Iran. So, I contacted a friend in Norway, he bought me a VOIP account with 20 Euro and I paid the price in Iranian currency to his father who lived in Iran. This VOIP account had the advantage that you could call landline telephones in the U.S. at no cost. I collected some landline numbers in the state of Pennsylvania and started making calls. I thought that with enough work, I would get what I wanted. But, things did not go that easy. First, I found that American citizens are annoyed by frequent calls which ask them to participate in a survey and there are even websites which give Americans cues to dodge survey phone calls. This was a big problem which made my progress very slow, but I was thinking that at least I could be sure I would get enough responses through time.

The second problem was that American respondents were unwilling to answer a phone call from someone they did not know or they could not see his number on their caller ID screen. American respondents told me they could not read my number, or, they asked me from where I did call them, and once I said from Iran, they became suspicious and many of them hung up. The third and most decisive problem, was that those American citizens who accepted to participate in my survey were trying to be nice and gave me answers that they thought would please me! They told me how wonderful Iranians are and that they did not believe what they saw in the media. This was not a problem that I could solve and therefore, after making more than 600 phone calls and getting only 10 answer –all of them were unnaturally positive towards Iranians- I announced to my supervisor that my project had failed.

As I was determined to do this project, I decided to try online survey. About 85% of Americans use Internet for some purpose and about 80% frequently use email. This is a good profile for someone who wants to do a cross country survey, but the problem was that this method would miss 20% and there will be always doubts if results could be generalized to the wider population. Moreover, there are always doubts about credibility and reliability of online surveys. Anyway, with the help of the same friend in Norway, I bought a software to find emails of U.S. citizens. This software was very slow because it needed a broadband Internet connection and we in Iran have limited bandwidth of about 100K/s. This made the process of email finding very slow and therefore I decided to start sending emails while more emails were being found. My questionnaire was short with about 24 questions. The most important questions were two open-ended questions: "when hearing the phrase 'an Iranian citizen,' what is the first image that comes to your mind?," and, "where did you get that impression?" When I started sending emails, new problems surfaced. I used Gmail, Yahoo and University of Tehran's emails. These email providers did not let clients send more than 500 emails a day and given tens of thousands of emails I got, I found I would not get anywhere if I were not to find a solution. Moreover, some respondents asked me to present my IRB certificate.

I asked my friends and relatives to help me on the first problem. I invited some of them to my home for dinner or launch and asked them to sign-in their emails. I send some emails and drafted many more and asked them to send some emails every day until all the drafts were sent. I also made a template and included with it groups of 150 emails for those whom I had not personal access and asked them send these emails according to instructions. More than 40 people helped me in this method and I could send all my emails. To solve the second problem, I started emailing some

American universities to issue an IRB certificate for my research. All of them politely rejected my request and said they could only issue such a certificate for professors and students at their university. Eventually, a kind person in University of Arizona asked for my documents and after finding a trusted Persian translator, they issued an IRB certificate for my project and the problem of possible ethical issues of this research, as far as safeguarding respondents was concerned, solved.

I had included in my online questionnaire in Google Drive a section in which respondents could enter their emails, had they had interest in knowing about the results. I received about 150 of such requests and some of them came up with their recommendations, encouragement or simply commented or further elaborated about their perception of Iranians. Moreover, as this questionnaire was sent by email, some people asked more information about different aspects of this project, before they decided to answer. Some correspondences included several emails. An estimated 1000 emails were sent or received by me in this course and this took a lot of time and energy. However, I committed myself to answer all emails properly and after completion of the project, those 150 respondents received a copy of my results and also my thanks for their cooperation.

In this project, I used a new sampling method named "reverse sampling" (I say new because this method was not widely used until recently). My approach was the one Abdollahyan and his colleagues developed in 2012. With this method, I estimated the required number of respondents based on the diversity of the respondent's responses. When the number of my responses reached 500, 700, and 900 I ran Abdollahyan's test and it was estimated that I needed 1106, 1121, and 1121 respondents respectively ($e = 0.05$ and $z = 1.96$).

Chapter 5

FINDINGS

In sum, I received 1752 answers from American citizens from 50 states. I codified findings of my qualitative answers and assigned each category a number. This gave me the opportunity to analyze my findings with SPSS. This, as we will see in this chapter and the next, yielded very interesting findings, though the statistical operations I was able to apply were limited. My primary factor which was different categories of cross cultural schemata as well as sources, was nominal. Therefore, although I had other variables in higher levels (like age, level of study etc.), in statistics we have a rule that when we want to study the relationship of two variables from two different levels, we are allowed to use tests which are relevant to the variable in the lower level, namely nominal level. We know that the number of tests we can apply at nominal level is small, but still the findings is valuable, particularly when linked to qualitative data.

In this chapter I will give a brief report about categories of cross cultural schemata Americans have of Iranians after a descriptive presentation of my findings. Then I will present my categorization of resources which my American respondents mentioned as the source for their cross cultural schemata of Iranians. I will include examples in each category because presenting firsthand accounts will have much to tell about how Americans think about sources of their perceptions about

Iranians. As cross cultural schemata yield more interesting information, I will come to detail with this subject in the next chapter. Allocating a whole chapter to these findings will give me more space to present the main focus of this book.

DEMOGRAPHICS

As I said, an overall number of 1752 participants accepted to fill my questionnaire. They were between 17 to 88 year old (mean = 45.5 and standard deviation = 14.85); I should add that 37 of my respondents did not mention their ages. This figure is near to the mean age of Americans over 18.

1737 respondents identified their gender. 946 (54.5%) were women and 791 (45.4%) were men. People of different levels of education participated in this study; their level of study included primary, high school, BA, MA and PhD with proportions of 0.4%, 8%, 28.2%, 33.6% and 29.8%, respectively. In levels of primary and PhD there were more men than women while at levels of high school, BA, and MA there were more women than men.

One of the important factors in social cognition in all cultures including United States is income. As questions regarding one's income might be sensitive for some respondents, rather than asking participants to write down their annual income, I asked them to mark a salary level. As I mentioned earlier, this did not negatively affect my analysis because the tests which I could use were limited to nominal tests. Here, 51 respondents (2.9%) said their annual income was less than 1000$ while 13.5% said they have a salary of more than 150,000$ a year. 125 respondents chose to mark "I would rather not to say," while 37 other did not answer this question at all. The highest frequency observed in the category "100,000$ to 150,000$" (22.5%) and the lowest frequency was of "1000$ to 19,999$" (2.7%). Based on this figures, more than 50% of the respondents reported they make more than 75,000$ a year.

In case of distribution, the respondents were scattered in all 50 states of the United States, though their quotas were not equal. Observed frequencies showed that Texas had the biggest representation in this study with 99 respondents (5.7%) followed by California (90 respondents), New Jersey (72 respondents) and Florida (63 respondents). States of West Virginia and Wyoming had the lowest rate of participation with only 5 participants each. 11 respondents said they lived in U.S. territories other than 50 states. This distribution gave this study an advantage to later claim the inferenced categories could be generalize to the American population. Further details have been brought in Table 1.

Table 1. Number of respondents in each state

	Frequency	Percent
Alabama	31	1.8
Alaska	13	.7
Arizona	51	2.9
Arkansas	20	1.1
California	90	5.1
Colorado	32	1.8
Connecticut	32	1.8
Delaware	14	.8
Florida	63	3.6
Georgia	18	1.0
Hawaii	6	.3
Idaho	15	.9
Illinois	23	1.3
Indiana	29	1.7
Iowa	20	1.1
Kansas	57	3.2
Kentucky	45	2.6
Louisiana	26	1.5
Maine	9	.5
Maryland	34	1.9
Massachusetts	45	2.6

Table 1. (Continued)

	Frequency	Percent
Michigan	49	2.8
Minnesota	59	3.4
Mississippi	24	1.4
Missouri	62	3.5
Montana	9	.5
Nebraska	28	1.6
Nevada	19	1.1
New Hampshire	10	.6
New Jersey	72	4.1
New Mexico	24	1.4
New York	59	3.4
North Carolina	26	1.5
North Dakota	49	2.8
Ohio	42	2.4
Oklahoma	44	2.5
Oregon	45	2.6
Pennsylvania	54	3.1
Rhode Island	10	.6
South Carolina	32	1.8
South Dakota	19	1.1
Tennessee	23	1.3
Texas	99	5.6
Utah	21	1.2
Vermont	10	.6
Virginia	52	3.0
Washington	35	2.0
West Virginia	5	.3
Wisconsin	56	3.2
Wyoming	5	.3
Z-Other U.S. Territories	11	.6
Total	1726	98.4
Missing System	28	1.6
Total	1754	100.0

AMERICAN CROSS CULTURAL SCHEMATA OF IRANIANS

As I said in the previous chapters, this book explores multiple tasks, one of the most important ones is to reveal cross cultural schemata Americans have of Iranians. A careful and well consulted categorization of qualitative answers of my American respondents yields six main categories: "Neutral," "Negative," "Positive," "No Cross Cultural Schemata," "Irrelevant or No Answer" and "Contradictory or Mixed." I say "careful" because I wanted to make sure that each answer is categorized inside the most relevant category. For example, I had a subcategory of "Brow Skin" and I did not know if this subcategory should be put into the "Negative," "neutral," or "Positive" category. I consulted my advisors and I started asking the opinion of my American friends. Professor Michael H. Prosser Professor Emeritus of the University of Virginia gave me the best answer. He said some 20 years ago this phrase could be understood as negative, but now as the society is more multicultural and there more minority population in the U.S., the phrase "Brown Skin" no longer has negative connotations and hence it should be put into the "Neutral" category. Therefore, of course there might be people in the U.S. who use this phrase to imply negative attitude or some people out there might not like to be called as someone with brown skin, but, in general I take it that this phrase is more neutral, rather than negative. I had similar cases like for example understanding Iranians as Arabs, hardworking, Muslim, Mahmoud Ahmadinejad etc.

After doing categorization and sub-categorizations, I codified my findings in a SPSS spreadsheet and calculated the weight of each category as well as the weight of each sub-category in its category and in overall categories.

My analysis revealed that negative cross cultural schemata of Iranians are about two times more prevalent among Americans than are positive cross cultural schemata. Moreover, about 6% of the respondents gave irrelevant answers to this questions or they blatantly said they had no idea of how an Iranian citizen might look like. As I mentioned in chapter 1, Americans have no clear and integrated image of Iranians. Here, in accordance with other studies, we can see that a majority of American people have negative perceptions about Iranians, but, not as negative as perceptions they have for Iranian political establishment. We will come back to the issue of cross cultural schemata as related to politics in more details in chapter 6.

SOURCES OF CROSS CULTURAL SCHEMATA

One of the open-ended question I asked the American respondents was about the source for their reported cross cultural schemata. Here again I used the categorization process to analyze my findings. As we can see in the below table, more than 41% of the respondents said their knowledge of the Iranian people comes directly from the media while only 19.6% of them said they know an Iranian in Person.

Source Category	Frequency	Valid Percent
Knowing someone in person	344	19.6
Seeing Iranians in Iran, U.S. or elsewhere	266	15.2
Media	728	41.5
Own thought and research	186	10.6
Don't know	19	1.1
No comment or not applicable	167	9.5
From the words "Citizen" or "Iran"	44	2.5
Total	1754	100.0

A considerable number of the respondents (9.5%) decided to remain silent on this question or gave irrelevant answer and 1.1% said they had no idea where their cross cultural schemata of Iranians came from. Let us review some examples of the sources my respondents mentioned.

Knowing Someone in Person

As we can see in the above table, 344 respondents (19.6%) said their knowledge came through knowing an Iranian citizen. This citizen could be someone they knew in the U.S. or met, befriended our perhaps troubled with in another country. As we will see in this chapter, this source is a powerful predictor of positive perceptions about Iranians. Examples in this category are:

Male	51	PhD	Florida	Personal interaction
Female	26	MA	Florida	I have friends from Iran and you can't tell them apart (sic) from others when we are all together. They each also have different ways of thinking and believe in different things so that is where I got the impression that everyone is unique -- that is why no specific images came to mind when I hear the phrase 'An Iranian Citizen'
Male	55	BA	New Jersey	I grew up with Iranian family by marriage, my Uncle Sal is the kindest person I have ever known and a Sufi Muslim. He has been one of the greatest influences on my life!!!
Male	67	BA	New Mexico	I had an Iranian (pre revolution) friend at school.
Male	44	MA	Oregon	I have met any many Iranians in Japan and the United States
Female	33	BA	North Dakota	As I have said, personal experience with work and school.
Female	34	BA	Texas	This is the impression that I've received from the Persians that I know and have had experiences with. Both male and female.
Female	62	MA	Texas	Back in the Shah's day I lived in DC and knew embassy kids quite well. I

				went to a public high school but we had kids from all over. One of them Fahranaz (sic) and I were into telling each other secrets on the phone at all hours of the night. I've worked with people who immigrated here in various ways over time. And who hasn't had a wonderful conversation with an Irani cab driver! I read the Economist weekly, read the NY Times and work at UH. Iran isn't all that far away, you know.
Female	28	BA	Arizona	I have a friend who is a first generation Iranian-American
Male	63	PhD	Massachusetts	I have had Iranian friends, first in graduate school, and several later on. People are people.
Male	57	PhD	Florida	All the Iranians I know have this appearance.
Female	32	BA	Kentucky	From the Iranian people I have known
Female	52	PhD	Ohio	A close friend from undergraduate school. He was from Iran and we became friends since we were both much younger than the other students in our dorm.
Female	36	MA	Iowa	I have a friend of Iranian decent
Female	29	PhD	Maryland	I know a number of Iranians, and they observe a variety of customs. Some women play soccer with me, others I have worked or gone to school with. I think of them has having the versatility as an American.
Male	67	PhD	Nebraska	Iranians I know
Female	24	MA	Mississippi	From previous encounters with Iranian people.

Male	64	PhD	Michigan	I've known several Iranian students.
Female	48	BA	New Mexico	Have interacted with Iranians in the past
Male		MA	Maryland	Several individual I know from Iran-Persian descent
Female	52	High School	Texas	Meet/great throught (sic) my adulthood. Co-workers.
Female	52	BA	Oregon	Two individuals of Persian descent who married into extended family.
Female	38	High School	Missouri	Working with an Iranian citizen.
Female	32	MA	Pennsylvania	Co-Workers
Female	57	MA		knowing Iranians
Female	57	BA	Missouri	two faculty, an ex-boyfriend and his family
Male	54	PhD	Massachusetts	Personal experience with persons from Iran.
Male	26	MA	Pennsylvania	I have met a number of Iranian citizens in the U.S. who have had a variety of viewpoints, characteristics, and so on. Furthermore, I spent time professsionally as a social studies teacher and taught about Iran and various events in its recent history.
Female	28	MA		The Iranians I have met tended to be so.
Female	40	BA	Maine	From people I have known.
Female	62	PhD	Georgia	Having met and worked with an Iranian male previously.
Female	63	PhD	Connecticut	From Iranian citizens who were my friends during undergraduate years, 1969-73.
Male	70	PhD	Florida	Contact wit (sic) Iranians dating back to the professional contwqacts (sic) and ISA students in the seventies, as well as reading and study

Female	62	PhD	Indiana	I have known a few Iranians - back in the 1970s, when we had many in ESL classes in the US. Hearing the news over the last many years, I know there have been many changes since the Shah left, since the Iran/Iraq conflict, and with the various internal arguments regarding religion and statehood.
Female	61	MA	Kansas	Several ways from years (sic) ago--In college, several students in my business classes were from Iran. For many years, my next door neighbor was the daughter of a military officer assigned to Iran. The family lived there while the Shah was in power. The history of Persia. Watching the religious and political leaders speak, position, posture.
Female	35	MA	Missouri	People I have known and been in contact with
Male	24	BA	New York	I work with him!
Female	58	MA	New York	Iranians I have know (sic) who self-identified at Persian.
Female	64	MA	Texas	I have known and worked with several Iranians during my life. As a very young person, I had a couple of pen-pals who lived in Iran. We found each other through a pen-pal exchange, and exchanged letters for a couple of years. We usually explained our various social and cultural events and habits with each other, along with some religious discussions. As an adult, I have also worked with several Iranians who have shared their thoughts and beliefs with me. The

				best way to get to know another culture, if you cannot visit the country, is through meeting and working with citizens of that country.
Male	40	BA	North Carolina	I worked with a guy named Amir who was all about some Persia. Very proud of his home country/culture. Smart guy, very nice.
Male	54	MA	Texas	I played soccer with Iranians who were classmates when I went to a small, private college in Kerrville, Texas in the late 1970s. I still remember the goalie's name, Hossein Haghigolem (sp). I have known many Iranians throughout my life and played in the Austin Men's Soccer Association with several of them on my Over 50 (everyone has to be over 50 years of age) soccer team. If I spoke Farsi I would understand what they were saying when they cursed
Female	29	BA	South Carolina	I receive that impression because of the Iranian Citizens that I interact with during my job. Most of the women I see are wearing vails over their face/head. The interaction with Iranian Citizens are the same as speaking with someone born in America except the accent is extremely thick and hard to understand.
Male	55	BA	California	I have worked with Iranians off and on most of my life. Persians in the US that I come in contact with, are generally first or second generation

dating from the fall of the Shaw. These people tend to be "cream of the crop" folks, who are not afflicted by religion or political over-zealousness. My impression of the people in Iran that make the news is the opposite of above.

Your first question below regarding US being exceptional - in what way? I think you should get a bit more specific with the wording of the questions.

Female	20	High School	Nevada	My mother's husband and his family are from Iran. They escaped shortly after the revolution. I know the history from about '75 to now--the Iranian people largely accepted an extremist government and a return to Sharia law, while most educated people got the fuck out before they could be persecuted.
Female	73	MA	Rhode Island	I've been privileged to meet people who are citizens of many countries, and have found that although they may have different backgrounds than I do, they all, if they are thoughtful people, want to learn about other cultures and try to foster common goals and interests -- strong family and community ties, a good life for their children, and a sense that since all parts of the world are not equally advantaged, trying to even things out would yield great benefits. I work in a "knowledge industry," with strong ties to academia, so my views are obviously biased by the

character of the people, mostly highly educated, I come in contact with.

"Seeing Iranians in Iran, U.S. or elsewhere" was predictive of relative positive cross cultural schemata of Iranians. 39% of people in this category reported positive cross cultural schemata while 35% of them reported neutral perceptions of Iranians. Another 16% had negative attitudes, 5% reported mixed or contradictory perceptions and less than 1% said they had no opinion on Iranians.

Male	41	PhD	Utah	Some people from Iran i know growing up in Canada
Female	22	High School	California	From my memory of people that I've encountered in my life that match the description above.
Male	22	BA	California	I've been to Iran
Female	73	PhD	Connecticut	previous experience
Male	18	High School	California	I know Iranian people
Female	20	High School	New Jersey	i (sic) work retail and we have many international customers, therefore i (sic) have been able to form my own observations.
Male	36	BA	Arizona	People I've met on the bus.
Female	51	BA	Florida	Knowledge of and experience of other nations.
Female	24	BA	Minnesota	My experience with dealing with anyone who has acheived (sic) dual status.
Male	23	BA	New York	From college where I did some work on helping to mend the different cultures of the middle east (sic). Many of the conflicts were around Iran, and dealt with different sects of the Muslim faith.

Male	33	High School	Tennessee	Society
Female	44	PhD	Illinois	I've met a small number of Iranians on university campuses, and I believe this image comes from those meetings. As mentioned above, my image of Iranians in Iran is less clear. However, I have watched the movie "A Separation," which was situationally sad and interesting to see a glimpse of what life might be like there.
Female	34	PhD	Oregon	interacting with international students
Female	34	High School	Texas	Just from day to day interactions.
Female	47	High School	Ohio	Most Iranians have dark hair that I've seen.
Female	54	PhD	North Dakota	Past students and peers
Male	57	BA	Alaska	I have lived in the Middle east for six years and in Europe for 15 years and as such it has given me a wide view of the world at large. People are just that people, they all want the same things for their families, communities and country.
Female	50	MA	Texas	The impression comes from understanding that the United States has several students and exchange visitor that enter the USA every days to study or do research.
Male	86	MA	California	Many floor covering stores are run by Iranians in this city
Female	37	High School	Virginia	people i (sic) see at stores, things ive (sic) seen on news most are isalm (sic).
Female	28	MA	Wisconsin	I'm not sure, general social

				exposure.
Female	38	BA	North Carolina	Personal travels to the region.
Female	25	BA	Texas	I've met a few people from Iran briefly on campus. Also, mainstream media playing up women's rights and voting (I'll admit to not being very educated in that regard or following media much).
Male	58	PhD	California Alabama	I try not to apply judgments to individuals I have not met. Since I have lived in many places in the US and around the world, and met people from many places, I realize that most of us have the same interests and ideas about how to live with our neighbors. I form opinions about people that I know from the news, however I know that the news portrays people with a bias and I try to avoid adopting that bias. Having said that, I would report a negative bias towards Hamas in Israel for sending rockets against civilians in Israel, but I do not think I have a negative bias towards all Gazans. Just like most Israelis they are innocent and interested in peace and prosperity.
Male	41	PhD	Utah	Some people from Iran i know growing up in Canada When I answer agree to hating the Islamic revolution it is because of the observation that it is willing to reduce freedom of speech and

democracy for its own people and it is willing to fund groups who attack people outside its territory. It is not unique in this regard and if you had asked me I would have said the US also attacks groups and people outside its own territory.

It is not because the US is exceptional that it must intervene. It is because it is powerful and has a vested interested in maintaining the status quo. Many of the places that it intervenes are not really necessary and sometimes harmful. I would say that the recent wars in Iraq have produced a lot of the instability we now have in the region. Chaos in any part of the world is bad for the whole world. Some intervention is necessary.

All countries that have nuclear capability have the ability to misuse it. The government of Iran has espoused policies that suggest they will not remain completely rational in the use of nuclear power. Neither has North Korea.

What does aggressive mean? Aggressive towards other countries? Then Iran is aggressive. Israel is aggressive. Sudan is aggressive.

The US is aggressive. Russia is aggressive. China is aggressive. This does not mean that the individual people in these countries are aggressive, or that countries can change their posture and become

Female	40	BA	Wisconsin	less threatening to their neighbors From growing up around immigrants from Iran
Female	64	PhD	Wisconsin	interactions with Iranian people in the USA
Male	30	MA	Texas	Having spoken too (sic) and met many from Iran.
Female	59	BA	Pennsyl-vania	encounters and television images
Male	66	PhD	Maine	My impressions come from personal interactions with recent emigrants and from historical reading.
Female		MA		I knew some people who fled during the Shah's reign.
Female	55	PhD	Connecticut	Iranians I have met and worked with.
Female	29	BA	Massa-chusetts	My work with international students. Most are very driven, highly educated, and in my experience I have found that their culture is very hospitable and warm.
Male	41	PhD	Washington	I have met many Iranians and seen some movies
Male	63	PhD	Tennessee	My experience with the Iranians who have come to the United States prompt this impression.
Female	63	BA	South Dakota	My opinion came from experience. Getting to know students from other parts of the world. 20 years ago, my opinion may have been very different-I have no way of knowing that for sure.
Female	44	MA	New York	I know some Iranians who fit the description and also know that there are a lot of young people in Iran.
Female	54	PhD	California	Experience as a professor.
Female	59	MA	Illinois	From students from Iran that came to this country to study.

Male	50	MA	Connecticut	working in academia
Female	60	MA	Virginia	I am an immigration lawyer and I know a lot of people from all over the world.
Female	50	PhD	Michigan	I have been exposed to many different kinds of people. And Armenians from that part of the world share many similar cultural values and behaviors to Iranians. I have a friend who is Iranian - a sort of new friend - and we share many similar values. So I would say it's my upbringing and friendships that shape my impressions.
Female	63	MA	Maryland	I have met and talk with Iranian women and always found them to be easy to talk with and I feel very comfortable around them. Iranian men, however, with the exception of one, I have felt uncomfortable around because of my experience with Iranian male students in college--they were aggressive and demanding towards me, especially when I would turn them down for dates. The one exception, I was at a New Year's Eve party in 1986 and met an Iranian male college student who told me the story of how his father got the rest of the family out of Iran because of the Ayotollah (sic) and so his sons would not have to serve on the front lines of the Iranian army. This person came across to me as just wanting to be a friend and I found his story compelling.

Female	42	PhD	Pennsylvania	My first thoughts are of the people I have met from Iran (or Iraq, which I know is not the same country, but they are linked in my mind). The little girl I met at summer camp during the Iranian hostage crisis of 1980. She told everyone she was from Persia but whispered the truth in my ear in that bathroom. The young men were my students, two in particular whom I really liked, who were both from Iran. The woman lying on bullets and the mute singing women are from an art exhibit by women of Islamic cultures that was on display at the Boston MFA last year. The angry images of young men in the streets come from TV and the movies
Male	64	PhD	New Jersey	Contact with Iranian citizens at conferences.

More than 66% of those who mentioned some type of media as the source for their perceptions about Iranians reported negative cross cultural schemata about Iranians. 18% of the respondents in this group had neutral cross cultural schemata and only 7% expressed positive comments about Iranians. Another 7% expressed mixed or contradictory comments about Iranian citizens.

Female	26	MA	South Carolina	I watch/read many news outlets, including those that are international. My husband's boss was born in Iran and moved to the US in the 1980s. I also saw the film "A Separation" a few years ago and wanted to more about

				Iran after watching the film and hearing about the censorship issues surrounding the director.
Male	69	PhD	Texas	From news sources along with visiting the country.
Female	25	BA	Massachusetts	Most likely I got that impression from the media.
Female	52	BA	Washington	Media, books, movies, cultural studies, students and citizens living in the USA
Female	80	High School	New Mexico	Our media makes them all appear to be wicked athiest (sic) and uneducated which is not true. Many are educated
Female	24	BA	Kansas	I've seen many Iranians on tv (sic), and the ones who stick in my mind are those speaking about international issues, how Iranian citizens see things, trying to explain their daily life and struggles.
Male	41	BA	Michigan	Dont (sic) know, tv (sic) i (sic) guess
Female	52	High School	Wisconsin	Visual impression only.
Female	56	PhD	Oklahoma	The only visual exposure I have for Iranian citizens is via the media and they oftentimes show males.
Female	53	BA	North Dakota	television, news reports
Female	35	BA	Oregon	Images from the news/other media.
Female	51	BA	Massachusetts	tv (sic)
Male	30	BA	Minnesota	Probably first from entertainment TV/movies, then from news television, then probably from my imagination filling in

				gaps from what I know of the climate in Iran, which is also second-hand knowledge.
Female	37	MA	Washington	movies, graphic novel persepolis (sic)
Female	55	BA	Utah	From what I have seen on TV and in magazines. Plus, I know a coupleof (sic) Iranians.
Female	62	PhD	Minnesota	television
Female	65	BA	North Dakota	news reports, TV, magazines, met some Iranians at the university
Female	35	MA	Colorado	Media images
Female	21	BA	Illinois	Pictures seen in the news of protests, violence, and citizens (doing good and bad things) from that country.
Male	56	PhD	Alaska	Seeing news and press conferences with Iranian leaders who tend to be dressed in western clothes, but otherwise not particularly different other than have a more Middle eastern appearance.
Male	33	BA	Missouri	TV
Female	66	MA	Connecticut	Media, some personal experiences
Male	57	PhD	Michigan	The only frame of reference that I have of Iranian people is what I saw on a US news show once, I beleive (sic) that it was 20/20. What impressed me about the program was how warm and friendly the general population, especially the youth appeared in interviews. They did not seem to be "anti-American" at all, but

				seemed as though they embraced a lot of western culture, and moderate views of the world that we share in the US. I also concluded that it was mostly individuals in the government that were extreme in some of their views that I as a US citizen am troubled by.
Male	49	MA	Kentucky	News
Female	67	MA	Kansas	Photographs and from personal interaction with students attending our university. (Looks like this submission included my edits. I was it listed me as being from California, not Kansas.)
Female	50	High School	Arkansas	Media, personal conversations
Female	67	MA	Idaho	As I have never been to Iran, it is probably from the media.
Female	59	MA	New Mexico	TV
Female	60	PhD	New York	Right now I think of the Youtube clip of "Happy in Tehran" with the young people dancing (and getting into trouble for making the video). Also from a friend who talked of his relatives in Tehran who have learned over several years how to make wine by drying their grapes on the balcony and then pressing them in the bathtub.
Male	38	BA	Wisconsin	News media, I presume.
Male	21	High School	Minnesota	Iranian films, American films providing depictions of Iranians. films like: Persepolis, Close-Up, Argo, etc.

Female	30	MA	Wisconsin	I think the general image is probably from news input or my impression of Iran and the Middle East having not been there.
Male	57	BA	Maryland	Mostly broadcast TV news reports.
Female	44	High School	Illinois	Probably the news media.
Male	17	Primary School	Minnesota	Probably from internet news sites and the few pictures I have seen online
Female	26	BA	Michigan	It's hard to picture "an Iranian citizen." I feel as though Iran is a shadow nation, always talked about in the news, but very rarely seen. I expect its people to look like those in other Arabic nations, but I don't believe I have a definite idea.
Female	20	High School	New Jersey	From the news+E1441
Male	47	MA	Missouri	News and geography
Female	50	MA	Michigan	My exposure to the notion of "Iranian citizen" would come from entertainment forms such as novels, films. I have read books and seen movies by Iranians. I have also seen films that were not created by Iranians but depicting them. I work at a University and we have Iranian faculty members. I try very hard to have an open mind and not generalize any people.

Female	45	BA	Nebraska	The news footage image comes from my childhood, and it's very vague and impressionistic. I saw a listing for a Rick Steves (sic) episode online recently and it looked good. Award-winning.
Female	26	MA	Texas	The news and other visual media. I do not think that this is a correct stereotype, and have not seen many "positive" Iranian representations in the American media. I have only met one person from Iran to my knowledge; he was just a normal guy.
Female	35	PhD	Washington	news general popular media
Female	57	High School	Alaska	The news
Male	38	BA	Delaware	News sources, reinforced by the lack of coverage

A group of the respondents mentioned sources which could be put into the category of "own thought and research." In this group, about 38% reported neutral comments about Iranians, 31% expressed negative cross cultural schemata and 19% expressed positive cross cultural schemata about Iranians. Less than 1% in this group gave irrelevant response and about 3% said they had no cross cultural schemata of Iranians.

Male	34	BA	Colorado	Personal reflection to counter my own inherent bias. Media.
Male	38	PhD	Indiana	I did not get any impressions from anybody.
Female	23	BA	Montana	My parents, who believe that we are all human beings, created the same way.
Female	36	PhD	North Dakota	My experience with many

				different cultures that every person has their own unique qualities.
Female	54	BA	North Carolina	I got it from my grandfather. He always told me that you should never judge people until you get to know them.
Female	48	MA	Oregon	Politics, novels, news
Female	33	BA	Oklahoma	I was brought up to keep an open mind about all people until you get to know them. I guess that is why this phrase makes me think of just another person I would run into from day to day.
Male	60	PhD	California	Logic and reason.
Male	69	High School	Pennsylvania	My church
Female	30	MA	California	we are all people and should not stereotypical views cloud our judgement
Female	72	PhD	New Mexico	God created all men equal
Male	66	PhD	Wisconsin	Early university education, research and reading, and personal interface with people who emigrated from Iran.
Male	61	PhD	Massachusetts	My religious belief
Female	30	MA	Louisiana	I see people as they are and not by sterotypes (sic).
Female	19	High School	Indiana	From what I've learned about the world in past classes and images I've seen on the news.
Female	23	BA	Iowa	I'm not entirely sure. Probably some assumption - Iran is in the Middle East, and people from the Middle East generally have darker skin (although I'm sure this isn't necessarily true).

Female	22	High School	Kentucky	I see them as human. It isn't right to stereotype them based on what we see/hear in the media.
Male	59	PhD	Massachusetts	As a student and teacher of history.
Female	39	MA	Indiana	That is my interpretation of Iranian... a person from Iran.
Male	24	BA	New Jersey	Thats (sic) just my perception.
Female	24	MA	Mississippi	Demographics
Male	61	PhD	New Jersey	geography
Male	67	PhD	New Jersey	60 years of experiences
Female	68	MA	North Dakota	I believe truly that each person is to be learned as stereotypes are part of our difficulty in the battles going on~ whether with people from East, blacks, Natives, Hispanics or whomever.
Male	55	PhD	North Dakota	Terminology commonly used in my environment or education while growing up (this person is a "Citizen of" a particular country).
Female	31	MA	Ohio	The book reading lolita (sic) in tehran (sic), persepolis (sic).
Male	66	MA	Vermont	Logic & education
Male	67	PhD	Oklahoma	I have studied ancient Greek and Roman history, and there were three great Persian Empires--the Achaemenid, the Arsacid, and Sasanid.
Female	35	BA	Washington	I associate Iran with Persia or the Persian Empire through pop culture such as literature, nonfiction, graphic novels, history books, etc., as well as restaurants that describe their cuisine as "Persian" vs.

				"Iranian."
Male	65	PhD	West Virginia	Teaching in college courses in the U.S. Over the years, I had a number of bright Iranian students. I taught at WVU for 45 years.
Male	52	PhD	Massachusetts	History
Male	44	PhD	Arizona	Just my opinion
Female	27	PhD	Virginia	My own curiosity about the tensions between Iraq and Iran.
Female	21	High School	Colorado	My Anthropology classes and interest in their culture and food.
Male	64	MA	Ohio	I use to teach elementary Social Studies. The stories that were presented in the textbook were always unbiased not like the media of today. In today's society we are forced to read what they want us to read and with that a lot of times opinions are often negative. Until I wear the shoes of an Iranian, my image will always be that of a middle easterner whose religious ties and beliefs are strong and a culture of close family ties.
Male	59	MA	North Carolina	Knowledge of world affairs primarily based on degree in history and the news.
Male	52	PhD	Pennsylvania	Studying history.
Male	46	MA	Louisiana	Self explanatory.
Male	31	BA	Arizona	Saddam Hussein biography
Male	22	BA	Connecticut	History
Female	59	MA	Missouri	I am not certain where that would come from. I suppose that I learned about Iran and the Muslim religion first when I was

				in elementary school at a Catholic school in St. Charles, MO. Then I would have studied religion in high school and college. I am sure that my image is also influenced by the media but I think my perceptions were embedded prior to the emphasis in the media.
Male	30	PhD	Delaware	World history and Taliban
Male	62	MA	Minnesota	Extensive reading, including Amir Taheri and Fouad Ajami.
Male	60	MA	Minnesota	There are multiple sources of information to include even National Geographic who ran a multi-page story about what has happened since the Shaw (sic) was ousted. Iran under the Shaw was an open cosmopolitan country embracing much of the ideals of the US. Women were not forced to wear Burqas, they could be Doctors, Lawyers, and own their own businesses etc. Why do I think the current government will use a nuclear bomb if they have it? Because that has been the case for all hard-line Islamic groups. Just look at Isis in northern Iraq. They are conducting the same campaign as the Arabs did when they rolled through what is now Croatia, Bosina & Herzegovina etc. 300 years ago. If you do not agree with their policy and you convert to their style of Islam,

they kill you. With the current bombing of Israel, by Isis, can anyone take a chance the if Iran develops a nuclear bomb that one might not find it's way to Isreal? If they do, then they have not studied history and watched the progress of Hitler, Stalin and many other dictators that came into power.

Additional discussions could be made on your questions, but to me they are too broad and can be misinterpreted in many different ways. I believe you should start over with a better description of what you are asking for.

Should the US take a role in the world? Yes. Not through force unless absolutely necessary. When the hard-line Islamic group stole +300 women in Africa, the US should have been the focal point to rally the other countries to track down this group and recover the women. What did Obama do? He went golfing. When the Egyptian people rejected the hard-line Islamist leader by protest, what did Obama do? He criticized them for getting rid of an elected leader even though the leader was not following the Egyptian constitution and trying to install Sharia law.

Male	39	BA	North Carolina	Reading on the history of the middle east, and national news
Male	69	PhD	West Virginia	Reading a lot of political history and sociology. I also know several Iranians in the United States and am good friends with several of them.

19 respondents said they don't know where their cross cultural schemata came from. 37% of people expressed negative comments about Iranians, 32% reported neutral perceptions and 11% of them were positive about the citizens of Iran.

Male	35	BA	Kansas	don't know
Female	27	BA	Ohio	I'm not sure.
Female	30	MA	Pennsylvania	I'm not sure, maybe cultural association
Female	26	MA	Nebraska	not sure
Male	35	BA	Utah	I don't know much about Iran specifically so I generalize the look of middle eastern (sic) people.
Female	35	MA	South Carolina	I don't know why. Maybe something I saw on tv (sic)
Female	35	MA	Montana	No idea why that popped into my head.
Male	44	BA	Rhode Island	??? No certain idea
Female	38	MA	Virginia	I have no idea.
Female	38	PhD	New York	I don't know where this idea comes from. I have an image of a sophisticated 50-something man with professional training who has come to the U.S. under difficult circumstances and opened a shop. I think this might be some mix of references from the movies Crash and Kiterunner

				(although Kiterunner, I know, is about a family from Afghanistan, not Iran, but somehow that's what comes to mind). Also Edward Said comes to mind. Again, he's not Iranian but... if I'm being honest, these are the things that come to mind.
Male	40	PhD	Oregon	I have no idea
Female	70	PhD	Connecticut	I don't know -- my education and current events, I suppose.

Some respondents did not mention any source for their cross cultural schemata or, their comments had nothing to do with some sort of source for any perception. 36% of these respondents had given irrelevant answers when they had been asked about their perception of Iranian citizens. About 22% of them gave neutral accounts, 19% reported negative perceptions and 8% had positive perception. More than 13% in this category had no cross cultural schemata of Iranians and less than 2% of them reported mixed or contradictory attitudes.

Male	40	PhD	Nebraska	Institutional envt (sic) (the legal system, democratic system, informal inst.) are obviously different in Iran. I do not see it as an open democratic system. And I think of legal system there as a sham mostly (but it is based on what we read in media, no firsthand experience)
Male	39	MA	Ohio	The quality of life.
Male	62	High School	California	seems obvious
Female	29	BA	Oklahoma	Darker complexion- shorter build-muscular- pretty hair-

Male	77	PhD	Mississippi	natural beauty- educated ?
Female	43	BA	Ohio	I have no preconceived notions
Female	49	PhD	Maryland	N/A
Male	68	BA	South Carolina	I make no particular association beyond the information supplied.
Female	39	MA	Virginia	I do not have any other impression until I meet and and (sic) or get to know them further.
Female	51	MA	South Carolina	I was taught to treat everyone the same.
Male	51	PhD	Michigan	It is true.
Male	63	MA	Illinois	From the presentation!
Female	38	PhD	Alabama	???
Male	46	High School	North Carolina	I simply have an impression of an Islamic society not being woman-friendly. I know there are accomplished, professional women there, but they aren't as free as men are.
Male	46	MA	Missouri	I tend to immediately think of a male, though I'm not sure why.
Male	40	MA	Arizona	Iran was part of Persia, Iranian do not like to be called Arabs.
Female	57	MA	New York	The streets of many urban cities in several countries
Female	59	BA	Alaska	War
Female	19	High School	Washington	Alot (sic) of people sterotype (sic) becuase (sic) of 9/11 even though it wasn't Iran's fault
Male	33	BA	Indiana	in the bed
Male	56	MA	California	The common dress is not an abaya
Male	22	BA	North Dakota	Islam is a very prominent religion in Iran. Iran also practices sharia law which is

				based heavily on the Islamic religion
Female	22	BA	Pennsylvania	The dress code is very different from ours, and it is enforced, which also makes it unusual, so it is what I noticed first.
Female	26	BA	Ohio	Unfortunately, because I do not know much about Iranians other than they come from a middle eastern country.
Female	19	High School	New Jersey	Iran is practically a desert and their people wear turbans
Female	51	MA	Connecticut	I tend to think more of woman and their struggles for recognition and rights. Muslim women from more conservative cultures wear burqa or hijab in my experience. These are also more common images in the media.
Female	21	BA	California	it is a muslim nation
Male	60	PhD	Missouri	a religious reason
Female	26	BA	Indiana	desert and heat- i (sic) think of the landscape that shaped people and culture (i (sic) could be totally wrong because my knowledge of Iran's geography isn't great)dark hair and eyes- i (sic) think of men with dark serious eyes and dark brown hair and women with longer dark brown hair and guarded eyes colorful clothing and culture- red and pink are just what come to mind. culture because a country what is in conflict, is more times than not in conflict because they

				have believes (which stem from culture) to fight for. hate and sorrow for 2 reasons. first is because for the actual conflicts going on, and the second because of the prejudice many people hold and the sorrow i (sic) feel know how cruel people can be. as for where I learned these impression, I would say media, and school both shaped them
Female	75	BA	New Mexico	There are to (sic) many uneducated people in the world who tell other uneducated people what should be done. People who are 35 years or older and have not been in a town 45 miles away, or have taken the time to read a book about other people from other places in this wonderful big world. You should see the look on their faces, when they find out I'm from Germany. (Or the blank look)
Male	40	MA	Utah	I have a general distaste for any government, including my own. I political hotspot like Iran is going to get more than their fair share of stupid governments trying to "fix" the problems they continually create. The suffering usually falls onto the citizens who have to bear the burden of the government oppression. I get

				that impression from looking at the history of mankind.
Female	27	PhD	Wyoming	NPR
Male	54	BA	Tennessee	Pretty single subject focused.
Female	23	BA	Texas	Not Applicable
Male	23	Primary School	Kansas	HGFHGFH

One category for the sources of perceptions about Iranians was "from the words "Citizen" or "Iran." It is interesting that 89% of these respondents reported neutral cross cultural schemata of Iranians, while 7% had negative perceptions of Iranians, only 2% had positive perceptions of Iranian citizens and another 2% gave irrelevant answers to this question.

Female	27	MA	California	A citizen implies a person and a person is human.
Female	22	High School	New Jersey	Just simply by the phrase.
Male	62	High School	Delaware	everyone hear (sic) is a US citizen
	75	High School	Texas	People are generally citizens of the place they are born in. So if the individual was born in Iran (sic) he's an Iranian Citizen.
Female	60	MA	Idaho	Just the definition of citizen.
Male	22	BA	California	I got that impression from the phrase "An Iranian Citizen" and my knowledge of the English language.
Female	67	PhD	Kansas	The phrase "An Iranian Citizen"
Female	47	PhD	Kentucky	To me it is like any country. An american (sic) is a person who has citizenship in the USA. Just something I was taught through school.
Male		PhD	Missouri	The construction of the phrase
Female	65	MA	New York	definition of citizenship.

Female	66	BA	North Dakota	The word "citizen" and not "resident" or "naturalized."
Male	45	BA	Virginia	The phrase is self explanatory
Male	47	BA	North Dakota	A citizen is one who exercises the rights and duties of citizenship of a state/country, so a citizen of Iran is no different than than (sic) a citizen of the U.S. or any other country.
Male	67	MA	Nevada	From the phrase "Iranian Citizen". I immediately believe the person is from Iran and the word citizen to me, means lives in that country.
Female	68	BA	South Carolina	From the words themselves... "Iranian Citizen" Doesn't say whether he's Muslim or Christian or Atheist or anything other than he/she's an Iranian citizen.
Female	71	BA	Florida	Just the same as a person born in American would be an American citizen
Female	47	MA	California Alabama	The word Iranian
Male	64	MA	Texas	Because that's what the words mean.
Female	58	BA	New York	I am an US citizen born in the United States, so my guess would be an Iranian Citizen is someone born in Iran
Female	56	PhD	Texas	a universal definition of citizenship
Female	31	BA	Texas	The idea of a citizen is someone who is born in whatever country they hold citizenship, whether it be America or Japan or Iran. If

				you are not born in that country but want to become a citizen you must first immigrate to that country and begin the naturalization process.
Male	69	MA	Massachusetts	Almost everyone is a citizen of some country and Iran is a country.
Female	24	MA	Maryland	The definition of the word "citizen".

Further analysis gave more interesting insights as I found people who draw on different sources, had different perceptions of Iranians. More than 45% of the people who mentioned their knowledge came through personal acquaintance with an Iranian person, reported positive cross cultural schemata, while only 13% of respondents in this category reported negative cross cultural schemata of Iranians.

OTHER FACTORS

In this study I wanted to see if there was any other factor affecting the way American public see Iranian citizens. One of these factors is "American exceptionalism." American exceptionalism is an idea which holds that United States has been built by special people, in a special time and in a special place and therefore this country is exceptional to the point that we cannot evaluate or judge it with conventional criteria. Many studies show that despite changes in the American society towards more global and universal values, there is still a great sense of exceptionalism among the American public. American exceptionalism is at the same time an intercultural stance, as being an "exceptional" nation needs some other non-exceptional nations. Therefore, this attitude can affect how American people view citizens of other nations which has many other implications that are not directly relevant to this study.

The results show that the highest rate of American exceptionalism is among those respondents who left our question regarding their perceptions about Iranians blank or those who gave irrelevant responses. The second rank in having American exceptionalism tenets belonged to the group of respondents who said they had no cross cultural schemata of Iranians. As it could be predicted, American respondents who had positive perceptions of Iranians had the lowest level American exceptionalism mindset in my sample.

One other factor that I studied in this project was the possible relationship between cross cultural schemata of Iranians and perception of the Iranian government. As it could be predicted, there was a strong relationship between negative perceptions of the Iranian government and cross cultural schemata Americans have for Iranians. In fact, the more a respondent had negative perception of the Iranian government, the more he or she was likely to see Iranian citizens negatively.

In order to study a possible relationship between gender and cross cultural schemata I redefined gender as a dummy variable. Analysis showed that men and women had a similar rate of neutral cross cultural schemata (26.8% and 27.8% respectively) while men reported more positive comments about Iranians than did women (22% and 19.6% respectively). Accordingly, women more than men reported negative cross cultural schemata of Iranians (40.3% and 36.7% respectively) but these slight differences showed that gender could not be considered as a predicting cross cultural schemata. Nevertheless, within each category of cross cultural schemata there was strong relationships between gender and some sub-categories. For example, women more than men were likely to see Iranians as subdued women, while men more than women were likely to see Iranians as politically aggressive (I will give more detail on this finding in the next chapter).

One other important factor in surveys is age. Age is predictive of attitudes on different issues like political attitude, marriage, capital punishment, economy, election etc. and one of these issues is intercultural perceptions. Here I found that older people were more likely to have mixed or contradictory attitudes, while younger respondents were found to have either no cross cultural schemata of Iranians or they gave irrelevant answers to the research question. It is important to say that the mean age of those who expressed positive comments about Iranians, were more than the mean age of those who had negative cross cultural schemata of Iranians (47.38 and 44.45 respectively).

One other possible factor to be included in this analysis was level of education. Education changed attitudes and visions (although this change is not always positive!) and hence I decided to find out how increase in the level of education would associate with changes in cross cultural schemata. 42% of those who had preliminary education had negative cross cultural schemata of Iranians and another 42% either gave irrelevant answers or said they had no perceptions of Iranians. Intriguingly, no one in this category had mixed or positive cross cultural schemata. Back to our theoretical section, we could see that cross cultural schemata needs additional mental work and brain as a human organ tries to be as economic as possible on mental activities. Therefore, as people with preliminary education see no importance in having cross cultural schemata of Iranians, they either do not bother themselves to think of it or follow media in how to think about other people.

More than 33% of those who reported they had high school diploma reported neutral cross cultural schemata of Iranians. 46% of these respondents had negative cross cultural schemata of Iranians and only 11% expressed positive comments about Iranian citizens. More than 43% of participants with BA degree or equivalent were negative about Iranians, 30% reported positive perceptions and 16% had positive cross cultural schemata about people of Iran. 38% of respondents with MA degree or equivalent had negative perceptions while 22% reported positive attitudes towards Iranians citizens. 27% of respondents in this category were neutral. 32% of respondents with PhD degree reported negative cross cultural schemata while 27% were positive about the Iranians people. 24% of these participants reported neutral cross cultural schemata of Iranians.

Further analysis using Cramer's V test showed that although negative cross cultural schemata in all education groups are more than positive cross cultural schemata, the overall distribution of these schemata in these education groups is not similar. It could be said, therefore, that increase in the level of education will be associated with decrease in negativity of perceptions about Iranian citizens.

Income is an important factor in many surveys, although this is very hard to determine if respondents have reported their true income. Income can predict many attitudes, including attitudes about other people, but, in this study I could not find a strong relationship between income level and cross cultural schemata about Iranians.

We saw in the previous sections that we had respondents across all 50 American States and perceptions of these respondents about Iranians were categorized into six main categories. I was interested to know how Americans in different states had different attitudes on Iranians and because studying all six categories in 50 states takes many space, here I concentrate on positive and negative cross cultural schemata which means I only include 1023 responses. In two American states (Massachusetts and Washington) the positive perceptions for Iranians consisted more than half of the responses (59% and 51% respectively). In the states of Florida, Georgia, Hawaii, New Hampshire, and West Virginia the number of positive and negative responses were approximately equal and in the remaining states there were more negative perceptions, and less positive cross cultural schemata. 100% of our respondents in the state of Wyoming were negative about Iranians. After Wyoming, Kentucky (more than 91%), Iowa (91%), North Carolina (87%), Arizona (83%), Arkansas (82%) and New Jersey (80%) were the most negative states about Iranians.

Chapter 6

CROSS CULTURAL SCHEMATA

The main aim of this project was to reveal the cross cultural schemata American people have of Iranians and that is why I am allocating a whole chapter to reports participants' answers about their perceptions of Iranians. Six main categories were recognized: "Neutral," "Negative," "Positive," "No Cross Cultural Schemata," "Irrelevant or No Answer" and "Contradictory or Mixed." We had a brief review of six main categories of perceptions and in this chapter we will focus mainly on comments of the participants. As I mentioned in the previous chapter, my approach is to do routine analyses and combine it with presenting the first hand perceptions as expressed by American participants.

The following table shows that we have 6 subcategories among which three categories of "Neutral," "Negative," and "Positive" have been further subcategorized. Neutral category has five subcategories, negative category has 10 subcategories, and positive category has 7 sub-categories. This gives the overall figure as 6 categories and 22 sub-categories which I will take as a framework to structure this chapter.

Category	Sub-Category	Frequency	Valid Percent
Neutral (27.3%)	People Like Every Body, Some Are Good And Some Are Bad	62	3.5
	Brown Skin, Dark Complected	119	6.8
	Citizen of Iran, Not American	164	9.4
	Muslim	39	2.2
	Middle Eastern	95	5.4
Negative (38.5%)	Subdued Women	47	2.7
	War Torn	62	3.5
	Arab (Negatively Viewed)	81	4.6
	Turban, Burqa, Robe, Hijab or Niqab	137	7.8
	Poverty, Bad Living Condition	56	3.2
	Intolerant, Aggressive	108	6.2
	Terrorist	29	1.7
	Hostage Crisis	18	1.0
	Ahmadinejad, bad Iranian Politicians	61	3.5
	Oppressed	75	4.3
Positive (20.7%)	Friend, classmate, Student or Colleague	93	5.3
	Cultural Aspects Emphasized	99	5.7
	Smart and Educated	79	4.5
	Relative	12	.7
	Physically Attractive	43	2.5
	Hardworking	24	1.4
	Victim of Media Bad-Representation	13	.7
No Cross Cultural Schemata (2.5%)	No Cross Cultural Schemata	44	2.5
No Comment or Not Applicable (3.8%)	No Comment or Not Applicable	63	3.6
Mixed and Contradictory Cross Cultural Schemata (7.2%)	Mixed and Contradictory Cross Cultural Schemata	127	7.2
	Total	1752	100.0

NEUTRAL

478 respondents (27.3%) out 1752 participants reported neutral cross cultural schemata of Iranians. Their answers to the question regarding their perceptions of Iranians were evaluated as neither positive nor negative. As I mentioned in the previous chapter, the neutrality of these responses were determined by careful examination of the language of the respondents and after a close consultation with some American sociologists or Iranian professors who had the experience of living and teaching in the United States. There were five subcategories in this category.

People Like Every Body, Some Are Good and Some Are Bad

62 respondents gave accounts which fell into the category of "People Like Every Body, Some Are Good And Some Are Bad." They consisted 13% in the neutral and 3.5% in all responses. This group of people held that Iranian people are like people of all other nations and there is nothing particularly good or bad about them. Examples include:

Male	35	BA	Kansas	They are people like everybody
Male	51	PhD	Florida	I'm a professor who works with students around the world, including Iranian citizens, thus they are just like other students.
Male	55	BA	New Jersey	Just another human being.
Male	34	BA	Colorado	Human being. Religious. Normal, which is to say both smart and ignorant.
Male	57	PhD	Idaho	Really not a lot. If I heard the phrase "Republican Guards," "Ayatollah," or even "Iran," then I would have a negative image of a country that seems to be hiding its nuclear program, persecuting

				certain of its own citizens, and funding Shiite terrorists, and has vowed to destroy another country. However, I have a neutral view of Iranian citizens themselves.
Male	38	PhD	Indiana	I've heard this phrase long time ago. What means to me -- a citizen of another country. Every country has good and bad people.
Female	58	BA	Kansas	A person that could be very much like me, but speak another language and have different religious beliefs. They would have a family and be concerned for their family like I am, but live in a different country.
Female	28	BA	Georgia	Iranian Citizen's look similar to American's. There are a few women who cover their hair with Hijab's but I have interacted with some that do not.
Female	54	MA	Kansas	I have a variety of images as I've had colleagues who are Iranian. But I've only met one actual Iranian citizen. Since I've lived in Egypt for seven years, I know that you can't categorize people under any one assumption.
Male	65	MA	Maryland	A person
Male	40	PhD	Nebraska	Just another person like me, but you live up in a different institutional envt (sic). I grew up in India which has historical influence from Persia etc., so I see Iranians as no different from me as human beings. We have same

				aspirations at an individual level; want health, happiness, job, family, career, education.
Female	23	BA	Montana	A human being.
Male	67	BA	New Mexico	People very much like me.
Male	46	PhD	New York	Nothing different than someone were to say "a Canadian citizen"
Male	44	MA	North Dakota	A persons ideology that is the polar opposite of Western culture and beliefs, keeping in mind that not all Iranians are the same, nor are all Westerners are the same
Male	30	BA	Utah	I think of the place I've seen and the people I've met from Iran. I think of "an Iranian citizen" as I think of all humans. We all want happiness, peace, and success for ourselves and our families.
Female	54	BA	North Carolina	no images - they are no different from any other "citizen" from any other part of the world. People are just people no matter where they are in this world.
Female	33	BA	Oklahoma	An everyday person you would meet on the street.
Male	44	MA	Oregon	I do not have a bad image of Iranian at all. There are good people and bad people everywhere.
Male	60	PhD	California	The same as any other citizen of any country based on a bell curve. Most citizens are essentially "cookie cutter" products of their culture and not able to go beyond the horizon of thinking beyond tradition of values exposed during early environment. Extremes of both positive and negative are in

				every culture.
Female	26	MA	South Carolina	I feel like the people who live in Iran are people, just like those who live anywhere else in the world. Many may be religious, many are not. Many are poor and many are not. Although the government may be considered heavy-handed, acting as it does through the Ministry of Culture and Islamic Guidance, there are many different and varied cultural/religious groups living within Iran.
Female	33	BA	North Dakota	I perceive Iranian citizens much like citizens in the US or other countries around the world. I have met people from Iran at conferences as well as attended university in the US with students from Iran and have no reason to think of them otherwise.
Male	57	MA	California	A person who has identical wants and needs as my own.

Brown Skin, Dark Complected

Here in Iran there is no notable racial difference. Therefore, we rarely describe each other by race and it is more common to describe people by their culture. When I studied responses, I found that these responses need a separate sub-category in which Iranians are described by their race which is most fit with the stereotype of "brown skin." 119 respondents' answers were subcategorized in this category and they consisted 24.9% responses of this category and 6.8% of all responses. Examples are:

Cross Cultural Schemata 165

Male		BA	Washington	Brown skin.
Female	30	MA	Louisiana	A person on Indian Descent with brown/tan skin and dark hair and dark eyes.
Female	42	BA	Virginia	dark hair and tan skin
Male	55	MA	Virginia	Dark hair and complexion.
Male	45	PhD	Colorado	The first images that I see are a woman and a child (maybe 5 or 6 years old) leaving their house. I cannot see the house, only the front door. I believe they are walking toward the car that is parked at the front of the house. Both mother and child have tanned skin, and she is wearing some type of head scarf.
Female	19	High School	Indiana	No clear image comes to mind as I know a large variety of people live there. I would imagine darker skin due to the climate tendencies?
Female	34	MA	Kansas	I first think of race…dark hair, brown eyes, darker skin than mine (I am very pale). For clothing I picture first someone in western clothes, like a button-down shirt tucked into pants. I picture a man first. For women, I picture someone who is young and pretty with their hair covered and wearing sunglasses, maybe because I have seen this type of photo in the media
Female	24	BA	Kansas	A Muslim person with dark hair, eyes, and complexion.
Female	23	BA	Iowa	Someone with darker skin, but not necessarily dressed differently

				from you or I.
Female	63	MA	Kentucky	Male---dark shin and beard
Female	50	MA	Kentucky	Swarthy complexion, black hair
Male	57	PhD	Florida	Mostly appearance - dark hair and eyes.
Female	35	MA	Iowa	Darker Skin Dark hair
Female	32	BA	Kentucky	A darker-skinned person with dark hair and eyes
Female	35	MA	Idaho	Just an image of someone with dark hair and darker skin. Nothing negative about personality.
Female	52	PhD	Ohio	A young man with very light brown skin, black hair and an aquiline nose.
Female	29	PhD	Maryland	Someone with slightly darker skin than I have, but other than that, nothing specific. No specific eye color or clothing, age, gender etc.
Female	43	MA	Indiana	Someone with dark skin and hair...a student.
Female	20	High School	Arkansas	- Dark skinned - Foriegn (sic) acent (sic)
Female	62	MA	Missouri	Dark-skinned person, maybe the woman wearing shawl over her head. Born in Iran.
Female	23	BA	Missouri	An individual with brown skin and dark hair
Female	57	BA	Missouri	a brown skinned person
Male	52	MA	Missouri	Brown hair, brown skin
Female	54	MA	Kentucky	Dark hair, darker, olive skin
Male	67	PhD	Nebraska	Dark hair Slender
Male	32	MA	Nebraska	A dark complected (sic) man, dark hair, dark facial hair. The

				man is a Muslim.
Male	41	BA	Michigan	Darker skin less than black, black hair, brown eyes
Female	24	MA	Mississippi	An individual whom is of dark complexion, black hair, and is of Indian descent.
Male	46	PhD	Oregon	Someone with darker skin, black hair, brown eyes
Female	52	High School	Wisconsin	A person of darker skin color and darker eye color.

Citizen of Iran, Not American

A group of respondents simply describe Iranians as someone who is the citizen of Iran or someone who is not the citizen of America. 164 responses fell into this category which means they consisted 34.3% of responses in this category and 9.4% of all responses. It seems that a considerable number of American respondents were not interested in making difference between Iranians and people of other nationalities. Examples are:

Female	47	MA	Louisiana	Different nationality
Female	25	High School	Louisiana	A citizen of Iran.
Male	57	PhD	Michigan	An individual that is a citizen of Iran?
Male	36	BA	Arizona	Someone of Persian ethnicity, probably Muslim, most likely either an older expat or a student.
Male	28	MA	Illinois	Persian.
Female	51	BA	Florida	An individual whose country of citizenship would be Iran.
	75	High School	Texas	Somebody that was born in Iran and is now in the USA.

Male	70	PhD	Florida	a person who comes from Iran, like Iranian friends, colleages (sic) and students
Female	60	MA	Idaho	A person who lives in Iran.
Male	22	BA	California	I picture a person of Iranian ethnicity who is a citizen of Iran.
Male	61	PhD	Texas	No particular image; simply, what the phrase states, i.e., a citizen of Iran.
Female	62	PhD	Indiana	A person who probably speaks Persian and is likely Muslim and someone who has gone through a lot of changes in the country in the last few years
Female	67	PhD	Kansas	Someone who is from Iran
Female	47	PhD	Kentucky	An person who is a citizen of Iran, this may be one that was born in Iran or imported to Iran and took up citizenship.
Female	22	High School	Kentucky	A person from Iran. I have no biases against people from Iran.
Female	67	MA	Kansas	Simply a person from Iran. As far as visual images, I think of somewhat darker skin and dark hair and women with covered heads. Intelligent people.
Female	24	BA	Minnesota	A person whom has earned dually citizenship from Iran and the country they are in. They are currently residing in the country they have citzenship (sic).
Male		PhD	Missouri	Simply, a citezen (sic) whose origin is from Iran
Male	44	BA	Iowa	A citizen of Iran.

Female	50	High School	Arkansas	in a broad sense culturally different from Americans
Male	59	PhD	Massachusetts	Someone from Iran, whose first language is Farsi, probably Muslim, but possibly Zoroastrian.
Male	23	BA	Indiana	Someone not from the U.S.
Male	42	PhD	Wisconsin	A person of Iranian descent.
Male	30	MA	Missouri	The Iranian capital of Tehran.
Female	52	BA	Missouri	A person who may have been born in the United States but is of Iranian descent (one or both parents are Iranian). Or a person who moved from an Iranian country and has earned citizenship in the United States.
Female	39	MA	Indiana	An image doesnt (sic) come to mind, but I think of someone that is born in Iran.
Male	54	PhD	Missouri	A person who lives in Iran.
Male	33	High School	Tennessee	A person from Iran with dark hair and medium stature.
Male	24	BA	New Jersey	A person of Persian decent. Similar to Arab, and yet different.
Male	77	PhD	Mississippi	An individual born and lived in Iran
Female	24	MA	Mississippi	A person in Iran.
Male	61	PhD	New Jersey	an iranian (sic)
Male	67	MA	New Jersey	An individual who lives in Iran legally.
Female	67	MA	Idaho	An image of someone who was born in Iran and may wear clothing unique to their culture, have darker skin than myself and speak another language.
Male	45	PhD	New York	A person who is from Iran.

Muslim

In Iran, we are used to think that most of the people we see in our daily encounters are Muslim (of course these days you might see some Iranians who identify themselves as "not religious" but even these people are most possibly children of a Muslims couple). Nevertheless, as United States is a country with high diversity, it is not uncommon that Americans identify other people by their religion. 38 responses fell into this sub-category which means they consist 7.9% of the responses in this subcategory and 2.2% of all responses. Examples are:

Male	31	PhD	Texas	Muslim
Male	75	PhD	Florida	Persian Muslim
Female	43	PhD	Missouri	A woman wearing makeup and a hijab - modern but visibly Muslim
Male	68	PhD	Rhode Island	A Moslem.
Female		BA	Wyoming	Religious Wealthy
Male	46	High School	North Carolina	An image of males in "western" style clothing, but women covered in modest garb.
Male	70	PhD	Wisconsin	Male with a beard.
Female	52	PhD	Virginia	A Muslim Male or Female in garb appropriate to their faith.
Female	36	MA	Rhode Island	Someone of the Muslim religion.
Male	50	MA		Muslim
Female	47	BA	California	someone who may believe in the Muslim faith.
Female	25	BA	Arizona	I think of a darker skinned individual who is Muslim
Female	20	High School	Oregon	Muslim, darker skin
Male	42	MA	Mississippi	muslim (sic), beard
Female	65	PhD	Indiana	I think the person might be Muslim, May have skin a shade of tan to medium brown, dark hair,

				dark eyes, slight build.
Male		PhD	Massachusetts	Muslim
Male	33	BA	Wisconsin	Women in headdress
Female	39	MA	Connecticut	most likely Shia Islam of persian (sic) decent
Female	44	BA	California	Different culture, likely Muslim
Female	65	BA	Connecticut	Islam

Middle Eastern

I already explained that race is a common feature when Americans want to refer to different people. One of the common themes in my responses was referring to Iranians as "Middle Eastern" people. In sum, 95 respondents gave accounts which were most related to this sub-category. They consisted 19.9% of the responses in this category and 5.4% in all categories. Examples include:

Male	37	BA	California	Assyrian Christian
Male	56	PhD	Michigan	A middle-eastern racial features
Female	44	High School	Virginia	dark hair, dark eyes an middle eastern look
Female	30	MA	Pennsylvania	Middle eastern
Male	38	MA	Georgia	A middle-eastern looking individual. I picture the men perhaps with a beard and the women likely wearing a hijab.
Female	49	PhD	Colorado	Middle eastern - skin darker than white- lighter than most Hispanics
Female	33	MA	Arizona	Middle eastern man.
Female	23	BA	Illinois	Middle eastern, Muslim, light skin
Male	21	BA	Kansas	Someone from the Middle East.
Female	36	High School	Florida	Middle Eastern, olive skin, dark eyes, women likely wear head scarves to cover their hair, modest dress, predominantly Muslim

Female	59	BA	Montana	a person from the middle-east
Male	37	BA	Kentucky	Someone of middle-eastern decent, who is likely Islamic by faith.
Female	43	High School	Missouri	Someone with middle eastern coloring and features
Female	26	MA	Nebraska	a citizen from the middle east
Male		BA	Kansas	Someone from the middle east. Or Muslim religion.
Male	28	BA	Michigan	Middle eastern, darker complected, clean, male w/ beard, light clothing.
Female	22	High School	Kansas	A Middle Eastern person.
Female	36	MA	Mississippi	Someone who look's middle eastern. A classmate from school.
Male	61	BA	Michigan	No real images other than that of a ethnic middle eastern person. Olive skin, dark hair.
Male	25	MA	Mississippi	Iranians are not monolithic. I think of the skin tone, the culturally appropriate dress, i think conservative; but all in the context of those not being the ONLY identities of Iranians.
Male	62	PhD	Montana	Someone of middle eastern decent.
Female	32	MA	North Carolina	I picture a middle eastern person that is an American citizen. Medium complexion wth (sic) black hair clearly not African Amercan (sic), Asian, or caucasian (sic).
Male	55	PhD	North Dakota	A person from the Middle East.
Female	21	High School	Colorado	Middle Eastern Culture
Male	64	MA	Ohio	Someone who comes from the Middle East. Someone whose

				culture is based with strong ties to their religion
Male	52	PhD	Pennsylvania	Persian, Middle East.
Male	65	BA	South Carolina	A person from the Middle East
Male	59	MA	Utah	Middle eastern ancestry. Muslim.
Male	58	MA	Pennsylvania	Middle Eastern possibly non Christian or Muslim.
Male	35	BA	Utah	A middle eastern looking man

NEGATIVE

In chapter 1 we saw that almost all previous studies of all kind show that American public are commonly negative about Iranians. Like the previous studies, this study shows that near 40% of American respondents are negative about Iranians while about 20% gave positive accounts about Iranians. The negative comments were categorized into 10 sub-categories and in this section I will present examples of perceptions in each category. These examples will show the nature of media representation of Iranians in the West, which as we saw in the previous chapter, is responsible for creating negative image of the Iranian people.

Subdued Women

The stereotype of Iranian woman as passive, victims and veiled is common in the West. Whenever I meet a Western scholar, one of the most recurring theme is the question of women in Iran. I always say that representation of Iranian women in the West is one sided and while it is true that some laws regarding women in Iran are unfair, women in Iran have their own sexist privileges. For example, each year tens of thousands of men are trialed for failing to pay their wives and thousands of them go to the jail. Moreover, it seems for Westerners that Iranian women are forced to wear hijab. Although a fraction of the society (who possibly have means to travel to West and have chance to talk to people in the West) do not believe in hijab, a considerable number of women still choose hijab (as was the case in the previous regime in which people were free to choose their appearance). Anyway, the stereotypes about Iranian women are visible in the comments of a group of respondents in this study.

47 respondents in this study gave comments in which women were portrayed as subdued subjects either to men or to the society. They consisted 7% of responses in this category and 2.7% of all responses across all categories. Examples include:

Female	35	BA	Kansas	Sympathy, empathy, images of a sad woman not allowed to vote or have any liberty
Female	62	BA	Michigan	Women who are forced to wear clothing that covers their entire body. I feel sorry for these women and I'm glad I was born in the United States so I am not subjected to this kind of oppression.
Female	55	BA	Florida	dark hair, olive skin, religious, head gear women, inequality for women
Male	30	MA	Illinois	Muslim culture, mistreatment of women.
Female	59	PhD	Florida	Muslim, prior to 1978 tradition of excellent higher education including for women. Post Shah the system may not be as interested in pursuit of science and not as supportive of women.
Male	64	PhD	Colorado	The Muslim religion. Oppression of women. Lack of individual freedom.
Female	50	High School	Kansas	Conflict. How women have to cover their faces and how they are

				being abused and treated.
Female	43	BA	Kentucky	Women in head scarves or burka, men in more modern dress, "western" business clothes, dark complexion, dark hair, facial hair on men. Women in submissive, servant like roles with authoritarian men.
Female	43	BA	Kentucky	I think, like children everywhere, it depends on the circumstances but with Iran in particular I think of whether the child is somewhere safe or in a war zone... either happy and bright eyed, curious... or shell shocked and scared
Female	35	BA	Kentucky	Middle Eastern person. Females with less rights then men and females mostly covered with at least a head scarf.
Female	50	PhD	Texas	a person like every other person in the world, except for women which are oppressed under Islamic rule.
Female	59	PhD	Maryland	it is a terrible tragedy that Iranian women, who used to be empowered and had extremely successful careers, are now subject to religiously imposed restrictions on their conduct and especially education and careers. This is a waste and a shame.
Female	26	MA	California	men extremely superior to women
Male	42	PhD	Massachusetts	Oppression, suppression, women treated like slaves, lack of freedom

Female	60	PhD	Massachusetts	oppressed women militant men poor children
Male	23	BA	Connecticut	Middle Eastern, dominant male figure.
Female	38	MA	New York	I feel a lot of sympathy. I think of women who don't have as many rights as I do. I think of the head scarves. I think of people living in unsafe conditions.
Female	50	MA	Michigan	Images of women in hijab, women not having equal access to laws, education, and careers, government oppression of some people.
Female	63	MA	Idaho	Desert, sand, white robes, sun tanned skin, primitive, women without equal rights and more subservient to men, political unrest.
Female	35	MA	Georgia	Dark hair and skin, traditional Iranian clothing. Male hierarchy.
Female	49	BA	North Dakota	Women who must cover their faces, look downward and walk behind the male family member escorting them. Giant pictures of the Ayatollah on the sides of buildings. Girls tortured for going to school.
Female	60	BA	Oklahoma	Muslim women -covered clothing
Female	59	BA	South Dakota	Americans most often see Iranians in television or internet news segments that cover the disagreements between the U.S. and Iran -- those images are most often groups of angry men. While those are negative images, we

Female	59	BA	South Dakota	understand that ordinary Iranians, like ordinary Americans, don't always agree with their political leaders and generally just want to have a good life for themselves and their families. Think women NEED MORE RIGHTS in Islamic countries, though!

War Torn

62 of our respondents reported cross cultural schemata which imagined Iran as a war torn country. They consist 9.2% of respondents in this category and 3.5% of all respondents. Examples include:

Female	41	High School	Utah	Muslim culture, war
Female	34	BA	Florida	a brown woman in a hijab, war zone
Male	56	PhD	Florida	The problems they face from war, internal conflict and terrorism.
Female	26	BA	Arizona	A picture of deployed soldiers/military
Female	23	BA	Kansas	War and refugees
Female	50	BA	Missouri	Different clothing. War.
Female	36	MA	Indiana	A person from Iran, war
Female	42	PhD	Texas	Middle East (sic), cover up, hot weather, bombs, wars
Female	28	MA	Maryland	War
Female	54	BA	Indiana	A person living in a war-torn country where each day could be their last.
Female	31	MA	Pennsylvania	Someone from Iran; someone

Male	63	PhD	Kansas	who is living in a war-torn middle-eastern country; women in beautiful head scarves; men in robes; Head covering, Muslim, conflict and strife, centuries of struggle dating back to Abraham.
Female	28	MA	Missouri	fight, headdress
	60	PhD	Missouri	fleeing families, cultural and political breakdown causing population victimization
Female	45	BA	Nebraska	News footage from 20 years ago and mention of a Rick Steves episode
Male	42	BA	Nebraska	Violence
Female	38	MA	Mississippi	War
Female	54	PhD	Mississippi	The War Zone Country that the Iranians live in.
Female	21	High School	Illinois	The conflict on television.
Female	57	PhD	Oregon	Poor women, children and elderly trying to survive a war torn country with few resources.
Female	57	BA	Wisconsin	A lot of strife ridden faces. Angry, sad war torn.
Female	58	MA	Oklahoma	A war torn country
Female	57	MA	Texas	Someone who might have had to leave their own country due to political unrest
Female	18	High School	Nevada	Terrorism, war, hunger
Male	22	BA	New York	A person struggling to maintain dignity, cultural and community identity in a region that is fractured by conflict.
Female	54	MA	Louisiana	Honestly, nothing. Maybe "Oh, I hope they don't go back" because

Cross Cultural Schemata 179

				of the unrest there.
Male	69	MA	Texas	A person from a country that has been in a state of civil unrest and military conflict for a long period of years. A person likely to have different religious and political views compared to western nations including America.
Female	26	MA	Texas	Darker complexion, the dessert, war.
Female	31	BA	Michigan	Oppression, war, anger & sadness
Female	40	MA	Oklahoma	News media images of conflict
Female	35	PhD	Washington	desert women with covered heads/faces war torn buildings
Female	40	PhD	Alabama	Fighting in the Middle East
Female	38	MA	Alabama	Someone who has witnessed a lot of warfare in their lifetime.
Female	57	High School	Alaska	Mideast Nation in turmoil
Male	38	BA	Delaware	Sadly, US Drone strikes
Female	58	High School	California	Images of turmoil and violence. These are problems that only their leaders and people of their region can resolve for themselves. There's too much in-fighting.
Male	33	BA	California	captured journalist the cast of the FOX TV show Tyrant the iran (sic) conflict troubled sad images of children in war zone
Female	42	BA	Arizona	War
Female	26	MA	Virginia	I'm ashamed to say I don't know too much about Iranian culture. What initially comes to mind are

				women in head coverings and a sense of fear for the citizens due to all the conflict in the middle east.
Female	19	High School	Washington	I think of war, and the soliders (sic) that fight constantly, I know some iranian (sic) soldiers are torchured (sic) and some Iranians are labeled in a negative way
Female	43	MA	Maine	Someone from Iran. Someone with a darker colored skin (deep tan) with brown eyes and dark hair. There seems to be a large amount of dust as well (the desert village). Unfortunately, with the way things are today, the very first image that comes to mind is that of someone living in a wartorn country - maybe displaced.
Female	26	MA	Pennsylvania	classmates from Temple, television shows, Iran/Iraq war,
Male	54	PhD	Alabama	War torn. Exploited by their own government and U.S. interest.
Female	43	PhD	Arizona	I usually envision impoverished women and children in a desert environment with war-torn buildings in the background.
Female	48	MA	New Jersey	Coming from a war zone.
Male	62	MA	Nebraska	Probably Muslim. From a wartorn country. Might or might not be sympathetic to European/ American points of view. A range of philosophical positions from first-world western to radical Islam.
Female	24	BA	Connecticut	Someone who is of the muslim

				(sic) faith and lives in a country of war
Female	33	High School	New Jersey	A person of Middle Eastern decent coming from the country of Iran. I wonder where in Iran they are from. How much of the war they have seen and how it has affected themselves and their families.
Female	64	High School	Oregon	Fear, war, demeaning to women, very backwords (sic), possibly not educated.

Arab (Negatively Viewed)

81 participants in this study had cross cultural schemata of Iranians as though Iranians are Arab people, but in a negative way. This negativity was determined by the language of the comments in the American context. These respondents consisted 12% of participants in this category and 4.6% of all participants. Examples include:

Male	32	MA	Florida	Tan skin, head dressing of some sort, hot living conditions.
Female	25	MA	Florida	I think of a (sic) older man in a white outfit with a white hat on. I aslo (sic) think of war and poverty.
Female	29	BA	Florida	a tall man with very tan skin, dark hair, and a beard
Female	43	PhD	Florida	The words: "diversity" and "religious conservatism" come to mind. Diversity means to me the practiced religions and degrees to which they are practiced. The images of a hijab for a woman

				who practices (or respects in public) Islam and a skullcap, fez, turban or headscarf for males of different religions are the images that come to my mind. Also, I think of someone Iranian as strong in beliefs and stature - as a citizen who has faced numerous difficulties as a result of living in a country for some time that has faced intense conflicts from outside and within.
Female	61	PhD	Tennessee	Someone with black hair, covered with material, dark skinned, dressed in a colorful robe.
Male	45	PhD	Florida	muslim (sic), arabic (sic) appearance, dark hair, dark eyes
Male	24	BA	Utah	A middle eastern person with slightly darker skin and dark features wearing slightly different clothes from western culture.
Female	40	MA	Maryland	Arab decent, muslim (sic)
Female	40	MA	California	Muslim, good food, possible radicals, Arabic.
Female	31	BA	Alaska	An Arabic person dressed conservatively
Male	25	BA	Arizona	Mustaches, dark skin, loose clothes
Male	35	MA	Idaho	Families, walking down a busy street, entering mosques, traditional ethnic clothes, etc.
Female	35	PhD	Tennessee	Women in long shirts and covered faces/hair with wraps carrying a child on her hip.
Male	30	BA	Kansas	A person of Arabian descent who is most likely a Muslim.
Female	62	BA	Maryland	Someone who generally looks

				Arabic (dark hair, dark eyes, Caucasian features, tannish skin color)
Male	48	MA	Kansas	Dark skin, beard or facial hair, blue long sleeve shirt with collar.
Male	84	PhD	Kansas	A bearded man wearing a white garment.
Female	67	PhD	Kentucky	body fully clothed
Male	60	BA	Kentucky	Desert wonderer (sic)
Female	32	MA	Kansas	Male, dark hair, dark eyes. Wearing a scarf (which a lot of guys in my area do not).
Female	53	MA	Kansas	An Arab man or woman that grew up in a (sic) area of the world that is mostly desert. Their skin is brown, and their clothes cover most of their body, despite the heat. I see a people that are deeply devote to their religion.
Female	47	BA	Nebraska	Dark complected, bearded man with traditional arabic (sic) head wrap/clothing
Male	25	BA	Michigan	A person holding an Iranian flag in a sandy desert wearing ropes and maybe a scarf.
Female	38	BA	Mississippi	Oil Turban 911
Male	57	BA	Texas	desert people
Female		MA	South Dakota	Muslim religion Women wearing Burka's Desert landscape Beards Strife from years of war Refugees
Female	42	MA	Oregon	a brown-skinned male with facial hair, wearing all white

Turban, Burqa, Robe, Hijab or Niqab

137 respondents referred to Islamic dress when they read phrase "an Iranian citizen" and therefore their responses were put into the category of "Turban, Burqa, Robe, Hijab or Niqab." Their accounts consisted 20.3% responses in this category and 7.8% of all responses. Examples are:

Male	27	MA	Kansas	Turban wearing men, veiled women. Dark complected skin and black hair.
Male	31	BA	Kansas	I think of a man or women with slightly tanned skin and dark hair. Females I imagine dressing according to Islamic tradition (Burka, hijab, etc.), while men may wear locally made (non-western fashion) pants and shirts.
Female	39	MA	Kansas	turban, beards, terrorism
Male	33	MA	Ohio	Middle eastern person with a turban
Male	29	MA	Kansas	Shawls over the face and complete coverage of the body for women
Female	63	High School	Iowa	males-head wrap on head & dark skin with white clothing females-dark skin with white dress and black mark on forehead.
Female	38	MA	Kentucky	Turbans, beards. Centuries-old culture, Middle East.
Female	26	BA	Nebraska	a dark complected person with a robe and turban
Female	61	MA	Missouri	A person in a chador.
Male	53	MA	Kentucky	Dark Hair Large, distinctive nose. Dressed in black burkah (if woman) Dressed in out of style (to me) jeans (if man)

Male	29	BA	Indiana	Turbin (sic). Beard. Long clothing.
Male	19	High School	Minnesota	A man with beard and a turban.
Female	69	MA	Colorado	Women wearing scarves and coverings.
Female	29	BA	Minnesota	young woman wearing a chador.
Female	23	BA	Nebraska	A Middle Eastern individual. A large number of Middle Eastern individuals follow the Islamic religion, so I might picture burqas or at least headscarves (for women).
Male	70	PhD	Wisconsin	A bearded Muslim man or a Muslim woman perhaps in a head cover.
Female	28	High School	Missouri	A woman in a chador.
Female	46	PhD	Minnesota	Oil, turbans, white clothing, and veiled women.
Female	56	MA	Missouri	Turbans on men black sarongs and head cover on women
Male	39	PhD	Missouri	Men who dress like Osma (sic) Bin Landen (beard and head dress) and women completely covered in dark clothing
Male	28	MA	Missouri	The image of a dark complected man pops into my mind. Sometimes he is wearing a turban, while other times he is not.
Female	25	BA	Missouri	Women in burkas, foreign accents
Female	29	BA	Missouri	Women in headscarves, dark skinned men with moustaches.
Female	19	High School	Minnesota	turbans
Female	30	MA	Washington	A woman with a head scarf.
Female	19	High School	Michigan	A woman in the hijab

Male	63	MA	Nebraska	Male>beard, open collar shirt, Female> scarf, covered dress, beautiful eyes
Male	61	BA	New Jersey	ladies wearing scarves over there face

Poverty, Bad Living Condition

56 people in this project reported poverty and bad living condition whenever they heard the phrase "an Iranian citizen." They consisted 8.3% of respondents in this category and 3.2% of all participants. Examples are:

Female	50	BA	Kansas	I feel sorry for the 90% that is taking the blunt of the anger from victims when it is only 10% that are causing the issues.
Male	65	MA	Missouri	the images from the media: they show the outdoor cafes which show groups of people in the lower class.
Female	21	High School	Texas	A person from Iran in need of safety.
Male	25	BA	Missouri	An image of village leaders.
	53	BA	Arkansas	Someone that has learn to adapt to a challenging environment.
Female	50	MA	Kansas	a victim who needs our help
Female	55	BA	Missouri	Middle Eastern, Muslim. Several family members in one household.
Female	61	PhD	Florida	People who are between worlds of power. I have sympathy for them and can't imagine what it would be like to live among violence.
Female	39	MA	North Dakota	An immigrant with a family coming to the US either for asylum or education

Female	58	BA	North Dakota	Family trying to escape tyranny, forced changes on women's lifestyle over my lifetime, and Americans and others trying to stick their noses in something to try to make a change where perhaps they should not be.
Female	45	High School	Colorado	Women dressed in black and people constantly having to live under the threat of violence.
Female	40	MA	Virginia	Pity, sorrow and fear. I feel like those poor people have suffered so much more than I will ever begin to know. I wonder how much one person can endure for their level is obviously going to be quite different than me. I think of arid lands with water being difficult to come by making food expensive because it is likely imported from other countries and the government may or may not have their hand in there selfishly inflating food costs, taxes, etc. I don't know what it is like to walk down the same streets as people carrying large artillery, or to walk by buildings that have been destroyed by mortars and just left to deteriorate.
Female	41	MA	Rhode Island	a citizen of a country that is more politically isolated and subject to international pressure
Female	39	BA	North Dakota	A foreign person living off our government.
Male	57	MA	South Carolina	Some one (sic) who has fled the conflict in Iran and become a US citizen....which elicits a positive feeling

Male	56	MA	Nevada	Young guy with beard looking for a job
Male	38	BA	Minnesota	Suffering
Male	57	BA	Rhode Island	A person living in the middle east under great duress due to continued religious infighting and world intervention.
Male	55	BA	California	depends on context. normal somewhat higher educated person for over here in the US. For a citizen in Iran: perhaps less to no education, with less to no material wealth.
Male	20	High School	Minnesota	An unhappy Muslim fellow.
Male	57	MA	Washington	Poor, plain clothing, women with heads covered.
Male	37	PhD	Washington	Oppressed, Muslim, poor
Male	20	High School	Alabama	A desert with white buildings and people walking through the town. Children playing soccer in the dirt/sand.
Male	62	PhD	Alabama	grieved
Female	56	PhD	Arkansas	Unfortunately it is negative. Either dire poverty or extremist
Female	35	PhD	South Dakota	Muslim--hajib, mosques, large rich/poor gap
Female	73	MA	Arizona	A person who struggles
Female	63	MA	California	Someone who suffers and lives in turmoil and oppression
Female	29	BA	California	Refugees

Intolerant, Aggressive

108 response were sub-categorized into this group which means these responses consisted 16% of responses in this category and 6.2% of all responses in this study. Examples include:

Male	38	BA	Louisiana	Hezbollah, Hamas, and a bunch of other radical fanatics that hate America.
Female	54	MA	Louisiana	Intolerance
Male	42	PhD	Kentucky	Rigid beliefs.
Male	42	MA	Washington	Dark haired, medium dark skin, Bearded Conservative Muslim who hates the US, considers women to be inferior to men (rights, respect, equality, etc.), and wants Islam to take over the world.
Male	46	MA	Louisiana	Images of Marjane Satrapi from her graphic novel Persepolis and the animated film of the same name.
Female	25	BA	Pennsylvania	1970's; the shah; oil; middle eastern appearance; mountain desert; middle aged man with a stern expression
Female	56	BA	Pennsylvania	Muslim, anti-america (sic), possibly dangerous
Male	31	BA	Arizona	harsh speaking, proud, engineer weapons out of anything, poor
Female	65	PhD	Arizona	hairy men, conservative women, non-Christian.
Male	53	BA	Arizona	Radical religious person that feel Americans are infidels
Female	31	High School	Arizona	Men & women carrying large guns.
Male	70	High School	New Hampshire	A Dark complected man, serious eyes, not very happy, maybe a bit edgy.
Female	50	MA	Arizona	Middle eastern Muslims radicles is someone who likes conflict.
Male	54	MA	Texas	
Male	63	MA		Hard to make an objective image. To be alert, careful and

				keep distance.
Male	22	Primary School	Washington	Wild bastards
Female	50	MA	Kentucky	A member of the Moslem religion. Intolerant of the idea of freedom for women. Prone to violent behaviors or erratic outbursts of emotion that are easily provoked.
Male	32	BA	Indiana	Loyal and hardworking. But loyal to a fault
Female	21	High School	Kentucky	Dark skinned and dark haired people who are a threat to the united states. And possibly of the same decent as the people who brought down the towers on 9-11
Male	57	PhD	Kentucky	Dark hair, praying toward Mecca, burka, degradation of women in their culture, intolerance of others outside the Muslim faith
Female	56	MA	Maryland	A crowd of people fighting in Iran and saying expletives that they hate Americans. Very militant type individuals whose purpose is to demise the United States and kill its Citizens in retaliation for all done wrong to Iran by the Americans. Bomb touting individuals who are prepared to die to make American's suffer.
Female	27	MA	Minnesota	Dark colored skin, head wraps, large guns (unfortunately), colorful clothing, small children who look very skinny, a country

Female	27	BA	Wisconsin	landscape with dry dirt ground, The extras in "Homeland," people in light, loose fitting clothing. Women with a scarf or shawl over their hair, men with beards.
Female	26	BA	Indiana	desert and heat dark hair and eyes sun darkened skin colorful clothing and culture hate and sorrow
Male	49	MA	Missouri	Middle East, dark skin, dark hair, hairy body, wearing traditional clothes of the culture, very religious, intolerant, male,
Female	47	MA	Missouri	I've had limited exposure to people who live in Iran. Images from long ago of people in Iran filling the streets in support of Khomeini after toppling the Shah are all I really have. That is pretty sad but true. I don't think it applies to current citizens, but it was the first thing I thought of.
Female	33	MA	Kansas	I think that I probably have an innately negative image of Iran and the Iranian people. However, I am able to shake that feeling if I take a second to think about it. I certainly wouldn't want another country to think that all Americans are like Rush Limbaugh, Kim Kardashian, or George W. Bush.
Male	56	PhD	New Jersey	fanatic Muslim

Female	70	PhD	New York	Jews that were forced to leave and have resettled here - people in Iran who are Moslem and hostile to Jews and to the US
Male	26	MA	New Mexico	Enemy of Israel
Male	59	BA	Texas	Anti-American Radical muslim (sic) I know that not all are that way but it's what jumps to mind.
Male	42	MA	North Dakota	Religious fanatics.
Female	47	PhD	Virginia	a woman in a black burqa, angry protesters, people with limited freedom
Female	39	BA	North Dakota	Muslim, poor, anti-american (sic), "old world" thinking, belligerent
Female	44	BA	New Mexico	Mistrust, crazed zealot
Female	22	BA	North Dakota	Someone, that would presumeably but not necessarily have tan skin and dark hair, and potentially be assertive in speaking mannerisms
Male	66	BA	North Dakota	Muslim, reactionary, emotional
Male	65	PhD	Oklahoma	not good unfortunately... I see constant fighting, anti-American, egotistical people that are hard to reason with
Female	59	MA	Missouri	I don't have an immediate image but if I think about it for a few minutes, I see a map of Iran and then people praying.
Female	46.602	MA	Louisiana	Intolerance

Terrorist

29 respondents directly or indirectly said when they wanted to imagine an Iranian citizen, the first thing that comes to their mind is a terrorist. Their responses consisted 4.3% of negative cross cultural schemata of Iranians and 1.7% of all responses in this study. Some of the examples of this sub-category are:

Female	60	BA	Ohio	terrorist
Female	34	MA	Kentucky	Someone with a gun
Male	68	PhD	Wisconsin	Muslim, terrorist,
Male	65	MA	Virginia	Islam, radical conservative, possibly terrorist
Female	50	High School	Indiana	Terroist (sic)
Male	51	BA	Iowa	Ter·ror·ist (sic)
Female	25	MA	Iowa	9/11. Terrorits (sic) attacks on U.S.
Female	51	MA	Kentucky	Seeing as how I do not have any acquaintances from Iran to help temper my stereotype, I do feel a little uneasy and my image immediately reflects back to 9/11.
Female	50	MA	Mississippi	terrorists
Male	54	PhD	New York	Terrorists. Islamic religious zealots who behead journalists.
Female	62	BA	Oklahoma	Terrorism, Middle East conflicts, illiteracy, suppression of women, violence
Male	66	BA	Virginia	9/11/2001
Male	17	High School	Arkansas	Woolwich murder
Male	55	BA	Vermont	terrorist
Female	54	MA	Wisconsin	The images shown on from TV after 911.
Male	60	MA	Tennessee	terrorist, war, religious zealous
Female	41	MA	Alabama	Taliban soldiers with guns

Female	50	MA	Oklahoma	Someone different, maybe terrorist
Male	58	PhD	California	Terrorism and oppression
Male	34	BA	Arizona	Terrorist
Female	42	BA	Michigan	Iran, "terrorists," war
Male	59	BA	Alabama	Are they terroist (sic)
Female	60	BA	North Dakota	person from a terrorist country with no respect for America

Hostage Crisis

18 respondents directly said that the image of an Iranian citizen is inextricably intertwined with their memoirs of Iranian Hostage Crisis. They consisted 2.7% the respondents in the negative category and 1% of all respondents in this study. Crosstabulation showed that these people tend to be older. Examples are:

Male	45	MA	Kentucky	Iranian Hostage Crisis
Male	56	PhD	Iowa	I still think back to the Iranian hostage situation during Jimmy Carter's administration
Female	53	BA	Nebraska	my high school friend whose father worked at the American embassy during the kidnapping under Khomeini's rule.
Male	49	MA	New York	Mostly fashionable young people held, and older original revolutionaries held hostage by the conservative mullahs.
Male	59	BA	North Carolina	Radical racists and hostage holder
Female	47	BA	Oregon	The image that comes to mind is that of the American diplomats that were held hostage during the late 70s and early 80s. I was a around 14 at the time and I remember not really

				understanding the crisis.
Male	51	BA	Pennsylvania	scenes from the Iranian hostage crisis; Ayatollah Khomeni
Male	56	BA	Tennessee	The Iranian government appears to dislike the U. S. Government and it international policies. I don't think the U. S. will forget the Iranian hostage crisis in my life time.
Male	53	PhD	Texas	The hostage crisis in the late 1970s. The ongoing tensions with Israel. Islamic extremism.
Male	66	BA	Texas	The Iranian hostage situation of the 80's. The Iranians beating themselves with chains across their backs. Holding the hostages at the political request (supposedly) of Mr. Reagan and to the detriment of Mr. Carter.
Male	49	PhD	North Carolina	Protestors outside the American Embassy during the Hostage crisis. As an adult, I worked with a number of Iranians and most of them preferred to be known as "Persians."
Male	55	PhD	Florida	The image I have is of mobs, backed by the government, storming the US Embassy in Tehran and taking diplomats hostage. The next image is of Neda Soltan being shot in the street by paramilitary created by the Islamic government. Watching this young woman die and then watching how the government blamed it on the BBC and US journalists angered me.
Female	61	PhD	New Jersey	I think about the Iranians holding Americans hostage for over one year.

Ahmadinejad, Bad Iranian Politicians

61% of the respondents referred to Iranian politicians and particularly Mahmoud Ahmadinejad when they read the phrase "an Iranian citizen." Their responses consisted 9.1% of the responses in this category and 3.5% of all responses in this study. Examples include:

Female	38	MA	Florida	I don't really have an image so to speak. I guess if I thought about it, probably a woman covered from head-to-toe or the former president Ahmadinejad. I'm sure that citizens of Iran look very different in terms of dress, language, and culture depending on which part of the country they live in (i.e., Rural vs. City).
Male	28	High School	Georgia	Hijabs. Facial hair. Ahmadinejad. Kufta.
				The differences in 1970s Tehran and 2010s Tehran.
Male	33	BA	Florida	Oil, Mahmoud Ahmadinejad, terror.
Male	60	PhD	Virginia	Ayatollah Khomeini
Male	63	PhD	Hawaii	Ahmedinijad
				The "Happy" tribute folks that got in trouble for that.
Male	25	MA	Arizona	The ongoing war/bombings occurring right now in Iraq (I understand its (sic) not Iran). The Iranian President who was trying to build a nuclear weapon. Also, the Iranian Hostage Crisis in the 1970's.
Male	21	High School	Iowa	Someone who looks like Mahmoud Ahmadinejad.
Male	72	PhD	Maryland	Difficulties that Iranians have with theocratic government, and nuclear

				enrichment activities in Iran.
Male	33	MA	Arizona	Mahmoud Ahmadinejad
Male	30	BA	Michigan	Iranian President Mahmoud Ahmadinejad
Male	65	PhD	New York	I have mixed images about the phrase "an Iranian citizen." I get the impression that the governmental leaders in Iran are more concerned about power in their country and their region than the regular citizens in that country.
Male	25	MA	Iowa	Mahmoud Ahmadinejad
Female	20	BA	Michigan	The middle east. Oil. Ahmenijab (sic). Nuclear programs.
Male	47	PhD	New Jersey	Mahmoud Ahmadinejad
Male	58	PhD	Maryland	President Ahamadinajad picture
Male	46	PhD	New Jersey	The former PM Ahmadinejad
Male	25	High School	New York	Red, white and green. Vocal minority of extremists. Oppression and narrowmindedness from the government.
Male	37	BA	New York	A person oppressed by a leader that is hell bent on destroying anyone who is not of his beliefs.
Male	53	PhD	New Jersey	Flag-waving citizens. Former President Ahmadinejad addressing the UN: gutsy, proud. My colleague's father, living in an apartment in Tehran by himself, a lonely, old Jew surrounded by books.
Male	35	BA	North Carolina	the Ayatollah
Male	52	BA	Oklahoma	I'm afraid my initial mental image is of Mahmoud Ahmadinejad -- short beard, no tie.

Male	37	PhD	Oregon	Ahmedinazad (sic)
Male	44	BA	North Carolina	A culture made up of happy caring individuals striving to westernize a bit (more individual freedoms), with authoritarian religious-based government suppressing them (irony understood if this is a legitimate survey). I also think the government tends to radicalize segments of the Iranian population to have anti-American sentiment, but I'm guessing it's probably not a majority of people.
Male	65	PhD	Tennessee	Antiquities, oil, Abolhassan Banisadr Mohammad-Ali Rajai Ali Khamenei, Iranian Revolution
Female	59	BA	Illinois	Burqhas and militant mullahs.
Female	48	MA	Minnesota	War, violence, military, fanatical Muslim leaders
Male	55	PhD	Oklahoma	Ayatollah Khomeini with a menacing grin. Former President A. stating teat tsic) the Holocaust never happened.
Male	50	PhD	Virginia	I am around students of many backgrounds all of the time, so the first thing that comes to mind is an Iranian. I do not have any negative images, except perhaps those of the former Ayatollah Khomeini from back in the Carter administration.
Female	58	BA	Arizona	Someone who has bad government in their country.
Male	21	High School	Tennessee	Desert, nuclear weapons conflict, Mahmoud Ahmedinejad
Male	62	MA	Minnesota	Khameini (sic) or Ahmadinejad.
Male	33	BA	Oklahoma	Mahmoud Ahmadinejad, Islamic Culture.

Male	60	MA	Minnesota	No bad connotations arise from the phrase "An Iranian Citizen" since that implies a citizenship for Iran requies (sic) something else than any other country. I find the following questions misleading and the answers can be interpreted many different ways. I believe the current leaders of Iran are not what the Iranian Citizens expected when the Shaw if Iran was ousted in the early 70's. The current un-rest of the citizens proves that but any public demonstration of it leads to their personal disappearance or harassment of their families.
Male	60	MA	Minnesota	Just like Iraq, they only way they will be disposed will be with outside assistance. The culture of Iran is vast and old and has had a great impact on the rest of the world. This is far different than the current climate where an American could not walk the streets if Iran with the current government in charge.
Male	66	High School	Oregon	People from the middle east, ruled by a extreme conservative religious government.
Female	56	MA	Michigan	bearded men. Persia. President Ahmadinejad.
Male	38	BA	Alaska	Ahmedinejad speaking at the U.N.
Male	57	PhD	Wyoming	People who like the United States but have some real crazy leaders.
Male	26	BA	Delaware	I usually have a mental image of a conservatively dressed person in a burqa or hijab or other religious garb

				(i.e., Ali Khamenei) or an "americanized" (sic) styled dress for males, much like Mahmoud Ahmadinejad. As a people I assumed that the population is more religious compared to the US, mostly consisting of Muslims.
Male	29	PhD	Delaware	Mahmoud Ahmadinejad

Oppressed

75 respondents said the image of an Iranian citizen in their mind is the image of an oppressed person. These respondents consisted 11.1% of the respondents in this category and 4.3% of all responses in this study. Examples are:

Female	50	High School	Iowa	Oppressed
Male	43	BA	Texas	A person from the oppressive nation of Iran. A person with no rights and afraid for his life if he is a Christian.
Male	60	PhD	Kansas	Suffers under dictatorship
Male	68	PhD	Ohio	someone living under a repressive gvernment (sic)
Male	45	BA	Louisiana	Someone that is trying to become free.
Female	52	MA	Kansas	someone from Iran. A closed off society.
Female	17	High School	Texas	A practicing Muslim, Persian background, most likely against the current governmental system
Male	34	MA	New Mexico	I think of peaceful citizens who are oppressed by political Islam.
Female	45	MA	Kentucky	That's difficult. I think Muslim, but that does not always equate to

				anything other than that. I think about the Iranian leadership and wonder how that affects its people.
Female	47	MA	Wisconsin	persecution. unrest
Female	39	MA	Minnesota	I think of a politically oppressed people, as well as a degree of religious extremism. I also think of the immense beauty of the country, and feel saddened for the people that are subjected to tyrannical rule.
Male		PhD	Minnesota	An educated individual who does not have the freedom to speak and act freely about his/her beliefs.
Male		PhD	Kansas	A middle-eastern country that has become more theocractic (sic) over the past few decades.
Male	33	MA	Arizona	Islam, protests, revolution, twitter, modernity repressed by state and religious values
Female	42	MA	Michigan	I don't really have an image - my mind looks at the long history of conflict in a country -that used be more liberal and now isn't
Female		MA	Illinois	An oppressed citizen
Male		BA	Georgia	Oppressed muslim (sic) forced to adhear (sic).
Male	54	PhD	North Dakota	Individuals with a true desire to operate in a fully integrated world, but who are prevented at home from expressing their opinions and desires openly for fear of governmental and religious retribution.
Male	40	MA	Utah	I think of a citizen living under a corrupt government with another layer of oppression from the US government meddling in their affairs and adding to the mess.

Male	51	MA	Oklahoma	I think if governments would get out of the way, all people would most likely get along and be friends. Someone who lives under a theocracy, who does not have the same freedoms as a US citizen.
Male	68	PhD	Ohio	A Persian living in a very restricted culture that once was expanding and acting more like a state that wanted to react with many other states in the world.
Male	55	PhD	Oklahoma	Someone who likely is oppressed by a totalitarian government.
Female	27	BA	Florida	A citizen who may be a practicing Muslim. Someone whose culture and history is important to them. Depending on the age of the citizen, I see those who wish to stay in a more close-minded society, while the younger generation wishes for change.
Male	50	PhD	South Carolina	Someone living under a repressive regime. (I hope that's not offensive. If so, I apologize.)
Male	66	PhD	Tennessee	A Persian who lives under an oppressive, theocratic Islamic regime.
Male	61	PhD	New York	under oppressive regime
Female	56	MA	Minnesota	Overall, people and families like us. I worry that Iranian citizens are oppressed by their government, and perhaps not fully informed of the reality of world events because of government media censorship.
Female	56	MA	Minnesota	Because of oppression, I think Iranian people are vulnerable to radical thinking against America, and public protests
Male	39	BA	North	A people who live in fear due to

			Carolina	government agendas
Male	39	MA	Wyoming	Suppressed people.
Male	48	BA	California	Very few freedoms/rights to think and speak freely or critisize political or religious leaders.
Male	36	BA	Arkansas	muslim (sic) culture, no freedoms
Female	30	BA	Oregon	Traditional women in chador, or modern women in hijab with blue jeans. Old men with turbans and long beards. "Morality police" with batons. Thousands of people protesting in the cities after the election in 2009.
Female	43	BA	Washington	Someone who is living in oppression and lack of freedom.
Female	65	PhD	North Carolina	Muslim, conservative, disempowered, lacking free access to information, talented, artistic, intelligent. Lack of meaningful participation by women and girls in making decisions and governing. Difficult for women and girls to have freedom to get an education or make choices about marriage - or divorce!
Male	69	PhD	West Virginia	I think about people who have been repressed in several ways by dictatorial regimes for about 60 years. I admire people who resisted those regimes. And while I am a U.S. citizen, I am totally opposed to the central role the U.S. government and its "security" forces played in the overthrow of Mohammed Mossadegh in 1953. I think it is quite similar to the role the U.S. played in other nations, such as in the Congo with the death of Patrick Lumumba and in Chile with the death of Salvador

Male	59	PhD	Wisconsin	Allende. caucasian (sic) features, slightly darker skin than most Europeans muslim (sic) cultural traditions repressive government
Female	51	BA	Minnesota	Someone who is oppressed by a religious group.
Female	33	MA	Colorado	The protests that happened a few years ago when the young woman was shot
Male	73	PhD	Massachusetts	A person from a very old and rich culture currently suppressed by religious ideology
Female	37	MA	Massachusetts	someone who has lived under an oppressive government.
Female	38	MA	Maryland	An indigenous community of people still fighting for religious freedoms.
Male	57	PhD	New York	An oppressed people
Male	58	PhD	North Carolina	Someone living in Iran, most likely oppressed by a tyrannical government.
Female	49	MA	Kentucky	For the younger individuals, a person wanting business and social reforms hindered by the leadership.
Male	30	BA	Massachusetts	someone with a closely cropped beard protesting election results in the streets
Male	76	PhD	Connecticut	A person who is living under a very repressive regime, with very little hope of a better life.
Male	30	BA	South Carolina	Persian, likely Muslim, living in a theocratic state. Religion is an important part of his or her daily life, although less important, on statistical average, than it is to an American. Free expression is limited in many areas, and women in particular are most affected by this, and are subject

to a sort of "modesty police" which keeps them from dressing in the way they choose. Is likely to harbor negative opinions of Americans and Westerners, probably due to what we did to them in the 1950s.

POSITIVE

In previous chapter we saw that 363 respondents or 20.7% of participants in this study reported positive cross cultural schemata of Iranians. Sub-categorization of responses in this category yielded 7 sub-categories.

Friend, Classmate, Student or Colleague

There are currently more than 10000 Iranians students in the U.S. This of course entail intercultural encounter that can shape perceptions. 93 responses fell into this subcategory which means they consisted 25.6% of responses in the positive category and 5.3% of all responses in this study. Examples are:

Male	20	BA	New York	My classmates.
Female	26	BA	California	Good friends, and good persian (sic) food.
Female	73	MA	Rhode Island	the faces of several acquaintances of Iranian descent, and the fact that I've been glad to make their acquaintance
Female	63	PhD	Virginia	A friend from college
Female	55	BA	New York	My friends from Iran, and Iranian cooking.
Male	39	PhD	Alaska	None for that phrase directly. It depends on context. If it is Iranian

Male	39	PhD	Alaska	citizen speaking of citizens of Iran then I think back to my favorite picture of all time which was a picture of a military parade in Tehran with a squad of women warriors marching and holding AK-47's. It's awesome. But I also think of some of the National Geographic images of Iranians in villages. If we talk about Iranians that are citizens of the US, then I think about some of my friends I knew in Chicago
Female	37	PhD	Hawaii	I have an Iranian friend
Female	32	MA	Florida	One my best friends from Shiraz.
Female	39	MA	Florida	I immediately think of my friend, Christy, who is half Iranian. I think of big brown eyes with soft billowy eyelashes, belly dancing, white robes, birkas, and lots of gold.
Male	66	PhD	Florida	The Iranian students I once had. Very nice, but a bit paranoid.
Female	49	BA	Washington	Our family has a close friend from Iran so I picture her and her family.
Female	57	PhD	Ohio	A young man who stayed with us once who was an Iranian citizen. He was a high school student, and he lived with us during the 1979 seizure of the people at the American Embassy. So that whole time period Comes to mind.
Female	24	MA	Arizona	My friend, Leila, who is an Iranian citizen.
Male	56	PhD	California	Soryia and Hamed. They are two colleagues of mine who did a sabbatical in my lab for one year. Very good people and scientists.
Female	60	PhD	Kentucky	My office mate who is an Iranian

				Citizen--a middle-aged woman, always dressed nicely who is very much into Science, Technology, Engineering and Math.
Female	49	BA	Virginia	No specific images except of a friend from childhood
Female	57	PhD	Missouri	A particular friend of mine
Female	43	MA	Kansas	I know many Iranians and Iranian Americans, so I tend to have a positive bias toward this group of people. All those I know are intelligent, curious, thoughtful, kind people. So, when I hear the phrase "an Iranian citizen" I tend to think of people who probably don't agree with their strict government, who want more freedom, and who are curious about the world.
Male	25	MA	California	Iranian friend I have
Male	48	MA	Nebraska	Student, small group of friends, cheerful
Female	45	PhD	Kentucky	Two dear friends of ours, a couple. She was from Argentina and he was from Iran.
Male	43	PhD	Missouri	I picture Iranians that I have met in school. Next, scenes from movies like A Separation and Persepolis.
Male	45	BA	California	My former boss at Sun Microsystems, who was an Iranian immigrant to the US.
Female	59	MA	Idaho	A wonderful neighbor I had that was from Iran.
Male	50	BA	Kansas	Farrokh Bulsara AKA Freddie Mercury.

Cultural Aspects Emphasized

99 responses fell into this subcategory which means they consisted 27.3% of responses in this category and 5.7% of all responses in this study. Examples include:

Male	60	MA	Arizona	Darker complexion, educated or seeking education, respectful, good family values, closed about religion discussions, good workers and employees, cautious about talking of cultural differences.
Male	31	MA	California	Someone born in the Islamic Republic of Iran. I guess I have a generally favorable view of the citizens and an unfavorable view of their government. One strong image is a man in a suit without a tie.
Male	28	BA	Kansas	Nice, family-oriented people.
Male	31	BA	Utah	Beautiful Countryside, well educated, rich culture, Farsi language, and stylish.
Female	50	MA	Missouri	A proud, attractive people, some of whom are proud of their Persian heritage as well as their Islamic nation.
Male	24	MA	Missouri	Strong cultural history. Pride. Struggle.
Female	26	BA	Utah	I imagine the food and smells that are so rich in the Middle East. I also think of a very friendly man, wearing a white abya, with a large smile.
Male	27	BA	Michigan	It reminds me of my time in Iraq due to how closely spelled Iran

				and Iraq are. Before my deployment, I would've associated Iranians or Iraqi's with terrorists, but then I found out that there are tons of really nice people who are just like us in the USA: they just want to live their lives in peace and want nothing to do with the political BS going on.
Female	55	High School	Texas	Respectful
Female	29	High School	Michigan	I think of a beautiful culture
Female	25	MA	Nebraska	Yummy food and very fun people.
Male	78	PhD	Michigan	Someone from a nation rich in history and culture.
Female	25	High School	Nevada	A close family group. Appearance-wise, tan skin; dark, typically thick/curly hair. Polite (more so than many Americans I've met).
Female	65	MA	Minnesota	deserts, non-western clothing styles, educated, handsome features with both men and women
Female	63	PhD	Montana	Open, generous, fun, and they have great cuisine. Loyal friends. Generally not religious, in my own experience. By the way, I am from a rather homogenous, geographically isolated state with a small population, much of it rural, where I was born and raised in a small town, although I attended graduate school in other states and in Italy, where I knew lots of Iranian students.
Female	63	PhD	Montana	My own ethnic background is English, Irish, Welsh, and Italian

	54	BA	Tennessee	Modern, civilized
Male	52	BA	New Mexico	Persia
Male	61	MA	New Mexico	Middle class family oriented but nationalistic individual with a strong sense of past history.
Male	37	MA	Oklahoma	Amazing Persian food.
Male	32	High School	Pennsylvania	Bazaars and markets, historical culture
Female	62	MA	Massachusetts	I have lived overseas for many years and have know (sic) a number of Iranians. I think of them as highly cultured, generous people.
Female	38	PhD	New York	Educated, sophisticated expatriate who appreciates style and the arts -- especially literary arts, fine architecture, and ancient culture.
Male	40	PhD	Colorado	Nice people
Female	25	BA	Texas	UTA, A woman voting, beautiful Persian calligraphy, and a lot of prominent folks in Persian history.
Male	21	High School	Oregon	When I hear the phrase, "An Iranian Citizen" I think about people with citizenship in Iran. I think about a culture of Islamic faith, which entails good will towards humanity. I think about Iranian food, and clothing styles.
Male	30	PhD	Pennsylvania	educated kind athletic passionate
Male	62	PhD	New York	A person who speaks Persian and belongs to an ancient and rich culture.
Female	42	MA	Florida	I would say that I do not have typical images of Iranian citizens

				because of my interactions with people and Persian culture on a volunteer basis. The images that come to my mind are Iranian people I have interacted with--my doctor (specialist) who is always so gentle with me despite my poor health decisions--he firmly tells me that I need to make changes for my good health. I think of a doctor that I used to work with in a museum (archaeological work) - he was a kind, gentle and intelligent man who encouraged volunteers at the museum, never making us feel inferior. I think of Darius and Cyrus - hard men, military men forging an empire, and unheard of tolerance of other religions. I think of the proud director of a film resurrecting Persepolis digitally. I think of the carvings at Persepolis, the marks of the carvers on the wall that denoted whose work it was. I think of the birth of writing, canals, postal service and extraordinary beauty.
Female	42	MA	Florida	I think of the lioness of Iran, saying My country/I will build you again/if needed, with bricks made of my life/the columns to hold the roof will be my bones (or something like that--I think of the soaring pillars of the thousand column hall. Unfortunately or fortunately, my images of Iran are

				only personal interactions or historical.
Male	33	BA	Minnesota	Prince of Persia
Female	63	MA	Oklahoma	Good people, interesting to talk to.
Male	57	BA	California	Pride in the heritage and culture

Smart and Educated

Iranians are among the most educated migrants to the U.S. Therefore, it is not surprising that 79 responses fell into this subcategory. They consisted 21.8% of responses in this category and 4.5% of all responses. Examples include:

Male	61	PhD	Washington	meek, mild kind and wise
Female	67	PhD	Florida	Progressive, peace-loving people.
Male	41	PhD	Hawaii	Educated, friendly and tolerant
Female	67	PhD	Missouri	I see a very intellectual and proud people.
Female	51	BA	Missouri	Intelligent, educated, culturally rich
Male	64	PhD	Kansas	Male, young, college student
Male	60	MA	Florida	Someone who lives in what was formerly Persia, well educated, friendly, likes to eat well, interested in world politics, genuine, warm
Female	66	MA	Iowa	An intelligent person who will make a good citizen.
Female	38	MA	Oregon	Great food, smart engineers, many female computer science PHDs
Male	77	PhD	Louisiana	Intelligent
Male	69	PhD	Kansas	Well educated; informed; devout; personable
Male	60	MA	New Mexico	Educated, technically adept.
Male	59	PhD	New Mexico	Western dress, intelligent, poly-lingual
Male	59	PhD	New	College student, physician,

Gender	Age	Degree	State	Response
			Hampshire	
Male	63	PhD	West Virginia	College Students
Male	48	PhD	North Dakota	Smart, loyal
Female	40	MA		I picture a younger (under 35 years old) person, who may be well-educated but perhaps under-employed. I generally feel that Iranians are mostly happy with their lives but would appreciate more economic opportunities and freedom of expression. I do not have any negative associations with "Iranian citizen," but I also believe my views may be different from the average American.
Male	63	MA	Tennessee	a very educated person, educated in the sciences
Female	44	PhD	Massachusetts	women I know from Iran, educated, poised, kind, professional
Female	63	BA	South Dakota	Because I work at a place where students are from all over the world, I usually just think that they are not American. I know many are well educated and for the most part very similar to the United States citizens.
Female	44	MA	New York	A young, educated person.
Female	54	PhD	California	In my experience someone visiting to complete graduate work in medicine or engineering.
Male	64	MA	South Carolina	Olive skin and an intelligent mind.
Male	47	BA	Minnesota	A business professional, often in computer science or engineering
Female	55	BA	Texas	college student
Female	32	MA	California	Highly educated. Los Angeles. Family is well off.

Female	63	BA	Vermont	Eudcated (sic), thoughtful, knows their ancient culture
Male	50	MA	Michigan	Western, educated, secular
Female	36	MA	South Carolina	A young educated Iranian, who is caught between tradition and modernization.
Male	21	BA	North Dakota	Very curious and knowledge seeking.
Male	52	BA	Pennsylvania	a wealthy, educated Muslim, probably a professor, scientist or teacher.
Male		PhD	North Dakota	More than likely an educated person, unlike many of the countries in the region, Iran has a long established propensity for having both men and women who are highly educated.
Female	48	MA	Michigan	A person of Persian origin. Probably well-educated.
Male	65	PhD	Wisconsin	A young man who has studied in the USA, 30 years old and dressed in a white shirt and dark pants.
Male	62	BA	Wisconsin	An intelligent individual.
Male	56	PhD	New York	I see the image of a well-educated, well-dressed person like former president Khatami.
Female	48	BA	Alabama	Someone who practices the Muslim faith, living in a urban environment and educated.
Female	51	PhD	Alaska	The Iranian road safety videos, and my Iranian friends who created them.
Female	63	PhD	Maryland	A person with dark hair, dark features and dark skin who is well educated and well to do.

Relative

The first known Iranian who travelled to U.S. came ashore in early 1830s. Since then, there has been a continuous flow of Iranian Immigration to the U.S. This is why instances of intercultural marriages take place and therefore we see here that 12 respondents said they think of a relative when they hear "an Iranian citizen." They consisted 3.3% of people in this category and 0.7% of all participants in this study. Examples are:

Female	51	PhD	New York	My partner, my mother-in-law, my grandmother-in-law, etc.
Female	54	MA	Oklahoma	My daughter in laws family; great joy!
Male	71	PhD	Oregon	My niece's husband, who is Iranian, and whose family I met at their wedding.
Female	38	PhD	Colorado	My good friend's ex-husband.
Female	59	PhD	New Hampshire	My brother married an Iranian American who came to this country when she was 11 years old. I am now raising her children because she cannot do so. She has an ongoing serious drug problem. Her family, however, is very successful and are prospering in this country. I also know an Iranian businessman here in NH who has helped me decorate my home. He is very friendly and I can call him anytime for help.
Female	25	MA	Ohio	My boyfriend - he is an Iranian-American who was born in the US to parents who immigrated to the US from Iran in the late 1970s. I imagine a household where families speak Farsi with one another when

				at home, but who are fluent in English as well.
Female	54	PhD	Massachusetts	my brother-in-law

Physically Attractive

43 respondents gave answers that referred to beauty or physical attractiveness of Iranian people. They consisted 11.8% participants in this category and 2.5% of all respondents in this study. Examples include:

Male	34	MA	Virginia	An individual with Caucasian features but brown skin, usually clean shaven, nicely dressed.
Female	31	MA	Florida	Dark hair, brown eyes, olive skin complexion
Female	26	BA	Georgia	My friend Mahsa from college, who was from Iran. She is beautiful, so then I think of beautiful Iranian women, then I picture women in black hijab, then men in white at sholat, then goat stew.
Male	55	PhD	Florida	An Iranian women who sublet a room that I stayed in when I was a graduate student. She was married to an American and was fairly nice. She was young and was an amateur belly dancer (her husband was a musician).
Female	41	MA	Florida	Someone that was born in the middle east and from Iran. Some with dark-brownish hair, usually brown eyes sometime those really pretty hazel blue eyes. Also skin tone of olive or brownish.

Female	63	MA	Colorado	Truly, my immediate image is of a beautiful Persian woman
Female	57	MA	Idaho	Dark skinned, attractive, we'll educated
	51	MA	Indiana	The immediate image is a person with darker skin than myself. I think of someone who is exotic and beautiful. I also think of Persia as many people I've met call themselves Persians.
Male	51	MA	Maine	Beautiful eyes and hair. Strong family ties. Intelligent.
Female	48	BA	Indiana	A lovely burka-clad woman or a mustachioed man, smiling
Female	53	PhD	Indiana	Beautiful olive skin toned people.
Female	39	MA	Missouri	When I hear the phrase "an Iranian citizen," I think of someone with beautiful skin and dark hair.
Female	33	BA	Texas	Good smile, tan/milky complexion, deep-set eyes, fairly short
Female	62	BA	Michigan	Women wearing burkas and beautiful eyes and men wearing white shirts with beards.
Female	41	MA	New Mexico	Good-looking darker skinned young man in black western suit
Female	43	MA	Oklahoma	beautiful skin
Female	62	PhD	Oregon	beautiful, complex
Female	58	High School	Tennessee	Dark haired, well dressed person.
Male	55	PhD	Oklahoma	A young man, neatly dressed in casual clothing, with a neatly-trimmed beard.
Male	53	PhD	Pennsylvania	A person with wavy black or dark hair and a darker complexion than a typical Caucasian but lighter complexion than a typical African American. The image I have is of

				someone who is fit and healthy - neither overweight nor underweight.
Female	52	MA	Virginia	An individual with beautiful dark eyes and dark hair. Hard workers, family oriented with strong family roots. The ones I have met are well educated.
Female	52	BA	New York	Beautiful dark skinned people. Head wraps, new food, different culture.
Female	64	MA	Washington	Dark hair. Beautiful eyes.
Female	52	High School	Virginia	Differene (sic) in clothing/dress. Beautiful women of color.
Female	74	MA	Michigan	The faces of beautiful and handsome people whom I've known for several years.
Female	33	PhD	Colorado	a pretty woman with dark eyes and hair and a lot of make up
Female	21	High School	Washington	Hajibs, beautiful exotic women, cultured, self-respectable, idealist, collective family setups.
Male	56	PhD	Nevada	A person with black hair and olive complexion with a melodic voice
Female	30	BA	Delaware	A pretty woman in a loose robe with a headscarf.
Female	31	BA	Arkansas	Gorgeous skin, Hijab's, nose piercings, lightweight clothes, wealth, educated
Male	43	MA	Indiana	beautiful brown skin women with head wraps made of what appears to be soft cotton. Icba, a former employee. Such a kind man.
Female	21	BA	Texas	Very beautiful women with pretty eyes.
Male	30	MA	Minnesota	Somebody beautiful. I don't really have connotations of Iranians

				beyond that.
Female	52	BA	Ohio	Black hair, fine features.
Female	37	PhD	Massachusetts	A beautiful woman wearing a headscarf.
Female	27	MA	Connecticut	Awesome culinary skills. Beautiful skin and eyes.
Female	43	BA	Colorado	Beautiful dark skin, dark hair
Female	70	PhD	New Jersey	Dark hair, good looking, citizen of Iran
Male	32	BA	Ohio	Tan complexion, dark hair, beautiful

Hardworking

24 Americans who participated in this study reported cross cultural schemata of Iranians in which Iranians are seen as hardworking people. These accounts consist 6.6% of responses in this category and 1.4% of all responses in this study. Examples are:

Male	19	High School	Florida	There is a family in my town the emigrated from Iran. They are hardworking, recently opening up their third business, and the food is great. I tend not to stereotype, but my interactions with this family and several of my college friends have bestowed upon me the "image" of a pioneering people.
Male	64	MA	Florida	Dark haired, dark eyed people, A conscientious and hardworking people who probably have some hesitation about the extremes of their own government.
Male	56	MA	Colorado	I was around many Iranian students during my undergrad

				years and that is my primary memory: Busy, tech oriented students who smoked and laughed a lot.
Male	41	BA	Wisconsin	Hard-working, honest.
Male	52	PhD	Texas	a hard working individual with high cuontry (sic) united.
Male		PhD		I am reminded of the hard working, studious people I met in my past university experiences.
Male	62	PhD	Maryland	Good neighbors, enjoyable to do business with, hard working.
Female	67	PhD	Oklahoma	Hard working but different ethical standards.
Male	50	MA	Oklahoma	Dark skin, hair and eyes. Quiet, studious.
Male	66	PhD	California	Bright, energetic, and work oriented.
Female	46	MA	California	Iraninan (sic) who leaves in United States. Educated, rich, smart and hard working.
Male	56	BA	South Dakota	The sweet older gentleman who lived next door for years. Hard working, generous and kind.
Female	61	PhD	California	Hard-working, sensitive, intelligent, good communicator, kind.
Male	60	BA	Washington	A hard working person like all other basic people in this world.
Male	66	PhD	Massachusetts	I have known 4 Iranians and all of them were exceptionally nice, intelligent, hardworking people. Based on that very small sample, I have a very positive impression of Iranians. Not a big fan of the government but I am not a big fan of what the US government has become either.

Female	56	PhD	Wisconsin	I think of an intelligent hard working person
Male	39	MA	Virginia	Hard working, smart, and passionate.
Male	49	MA	Mississippi	I have friends that are "Persian" or Iranian Citizens. So when I think of American Iranians I think of nice hardworking people. When I think of Iranian Citizens in Iran I think they are generally good people that are afraid to stand up due to the outside influences.
Female	40	PhD	New York	I only know a few Iranians, and they have been graduate students at my University. I think of assertive (in a good way) and motivated people. They students I have met have been well educated and are confident.
Male	36	MA	California	responsible
Male	37	BA	California	Hard-working, family oriented, focused individual who struggle daily to overcome some negative "images".
Female	20	High School	New Jersey	A hard working individual who does not receive everything they deserve.

Victim of Media Bad-Representation

13 respondents said for them Iranians are victims of malevolent media representation. They consisted 3.6% of participants with positive cross cultural schemata of Iranians and 0.7% of all respondents in this study. Examples are:

Male	30	MA	Florida	An image of someone who is misunderstood.
Male	45	PhD	Virginia	A human a friend someone who has been screwed over by the media by showing the bad side of a population
Male	39	PhD	Arizona	Stereotypical image of Muslim person, darker skin, skinny, male.
Female	23	BA	Pennsylvania	Unsure how to answer as I only have been exposed to a one-sided view and have not met an Iranian citizen only Americans of Iranian descent.
Male	56	BA	Minnesota	I think of an american (sic) citizen of Iranian nationality or an Iranian citizen; no other impressions. however, the american (sic) media does not tend to portray them kindly at times.
Male	32	MA	California	Misunderstood.
Male	75	PhD	California	A better educated, more sophisticated individual than usually portrayed in US media.
Female	32	MA	California	Outspoken people, not very well represented in the media.
Female	35	MA	Virginia	thoughtful, kind, often unfairly judged and profiled by others
Male	67	PhD	Louisiana	A misunderstood person in the United States.
Female	20	BA	New Jersey	some who is misunderstood as a terrorist, also a girl i (sic) went to high school with

NO CROSS CULTURAL SCHEMATA

44 American citizens who participated in this study (3.6% of all participants) said they have nothing in mind when the phrase "an Iranian

citizen" is heard. This finding was previously reported (for example in Shahghasemi and Heisey (2009)) which emphasize on Americans' unawareness of serious matters. Examples are:

Female	19	BA	South Dakota	Nothing
Female	45	PhD	Louisiana	none have been taught not to be bias
Female	27	PhD	Florida	no images come to mind
Male	44	PhD	Idaho	No particular image comes to mind immediately.
Male	39	PhD	Iowa	I don't think I have a particular image.
Female	60	MA	Kentucky	no images-
Female	24	BA	Maryland	When I think of an "Iranian" citizen, I think about what kind of history and background that will come with the culture. I would love to learn about the culture, but also how different it is from my culture.
Male	61	PhD	Kansas	I have no definitive (sic) image
Male	49	PhD	Pennsylvania	No image
Male	53	MA	Illinois	nothing in particular
Female	59	BA	New Hampshire	No particular image.
Male	52	PhD	North Dakota	A person from Iran, nothing special
Female	38	PhD	Mississippi	nothing
Female	58	BA	Washington	What is the food like there?
Female	43	High School	South Dakota	I really have no impression that would naturally come to mind.
Male	46	PhD	Pennsylvania	None
Female	51	PhD	Virginia	No image comes into mind other than a person with a different culture. While they may be dressed in a different way than the social norm for the generation, or in their

Female	37	MA	Florida	cultural dress, I find that people are people and have no set image in my mind when I hear the phrase. I don't really have an image that comes into mind with I hear this phrase.
Female	51	High School	Oklahoma	I really don't have anything that comes to mind. I don't watch the news when it comes to that.
Female	28	High School	North Dakota	Just hearing the phrase "Iranian Citizen," does not bring any images to mind; honestly, I need to know more information about a person to form any opinion. I am a people-first language individual.
Female	35	MA	Colorado	I do not think I know any Iranians. I know some Syrian's I assume Iranians and Syrians share some cultural similarities. I think most of Iranians speak Arabic. I think most of them are Muslim. Honestly I do not know enough about them to think anything about them. If I were to think about an Iranian Citizen in their home country I imagine they are trying to live there day to day life in a country that I think has some instability.
Female	35	MA	Colorado	If I were to think about an Iranian citizen in another country I would assume like most immigrants the moved for a better life.
Male		PhD	Michigan	None in particular.
Male	37	MA	Missouri	Nothing really
Male	58	BA	South Carolina	Nothing

Cross Cultural Schemata 225

Female	67	MA	Nevada	I don't think of anything at all. I have worked with lots of people from everywhere and lived in Trinidad for a short while. I don't know the person so I don't know what he/she will be like.
Female	63	PhD	Ohio	I do not have an image. I do not categorize people by physical images.
Male	59	PhD	Wisconsin	Do not have a specific image.
Male	59	MA	Alabama	Neutral
Male	67	PhD	Wisconsin	Nothing much in particular.
Female	24	MA	Massachusetts	No specific images come to mind.
Female	23	BA	Texas	Honestly, I have never heard that phrase before.
Female	30	PhD	Massachusetts	No particular good or bad impression
Male	31	PhD	Alabama	Nothing imparticular, (sic) I try not to judge a person simply off of where they are from.
Female	62	BA	New Jersey	Nothing in particular--mustache
Male	49	BA	California	none
Female	73	PhD		nothing in particular. Just concern about the years of struggle
Female	33	MA	Minnesota	I don't have any preconceived notions for images of an Iranian Citizen.
Female	38	MA	Connecticut	i (sic) don't have a clear impression
Male	54	PhD	New Jersey	nothing in particular

NO COMMENT OR NOT APPLICABLE

66 respondents (3.8% of all participants) either left the question unanswered or gave irrelevant answers. Examples include:

Female	44	MA	Mississippi	Are they christian (sic) or Muslim?
Male	44	PhD	Pennsylvania	You are from Iran
Male	70	MA	Virginia	More information is needed to determine whether the subject is peace loving or militant.
Female	34	PhD	Pennsylvania	I don't know how to answer this question, by asking it, I imagine you want me to give a stereotypical answer.
Female	56	PhD	Texas	I have no biased opinion toward people from any nation.
Male	23	Primary School	Kansas	FDGDHFD
Male	62	BA	Texas	I can't answer due to a lack of context.

MIXED AND CONTRADICTORY CROSS CULTURAL SCHEMATA

In sum, 127 responses (7.2% of all responses to the first question of this study) gave mixed or contradictory responses. This answers were more sophisticated and longer and as it can be seen below, they are better articulated in comparison with other responses.

Male	38	MA	Kentucky	Devout Traditional Passive females Dominant males Intelligent
Female	54	MA	Texas	good food, nice people, attractive, sad for the people who are not free to express their opinion
Male	61	PhD	Kentucky	I have two images that conflict: (1) I know several Iranians very well and find them to be decent,

				intelligent and honest. They are good friends. (2) I never really thought much about Iran before the taking of American hostages during the late 1970s. Since then, the constant vitriol from Iranian political and religious leaders has given me a bad impression. I realize a lot of this animosity has a basis, but it does seem Iran has had more than its share of zealots.
Female	70	MA	Florida	Nothing too specific but I Iran is a Muslim country with Shia, Kurds and Sunnis and struggles to have in inclusive government. It is suffering from US sanctions over its nuclear program. The Ayatollah is the leader and there is a prime minister- Maliki that has fallen out of favor. Persia has a great and glorious history and produced great art.
Male	50	PhD	Florida	I see two conflicting images, one is radical, militant, haters of isreal(sic) and sponsor of terroist. (sic) The other image is doctors, educated young society seaking (sic) place in the world.
Male	44	PhD	Indiana	I imagine a young bearded man, EITHER very angry at the West (especially the USA) and Israel OR very discontent at religious fundamentalism in the Iranian government and society.
Male	50	BA	Nebraska	many images----modern citizens in Tehran----religious leaders----"frightening" government figures----

				repressed political figures----poor citizens in countryside----fanatic soldiers in 1980s Iran/Iraq War----too many other images to list
Female	65	PhD	Indiana	Two images come to mind: 1. A bearded cleric spouting hate speech 2. A progressive woman, one who is hesitant to speak out
Male	62	BA	Maryland	I don't get a particular image. Rather a stream of images of different sorts.
Male	68	MA	Kentucky	My friend Mihan Mihankhah and family. My uncle's tour with U.S. Army in Iran in 1960's War between Iran and Iraq that killed more than 1000000 people
Male	68	MA	Kentucky	President Carter and President Reagan dealings with hostages from U.S. Consulate Radicalization of government with respect to cultural/religious constraints in the not too distant past
Female	46	MA	Maryland	good food, large family gatherings, people forced to lead double life: outwardly having to be very careful about what they say, what they wear, their conduct; in their home much more open and free.
Female	41	PhD	Virginia	I think of Persians, I think of rich heritage, I think of poverty, I think of women with limited rights to health care and education.
Male	39	MA	Kansas	Oppressed, Highly Educated, Muslim, Dictator, Anti-U.S.,
Male	33	MA	Kansas	For men, the former president,

				Ahmadinejad in a khaki jacket. For women, sometimes head scarves, sometimes not, often very pretty. Bad techno music in modified street racing cars. An Iranian restaurant in my old neighbourhood (sic) in Toronto that had awesome shawarma. A former stats professor, who was in his 60s, but ran marathons in every state -tall, thin, bald, and wearing glasses. It's hard to picture a typical "Iranian citizen." Since there are so many different and unique individual Iranians.
Female	48	MA	Kentucky	On one hand, I think "war-torn" country that has remnants of bombed buildings. Lots of protests, primarily against America. On the other hand, because I know people from Iran, I am told that Iran has beautiful countryside and is quite modern.
Male	53	PhD	Wisconsin	Unfortunately, one of defiance and religious fanaticism. An underlying hatred for the USA and a lack of scientific, medical and technological sophistication. In reference to a later question, I do have personal experience with agriculture scientists from Iran who do not fit this definition. And I am sure that the majority of Iranians are peace loving families just trying to make their way in the world and who do not understand us any better than we understand them. The

				scientists I have dealt with have all been polite, courteous, respectful and genuinely interested in making their lives and the lives of others in Iran better. In that respect they were very similar to us in many ways.
Female	24	MA	Arizona	Women and children outside crying outside of a destroyed shack. (Pics shown in news). And wealthy Iranian friends from San Fran & Scottsdale. BMW. Dentists. Surgeons. Lawyers.
Female	52	PhD	Massachusetts	A person with strong Islamic religious beliefs; a person who has lived a life under a difficult social and political environment. If the citizen is a woman, what comes to my mind is a victim of social repression. The person is very kind and family oriented.
Female	23	BA	Michigan	My dear friend from the University of Michigan and the struggles she had to endure in Iran to obtain an education. She faced a great deal of discrimination because of her status as a religious minority and because of her advocacy for HIV/AIDS research. She is one of the funniest, most intelligent, and kind-hearted people I know. I am fortunate to know her and talk to her about her experiences.
Female	63	MA	Maryland	Iranian women and how beautiful they are. But, unfortunately, my perception of Iranian men is of religious, political, and cultural fanatics.

Female	58	PhD	Indiana	Someone from Iran, formerly known as Persia. Persian food and music, Rumi! All of those things before the revolution, which happened when I was an undergrad.
Female	42	PhD	Pennsylvania	A frightened but proud little girl, looking at me through the bathroom mirror in a public place. Two earnest young men with books. A woman dressed in gold, lying on bullets. Mute video of women with covered hair, singing. Lastly, images of angry young men in the streets.
Male	59	PhD	Texas	A young lady whom I was in graduate school, who identified herself as "Persian". Her PhD was in Peace Education - this was after the revolution. 2 male students I worked with in fast food restaurant who were majoring in petroleum engineering - before the revolution. All were pleasant, engaging, intelligent and not overtly religious. The young in your country who are trying to live a modern life without extreme religious strictures being put upon them. Old religious leaders imposing 400 year old rules on the populous. Islamic extremist who will travel where ever there is a fight against what ever (sic) they think is the 'true' interpretation of the Koran, and will happily die trying to kill anyone who disagrees with the 'true' interpretation.

Male	31	MA	Illinois	Some are modern and some are hard line islamics. (sic)
Female	53	PhD	Kansas	The Shah Pahlavi, Ayatollah Khomeini, Marjane Satrapi, a young woman I know who has been studying in the States. --handsome uniformed man with a shadowy human rights record.
Male	48	PhD	Nebraska	The Shah My friend in Cairo An Iranian I saw on TV about 10 years ago -- very educated, knowledgeable who spoke perfect English Women wearing viels (sic)
Male	67	PhD	Kansas	mixed thoughts. the iranian (sic) government is presented as being very anti-American, which creates an initial negative bias. but what i (sic) know of individual iranians (sic) is quite different, but then we do not see many pro-government iranians (sic) in the US.
Male	46	MA	Washington	I think of my friend, M, who is a smart, beautiful, inquisitive 30 year old woman... and then I think of the culture she lives in the prevents her from doing the work she is trained for, and loves.
Female	64	BA	Michigan	Persian, well educated, entrepreneurial . . . unless you mean a citizen of Iran, in which case my view might be slightly altered - less well-rounded in education, less likely to speak Farsi and more likely to be culturally/ethnically polarized.

Female	67	BA	Louisiana	I think of a person from a country, different from mine, where the average person works hard, children learn in school, and one's family comes first. Like in every country, there are people who cause dissent, are greedy, and expect everyone to follow their lead, but the typical citizen leads a life similar to people all over the world.
Female	59	MA	Minnesota	muslim (sic) religion Persia 1,001 Arabian Nights coming from a war-torn country hopefully has no terrorist connections
Female	46	High School	Delaware	A human being first. Somebody tired of their country and families being torn apart over money and people who extort the resources there. Sadness and despair. But I also feel that they are loving, kind and hard-working people who worry about the future for their children there. I think they're constantly fighting for their lives and the few make it bad for the majority, just like over here in America.
Female	27	MA	California	My good friend Minhaz, (sic) with his head in hands and an ankle bracelet on before ICE tried to deport him. Or another friend enthusiastically cooking and sharing some of the best food I have ever had.
Female	27	MA	California	Or another friend who crashed at my apartment after a late night study

				session, coming into my room in the early morning light to say her morning prayers. I pretended to be asleep still so I wouldn't disturb her, but will never forget how beautiful she looked. I think about the same friend sharing dates with me as she broke her fast and explained the significance of the holy month. I think about the same friend expressing with tears in her eyes how she used to do ballet, but was forced to quit in her late teens because her parents thought it might be too provocative for her to be on stage (I too, was a ballerina, (sic) so I cried with her).
Male	72	PhD	New York	i think of my many Iranian friends, of Shoulet and Jusuf and Amir and Reza and Hamid and Shiva Mehdi Farbod, Azadeh Nassar etc. They are wonderful. When I think of Iranian citizens in general I imagine they represent an incredible range of ethnicities, ideologies, discourses, etc. I also think of the ways that Iranican (sic)-American citizens are harassed in the US
Male	31	MA	North Dakota	Someone of slightly darker complexion than a person who is white. As a culture they seem to only want the respect of others in the world and tend to call out nations that are expressing double standards when it includes topics that are going on inside of Iran. I

				know they support groups that are suspected/done significant attacks on US interest but this is not the first image that comes to mind however, it is one of them.
Female	60	BA	North Dakota	I think of 2 very opposing images one which is much like all citizens who are raising a family and want a good job and their kids to be safe and happy and the opposing one which is an extremist who can destroy in the name of religion.
Male	43	MA	New Mexico	One of my favorite WWF wrestlers, the Iron Shiek or some of my friends from graduate school...then.....an oppressed people who when empowered can make a positive difference in the world.
Female	48	MA	Utah	The students and/or colleague friends that I have worked with over the years who are from Iran. I picture Fahkri's beautiful hands, Fereshtah's smile and laugh, These are the first images. Secondary images are from my youth, when the news of Iran was the fall of the Shah, the rise of the Ayatolla Kohmeini, the embassy hostages. These were the images I had before I had the opportunity to actually meet and get to know Iranian citizens.
Female	49	BA	North Dakota	It depends because I have a couple friends who are originally from Iran but have been US citizens all their life so have no influence from the current state of Iran culture. If we are talking about those images then I

				would say friendly, considerate and hardworking individuals. If you are talking about current residents of Iran and surrounding areas then either it is victims of religous persecution or radical Islamic crazy people who hate the west (USA in particular) and christianity (sic) in general.
Female	31	High School	Oklahoma	Turban, Long white coats, hot weather, sand, Ladies in covers, Smiling cute kids, sand colored houses
Male	24	BA	Oklahoma	I would like to meet them and get to know them. Obviously, Iran is a controversial country, so the media has portrayed certain things about Iran. I would like have friendship with "an Iranian citizen.
Female	34	PhD	Oregon	Politically controlled. Repressed by governmental control. Personal lives are challenged by sanctions. Experienced traumatic events. Proud and strong-willed. Desires opportunities.
Male	42	MA	South Carolina	Educated, temperamental, irrational, cold, beards (black or grey), men over 50, young people chanting and walking, women with long black hair, uneasy, passionate, Islam, jihad
Male	57	PhD	Oklahoma	The Iranian/Persians I know: Mahmood, Hossein and Mostafa (deceased) and several others. They are a varied group. Mahmood is highly principled and honest as is his wife. Just lovely people to

				socialize and work with. Hossein is a merciless, very smart and nasty individual - one of the Shah's men and quite proud of what they did to the opposition during the Shah's rule. He is, unsurprisingly, socially adept. Mostafa was a paradox - in some ways a hippie and an excellent painter. He was also economically, extremely conservative. The other Persian I know reasonably well is a very socially liberal man and an absolute riot to hang around with. He's also very smart.
Female	49	PhD	Tennessee	I think of beautiful Persian people. I think of citizens who have a rich history and who value art, education, good food, good wine, and freedom from oppression. I think of educated women who want to have a voice in politics and reform.
Male	46	PhD	New York	A Shia muslim, (sic) a Persian, with a rich cultural heritage going back thousands of years, a Farsi speaker (probably also competent in English). Unfortunately, at present Iran's leadership is (to put it as mildly as possible) not a force for good in the world. But its people seem to be far more cosmopolitan and enlightened, and the recent uprisings (brutally suppressed by the regime) show that a great many of them would like to see a change.
Male	73	PhD	Utah	Someone who is intelligent and capable of teaching led by a group

Male	44	MA	Texas	of political leaders who are unrealistic in their expectations. Generally educated person living a lower middle class lifestyle but w/ very little ability to speak his/her mind or to live a lifestyle he/she chooses
Male	55	PhD	Iowa	Literate, well-educated individuals. Likely to have a strong science background, and to be cultured, sophisticated, and benefiting from strong family connections, but personsal (sic) liberty constrained by an authoritarian theocracy. Likely younger than the generation of the Iranian revolution or Iraq-Iran War, so maybe some of the old grievances are less meaningful than current worries about economic and social mobility. Persian history makes Iranian culture different than and distinctive from Arabic Islamic countries or cultures. Iran seems to highly value education. Respect is an important desire (not uncommon in cultures with a history of great empires).
Female	28	PhD	Iowa	cafes in city of Tehran that are gender segregated, pretty Persian women in head scarves
Male	57	PhD	New Hampshire	Funny, passionate, smart, kind. (from personal experience). A mix of hot headed, extremists and struggling, educated but squabbling moderates (from the media) I generally perceive a difference of generation: between younger,

				educated Iranians and older more traditional ones.
Male	53	MA	Kansas	intelligent, educated, urban, unhappy
Male	66	PhD	Oklahoma	A wonderful intelligent kind person who is lacking freedom due to the theocracy in power.
Male	30	BA	Texas	Interviews that i have seen with people on the streets that prove them to be normal people, perhaps trapped in an oppressive style of political governing. The people of Iran seem to think highly of Americans, and be a very nice people overall.

It is intriguing that in the firsthand accounts of American citizens, we can see the importance of the media in constructing their world. An independent study on this data will yield interesting outcomes. The other studies I have done on cross cultural schemata Iranians have for Americans, respondents have generally shown more favorable, realistic, and unmediatized perceptions. Anyway, though media are very important in shaping Americans' perception for Iranians, we should not only blame media for this matter, as media themselves are working in the wider political, social, cultural and even geographical sphere.

CONCLUSION

Whenever "Iran" and "US" is mentioned in a text or image, we are used to think of politics. And, we are less likely to think of their relationship in a historical context in which as (Badiozamani & Badiozamani (2005) call it, these two nations were "in love" with each other for most of their history of relationship. A complex set of events and factors have contributed to the current enmity and pessimism, and until these factors are in play, these problems will persist.

I don't buy into naïvely thinking that a well-planned cultural program will help in creating better intercultural communication between people of the two nations because these efforts are very weak and vulnerable in comparison with the competing forces. For example, after former Iranian president Mohammad Khatami favored normalized relationships with U.S and articulated the notion of Dialogue Among Civilizations, UN took the idea and the year 2001 was named the United Nations Year of Dialogue among Civilizations; it was somehow a reflection to Samuel P. Huntington's theory of a Clash of Civilizations. Ironically, in the very year of Dialogue among Civilizations, the events of 9/11 happened. Realities do not care about our fantasies.

One can say Iran and America are still in a secret love affair, but not in the kind of love affair that conspiracy theorists insist upon. United States need a ferocious enemy in the Middle East to justify her military presence in the region. Moreover, an always intimidating Iran will force Arab nations to urge U.S. to strengthen her presence in the Persian Gulf. The U.S. is very happy with this situation because she wants to retain her surveillance over the flow of oil, which means she will retain her global hegemony by protecting the economic advantage of the dollar.

On the other side, Iran is much happy with American enmity. Middle East is hard to be grasped by the people who have never lived here. Middle East is complicated and it is the place in which complicated people live. Having an enemy that is the sole superpower, is an advantage which creates popularity. This is why Saddam Hussain, Bashar al-Asad, Jabhat al-Nusrah, Daesh, Taliban, Iran and many other countries and groups who are fighting each other say America is their enemy while accuse the other parties of being puppets of the U.S. Moreover, there are some political rivalries in Iran that necessitates the existence of an outside enemy. The greater the enemy is, the greater the need to have internal solidarity will be. This has been an equilibrium for the last four decades. At times, both Iran and U.S. have found themselves in the same front. Both of them were fighting Saddam and Taliban and America removed these two great enemies of Iran. Until this equilibrium is working, there will be no great change in intercultural condition.

Nevertheless, this does not mean there is nothing people in Iran and U.S. can do in order to create a better understanding of each other. The most favorable image of American people in the Middle East exists in Iran. Iran is possibly the only country in the Middle East in which American visitor are welcome by ordinary people. There are numerous recent examples in which American travelers who visited Iran gave an extraordinary account of Iranian people's friendliness. In this context, and with the spread of social media networks, an intercultural dialogue between citizens of both countries can be helpful.

Intriguingly, in American political side we are seeing this approach, though for the purpose of propaganda. First-ever Persian language spokesperson of the United States Department of State, Alan Eyre played a wonderful role in creating a better image of America in Iran. His Facebook page has more than 100000 likes, even after he lost his position. In the posts on his page, Eyre asks about everyday life, art, poetry and literature in Iran and after Iranians reply (I am sure Eyre receives many Green Card requests!), Eyre thanks them. By speaking Persian and reading poems of Persian poetry like Hafez's poems, Eyre has gained popularity in Iran, though a Wikileaks document reveals "Hafez Khani" is not the only thing Eyre is doing in Iran! Anyway, the Iranian government has not shown a similar interest in reaching out to the American public, and I am sure the Iranian official who creates a page similar to that of Eyre will soon be criticized from inside.

A more effective strategy by Islamic Republic of Iran Broadcasting might be helpful. Iran already sponsors some TV channel to communicate with the Western people, but these outlets have an ineffective approach and so far, the only Iranian TV channel that has been successful outside Iran has been Ifilm. Ifilm continuously broadcasts Iranian TV series. Iranian directors are professional and well experienced. Many of these TV series have been produced aptly and are family oriented. These TV series have been dubbed into other languages and therefore Ifilm has had a phenomenal success in the Islamic countries. But, these TV series are mainly ideologically loaded and Western audience does not generally like any ideology but that of capitalism.

Fiske, S. T., & Linville, P. W. (1980). What does the Schema Concept Buy us? *Personality and Social Psychology Bulletin, 6*, 543-557.

Fiske, S. T., & Taylor, S. E. (1991). *Social cognition.* New York: McGraw-Hill.

Foldy, E. G. (2006). Dueling schemata: Dialectical sensemaking about gender. *Human Resources Abstracts, 42*(3), 350-372.

Forrest, A. I. (2006). *The soldiers of the revolution and empire.* London: MPG Books.

Fozooni, B. (2004). Religion, politics and class: Conflict and contestation in the development of football in Iran. *Soccer & Society, 5*(3), 356-370.

Frends to Evangelical Truth. (1806). *The Panoplist (and Missionary magazine) conducted by an association of.* Boston: E. Lincoln, Water-Street.

Frye, R. N. (2003). Persia in the mind of the West. *Islam and Christian-Muslim Relations, 14*, 403-406.

Gable, R. W. (1959). Culture and administration in Iran. *Middle East Journal, 13*(4), 407-421.

Garret-Rempel, D. (2008). The end of British empire in Iran: An Anglo-American sleight of hand. *the Clearihue Review, 2*(1), 45-55.

Gastil, R. D. (1958). Middle class impediments to Iranian modernization. *The Public Opinion Quarterly, 22*(3), 325-329.

Gerges, F. A. (2003). Islam and Muslims in the mind of America. *The ANNALS of the American Academy of Political and Social Science, 588*, 73-89.

Gibson, D. (2004). *Communication, power, and media.* New York: Nova Science Publishers.

Goode, E., & Ben-Yehuda, N. (2009). *Moral panics: The social construction of deviance.* Chichester: Wiley-Blackwell.

Grant, A. (1841). *The Nestorians, or, The lost tribes.* New York: Harper.

Hansen, B. (2001). Learning to Tax: The political economy of the opium trade in Iran, 1921-1941. *The Journal of Economic History, 61*(1), 95-113.

Daniel, R. L. (1964). American Influences in the Near East before 1861. *American Quarterly, 16*(1), 72-84.

Daryaee, T. (2012). *The Oxford Handbook of Iranian History.* Oxford ; New York: Oxford University Press.

Davids , J., & Nielson, J. M. (2002). Extraterritoriality. In A. DeConde, R. D. Burns, & F. Logevall, *Encyclopedia of American foreign policy / Vol. 2, E-N* (pp. 81-92). New York: Charles Scribner's Sons.

Davis, C. D. (2002). Arbitration, mediation, and conciliation. In T. G. Paterson, J. G. Clifford, & K. J. Hagan, *Encyclopedia of American foreign policy / Vol. 1 , A-D* (pp. 61-72). New York: Charles Scribner's Sons.

DeConde, A., Burns, R. D., & Logevall, F. (2002). *Encyclopedia of American foreign policy / Vol. 1 , A-D.* New York: Charles Scribner's Sons.

Dodge, B. (1972). American Educational and Missionary Efforts in the Nineteenth and Early Twentieth Centuries. *The ANNALS of the American Academy of Political and Social Science, 401.*

Douglas, W. O. (1951). *Strange Lands and Friendly People.* New York: Harper & Brothers Publishers.

Elder, J. (1960). *History of the American Presbyterian Mission to Iran.* Tehran: Literature Committee of the Church Council of Iran.

Endicott, L., Bock, T., & Narváez, D. (2003). Moral reasoning, intercultural development, and multicultural experiences : relations and cognitive underpinnings. *International Journal of Intercultural Relations, 27*, 403-419.

Farmanfarmaian, R. (2008). *War and peace in Qajar Persia : implications past and present.* London and New York: Routledge.

Fazeli, N. (2006). *Politics of culture in Iran: Anthropology, politics and society in the twentieth century.* London and New York: Routledge.

Ferraro, G. P., & Andreatt, S. (2011). *Cultural Anthropology: An Applied Perspective.* Belmont: Wadsworth.

Fiske, S. T., & Linville, P. W. (1980). What does the schema concept buy us? *Personality and Social Psychology Bulletin, 6*, 543-557.

Celmer, M. C. (1987). *Terrorism, U.S. strategy, and Reagan policies.* New York: Greenwood Press.

Chapman, C. (2011). Christians in the Middle East - past, present and future. *Transformation: An International Journal of Holistic Mission Studies, 29*, 90-110.

Clark, L. S. (2008). Reflections on Iran. *Journal of Media and Religion, 7*(1-2), 96-99.

Coan, F. G. (1939). *Yesterdays in Persia and Kurdistan.* Claremont: Saunders studio Press.

Cohen, J. M. (2008). *A history of Western literature : from medieval epic to modern poetry.* Piscataway: AldineTransaction.

Colby, F. M., & Williams, T. (1925). *The new international encyclopaedia* (Vol. I). New York: Dodd, Mead and Co.

Cole, J. R. (2005). The evolution of charismatic authority in the Bahai faith. In R. Gleave, *Religion and Society in Qajar Iran* (pp. 311-345). London: RoutledgeCurzon.

Collier , D. R. (2013). To Prevent a Revolution: John F. Kennedy and the Promotion of Democracy in Iran. *Diplomacy and Statecraft, 24*(3), 456-475.

Cook, A. H., & Rawshandil, J. (2009). *The United States and Iran : policy challenges and opportunities.* New York: Palgrave Macmillan.

Cooke, S. (2013). *Travellers' tales of wonder : Chatwin, Naipaul, Sebald.* Edinburgh: Edinburgh University Press.

Corte, C. (2007). Schema model of the self-concept to examine the role of the self-concept in alcohol dependence and recovery. *Journal of the American Psychiatric Nurses Association, 13*(1), 31-41.

Cottam, R. W. (1979). *Nationalism in Iran: Updated through 1978.* Pittsburgh: University of Pittsburgh Press.

Cyrino, S. M. (2010). "This is sparta!": The reinvention of the epic in. In R. Burgoyne, *The epic film in world* (pp. 19-38). New York: Routledge.

Dallalfar, S., & Movahedi, S. (1996). Women in multinational corporations: Old myths, new constructions and some deconstruction. *Organization, 3*(4), 546-559.

Bartlotti, L. N. (2001). Open access in closed societies: Theological education in Muslim contexts. *Transformation: An International Journal of Holistic Mission Studies, 18*(2), 99–113.

Bassett, J. (1886). *Persia: the land of the imams. A narrative of travel and residence, 1871-1885.* New York: Scribner.

Bateson, M. C. (1979). "This Figure of Tinsel": A Study of Themes of Hypocrisy and Pessimism in Iranian Culture. *Daedalus, 108*(3), 125-134.

Beattie, G. W., Agahi, C., & Spencer, C. (1982). Social stereotypes held by different occupational groups in post-revolutionary Iran. *European Journal of Social Psychology, 12*(1), 75-87.

Benjamin, S. G. (1886). Persia and the Persians. *Journal of the American Geographical Society of New York, 18*, 27-66.

Benjamin, S. G. (1887). *The story of the nations: Persia.* London and New York: Putnam's Sons.

Bill, J. A. (1988). *The Eagle and the Lion: The tragedy of American-Iranian relations.* New Heaven and London: Yale University Press.

Bonakdarian, M. (2007). US-Iranian relations, 1911–1951. In A. Amanat, & M. T. Bernhardsson, *U.S.-Middle East historical encounters* (pp. 121-141). Tallahassee: University Press of Florida.

Bozorgmehr, M. (1998). From Iranian studies to studies of Iranians in the United States. *Iranian Studies, 31*(1), 4-30.

Brock, S. P., & Witakowski, W. (2001). *At the turn of the third millennium: The Syrian Orthodox witness.* Roma: Trans World Film Italia.

Browne, E. G. (1893). *A year amongst the Persians : impressions as to the life, character, and thought of the people of Persia, received during twelve months' residence in that country in the years 1887-8.* London: A. and C. Black.

Campbell, J. (1995). Portrayal of Iranians in U.S. motion pictures. In Y. R. Kamalipour, *The U.S. media and the Middle East: Image and perception* (pp. 177-186). Westport: Greenwood Press.

Carter, R., & McRae, J. (2001). *The Routledge history of literature in English : Britain and Ireland.* London: Routledge.

Iranians. doi:http://ameli-saied.com/farsi/index.php?op = sarticles& group = 6.

Ahmad-Zadeh-Namvar, F. (2008). *Studying intercultural relations between Iran and the US emphasizing Schema and Intercultural Sensitivity theories.* Tehran: MA thesis in Communication, University of Tehran.

Alexander, Y., & Nanes, A. S. (1980). *The United States and Iran: A documentary history.* Frederick: Aletheia Books.

Alloy, L. B., Clements, C. M., & Koenig, L. J. (1993). Perceptions of control: Determinants and mechanisms. In G. Weary, F. Gleicher, & K. L. Marsh, *Control motivation and social cognition* (pp. 33-73). New York: Springer-Verlag.

Amanat, A. (1997). *Pivot of the universe: Nasir al-Din Shah Qajar and the Iranian Monarchy, 1831-1896.* Berkeley: University of California Press.

Ameli, S. R. & Shahghasemi, E. (2017). Americans' cross-cultural schemata of Iranians: an online survey, *Cross Cultural & Strategic Management*, 24(4), https://doi.org/10.1108/CCSM-10-2016-0176

Ameli, S. R. (2012). *Bibliographical Discourse Analysis: The Western Academic Perspective on Islam. 1, Muslims and Islamic Countries: 1949-1979.* London: Islamic Human Rights Commission.

Ameli, S. R., Mohseni, E., & Merali, A. (2013). *Once Upon a Hatred : Anti-muslim Experiences in the USA.* London: Once Upon a Hatred : Anti-muslim Experiences in the USA.

Andersen, H. C. (2012). *The Wild Swans and Other Tales.* London: Sovereign.

Anderson, G. H. (1998). *Biographical dictionary of Christian missions.* New York: Macmillan Reference.

Anderson, G. H. (1999). *Biographical dictionary of Christian missions.* New York: Macmillan Reference.

Asgard, R. (2010). U.S.-Iran cultural diplomacy: A historical perspective. *al Nakhlah*.

Badiozamani, B., & Badiozamani, G. (2005). *Iran and America: Re-kind[l]ing a love lost.* California: East-West Understanding Press.

BIBLIOGRAPHY

ABCFM. (1819). *The Panoplist, and Missionary Herald, Volume 15.* Boston: Samuel T. Armstrong.

ABCFM. (1825). *The Missionary herald XXI.* Boston: Crocker & Brewster.

ABCFM. (1834). *The Missionary Herald, Volume 30.* Boston: Crocker and Brewster.

Abrahamian, E. (1982). *Iran between two revolutions.* Princeton: Princeton University Press.

Abrahamian, E. (2004). Empire strikes back: Iran in U.S. sights . In B. Cumings, E. Abrahamian, & M. Ma'oz, *Inventing the axis of evil : the truth about North Korea, Iran, and Syria* (pp. 93-156). New York: New Press.

Abrahamian, E. (2008). *A history of modern Iran.* Cambridge, U.K. ; New York: Cambridge University Press.

Adolphs, R. (2001). The neurobiology of social cognition. *Current Opinion in Neurobiology, 11*(2), 231–239.

Afary, J. (1996). *The Iranian constitutional revolution, 1906-1911: Grassroots democracy, social democracy & the origins of feminism.* New York: Columbia University Press.

Ahmadzadeh, M., Sabaghi, A., Motamedi, B., & Esmaeili, A. (2005). *Assessing the intercultural sensitivity of Americans toward the*

Hassler-Forest, D. (2010). The 300 controvercy: A case study in the politics of adaptation. In J. Goggin, & D. Hassler-Forest, *The rise and reason of comics and graphic literature: Critical essays on the form* (pp. 119-127). United States of America: McFarland.

Haynes-Peterson, R. (2014, August 10). *Examiner*. Retrieved Spetember 1, 2014, from Anthony Bourdain kicks off chef talks at Long Island's Guild Hall: http://www.examiner.com/article/anthony-bourdain-kicks-off-chef-talks-at-long-island-s-guild-hall.

Heisey, D. R. (2008). *'The Great Satan' vs. An Axis of Evil': Perceptions Iranians and Americans have of each other.*" Hiram, Ohio, U.S.

Heisey, D. R., & Sharifzadeh, M. (2011). *The visual and artistic rhetoric of Americans and Iranians of each other impacted by media*. Phi Beta Delta. Philadelphia.

Hellot, F. (2005). The Western missionaries in Azerbaijani society (1835-1914). In R. Gleave, *Religion and Society in Qajar Iran* (pp. 270-292). London: Routledge Curzon.

Heradstveit, D., & Bonham, G. M. (2007). What the axis of evil metaphor did to Iran. *Middle East Journal, 61*(3), 421-441.

Heravi, M. (1999). *Iranian-American Diplomacy*. United States of American: Ibex Publishers.

Herman, E. S., & Chomsky, N. (2002). *Manufacturing consent: The political economy of the mass media*. New York: Pantheon Books.

Heubeck , A., & Hoekstra, A. (1990). *A Commentary on Homer's Odyssey*. Oxford: Oxford University Press.

Heuser, F. J. (1988). *A guide to foreign missionary manuscripts in the Presbyterian Historical Society*. New York: Greenwood Press.

Holliday, A., Kullman, J., & Hyde, M. (2004). *Intercultural communication, an advanced resource book*. London; New York: Routledge.

Hoover, S. M. (2008). Surprises and Learnings from the Tehran Conference. *Journal of Media and Religion, 7*(1-2), 100-102.

Hulme, P., & Youngs, T. (2002). *The Cambridge Companion to Travel Writing*. Cambridge, U.K.; New York: Cambridge University Press.

Imamoğlu, C. (2007). Assisted living as a new place schema. *Environment and Behavior, 39*(2), 246-268.

Iriye, A. (2002). Cultural relations and politics. In A. DeConde, R. D. Burns, & F. Logevall, *Encyclopedia of American foreign policy / Vol. 1 , A-D* (pp. 409-426). New York: Charles Scribner's Sons.

Israel, J., & Anderson, D. L. (2002). Department of state. In A. DeConde, R. D. Burns, & F. Logevall, *Encyclopedia of American foreign policy / Vol. 1, E-N* (Vol. 1, pp. 451-462). New York: Charles Scribner's Sons.

Ito, T. A. (2011). Perceiving social category information from faces: Using ERPs to study person perception. In A. B. Todorov, S. T. Fiske, & D. A. Prentice, *Social neuroscience: Toward understanding the underpinnings of the social mind* (pp. 85-100). Oxford; New York: Oxford University Press.

Johnston Conover, P., Mingst, K. A., & Sigelman, L. (1980). Mirror images in Americans' perceptions of nations and leaders during the Iranian hostage crisis. *Journal of Peace Research, 4*, 325-337.

Kambin, P. (2011). *A history of the Iranian Plateau: Rise and fall of an empire.* Bloomington: IUniverse Inc.

Kedie, N. R. (1988). Iranian revolutions in comparative perspectives. In E. Burke, E. Abrahamian, & I. M. Lapidu, *Islam, Politics, and Social Movements* (pp. 298-314). Berkeley: University of California Press.

Kellogg, R. T. (1997). *Cognitive psychology.* Thousand Oaks: Sage Publications.

Keshishian, F. (2000). Acculturation, communication, and the U.S. mass media: The experience of an Iranian immigrant. *Howard Journal of, 11*(2), 93-106.

Khatib-Shahidi, R. (2013). *German foreign policy towards Iran before World War II: Political relations, economic influence and the National Bank of Persia.* London: I.B. Tauris.

Kim, S.-B. D. (2013). Changes and trends in world Christianity. *Transformation: An International Journal of Holistic Mission Studies, 30*(4), 257-266.

Kimball, W. F. (2002). Alliances, coalitions, and entents. In A. DeConde, R. D. Burns, & F. Logevall, *Encyclopedia of American foreign policy / Vol. 1 , A-D* (pp. 13-28). New York: Charles Scribner's Sons.

Kinney, A. F. (2012). *The Oxford handbook of Shakespeare*. Oxford: Oxford University Press.

Kinzer, S. (2011). *All the Shah's men : An American coup and the roots of Middle East terror*. New Jersey: John Wiley & Sons, Inc.

Klare, M. T. (2002). Arms transfers and trade. In A. DeConde, R. D. Burns, & F. Logevall, *Encyclopedia of American foreign policy / Vol. 1 , A-D* (pp. 105-116). New York: Charles Scribner's Sons.

Kovacs, M. G. (1989). *The epic of Gilgamesh*. Stanford, Calif: Stanford University Press.

Kull, S. (2007). *Public opinion in Iran and America on key international issues*. World Public Opinion. Retrieved from http://www.worldpublicopinion.org/pipa/pdf/jan07/Iran_Jan07_rpt.pdf.

Lane, C. (1995). Germany's New Ostpolitik. *Foreign Affairs, 74*(6), 77-89.

Laurie, T. (1853). *Dr. Grant and the mountain Nestorians*. Boston: Gould and Lincoln.

Laurie, T. (1863). *Woman and her saviour in Persia*. Boston: Gould and Lincoln.

Laurie, T. (1887). *Woman and the gospel in Persia*. Chicago: Woman's Presbyterian Board of Missions of the Northwest.

Lauwers, J., Dhont, M., & Huybrecht, X. (2012). "This is Sparta!:" Discourse, gender, and the Orient in Zack Snyder's 300. In A.-B. Renger, & J. Solomon, *Ancient worlds in film and television: Gender and politics* (pp. 79-94). Boston: Brill.

Lee, K. (2003). *Health impacts of globalization: Towards global governance*. New York: Palgrave Macmillan.

Llewellyn-Jones, L., & Robson, J. (2010). *Ctesias' History of Persia: Tales of the Orient*. New York: Routledge.

Llobera, J. R. (2003). *An invitation to anthropology : the structure, evolution, and cultural identity of human societies*. New York: Berghahn Books.

Lorentz, J. H. (2010). *The A to Z of Iran*. Lanham: Scarecrow Press.

Macuch, R. (1987). Assyrians in Iran. In E. Yarshater, *Encyclopaedia Iranica* (Vol. II, pp. 820-842). London; Boston: Routledge & Kegan Paul.

Maghsoudlou, B. (2009). *Grass: Untold Stories.* Costa Mesa: Mazda Publishers.

Mahdavi, S. (2005). Shahs, doctors, diplomats and missionaries in 19th century Iran. *British Journal of Middle Eastern Studies, 32*(2), 169-191.

Malcolm, I., & Sharifian, F. (2002). Aspects of aboriginal English oral discourse: An application of cultural schema theory. *Discourse Studies, 4*(2), 169-181.

Malick, D. G. (2008). *The American mission press : A preliminary bibliography.* Chicago: Atour Publications.

Mansoori, A. (1986). *American missionaries in Iran, 1834-1934.* Muncie: Ball State University.

Marr, T. (2006). "Drying up the Euphrates": Muslims, Millennialism, and early American missionary enterprise. In T. Marr, *The cultural roots of American Islamicism* (pp. 130-149). Cambridge ; New York: Cambridge University Press.

Marr, T. (2006). *The cultural roots of American Islamicism.* Cambridge: Cambridge University Press.

Mayer, J. D., Rapp, H. C., & Williams, U. (1993). Individual differences in behavioral prediction: The acquisition of personal-action schemata. *Personality and Social Psychology Bulletin, 19*(4), 443-451.

McCrisken, T. B. (2002). Foreign aid. In A. DeConde, R. D. Burns, & F. Logevall, *Encyclopedia of American foreign policy / Vol. 2, E-N* (pp. 93-11). New York: Charles Scribner's Sons.

McGlinchey, S. (2013). Lyndon B. Johnson and arms credit sales to Iran 1964-1968. *Middle East Journal, 67*(2), 229-247.

McVee, M. B., Dunsmore, K., & Gavelek, J. R. (2005). Schema theory revisited. *Review of Educational Research, 75*(4), 531-566.

Merrick, J. L. (1847). *The pilgrim's harp.* Boston: Crocker and Brewster.

Millspaugh, A. C. (1925). *The American task in Persia.* New York ; London: Century Co.

Millward, W. G. (1975). The social psychology of anti-Iranology. *Iranian Studies, 8*(1/2), 48-69.

Mirani, G., Soofi, M., Ahmadzadeh Namvar, F., & Haghboei, A. (2006). *The shadow of schema over intercultural communications: A research on Iran-USA case.* doi:http://ameli-saied.com/english/index.php?op=sarticles&group=9.

Mobasher, M. M. (2012). *Iranians in Texas : Migration, politics, and ethnic identity.* Austin: University of Texas Press.

Mobasher, M. M. (2012). *Iranians in Texas: Migration, politics, and ethnic identity.* Austin: University of Texas Press.

Momen, M. (2005). The role of women in the Iranian Bahai community. In R. Gleave, *Religion and society in Qajar Iran* (pp. 346-370). London: RoutledgeCurzon.

Morier, J. J. (1812). *A journey through Persia, Armenia, and Asia Minor, to Constantinople, in the years 1808 and 1809 : in which is included, some account of the proceedings of His Majesty's mission, under Sir Harford Jones, Bart. K. C. to the court of the King of Persia.* London: Longman.

Morton, D. O. (1832). *Memoir of the Rev. Levi Parsons, first missionary to Palestine from the United States (1832).* Edinburgh: Edinburgh.

Moskowitz, G. B. (2005). *Social cognition: Understanding self and others.* New York: Guilford Press.

Movahedi, S. (1985). The social psychology of foreign policy and the politics of international images. *Human Affairs, 8,* 1-11.

Mullen, A. (2010). Bringing power back in: The Herman-Chomsky propaganda model, 1988-2008. In J. Klaehn, *The political economy of media and power* (pp. 207-228). New York: Peter Lang.

Murre-van den Berg, H. (1996). The Missionaries' Assistants: The Role of Assyrians in the Development of Written Urmia Aramaic. *Journal of the Assyrian Academic Society*(2), 3 - 17.

Murre-van den Berg, H. (2005). Nineteenth-century Protestant Missions and Middle-Eastern women: An overview. In I. M. Okkenhaug, & I. Flaskerud, *Gender, Religion and Change in the Middle East. Two*

Hundred Years of History. (pp. 103-122). Oxford and New York: BERG.

Nategh, H. (1996). *Karnameye farhangie farangi.* Paris: Khavaran.

Newcomb, H. (1854). *Cyclopedia of missions ; containing a comprehensive view of missionary operations throughout the world; with geographical descriptions, and accounts of the social, moral, and religious condition of the people.* New York: C. Scribner.

Nishida, H. (1999). A cognitive approach to intercultural communication based on schema theory. *International Journal of Intercultural Relations, 23*(5), 753-777.

Nye, J. S. (2013). *Presidential leadership and the creation of the American era.* Princeton, New Jersey: Princeton University Press.

Oller, J. W. (1995). Adding Abstract to Formal and Content Schemata: Results of Recent Work in Peircean Semiotics. *Applied Linguistics, 16*(3), 273-306.

Pazy, A. (1994). Cognitive schemata of professional obsolescence. *Human Relations, 47*(10), 1167-1199.

Pennington, D. C. (2000). *Social cognition.* London and Philadelphia: Routledge.

Perkins, H. M. (1887). *Life of Rev. Justin Perkins, D. D., Pioneer missionary to Persia.* Chicago: Woman's Pbesbyterian Board of Missions.

Perkins, J. (1843). *A Residence of Eight Years in Persia among the Nestorian Christians with Notices of the Muhammedans.* New York: Allen, Morrill & Wardwell.

Perkins, J. (1853). *The Persian flower: A memoir of Judith Grant Perkins, of Oroomiah, Persia.* Boston: American Tract Society.

Public Affairs Alliance of Iranian Americans. (2008). *Public opinion survey of American Perceptions of Iranian Americans.* Public Affairs Alliance of Iranian Americans. Retrieved September 22, 2013, from http://www.paaia.org/CMS/survey-of-american-perceptions-of-iranian-americans.aspx.

Rivas, D. (2002). Humanitarian intervention and relief. In A. DeConde, R. D. Burns, & F. Logevall, *Encyclopedia of American foreign policy / Vol. 2, E-N* (pp. 151-172). New York: Charles Scribner's Sons.

Saïd, S. (2011). *Homer and the Odyssey*. Oxford; New York: Oxford University Press.

Sajjādī, Ṣ. (1989). BĪMĀRESTĀN. In E. Yar-Shater, *Encyclopædia Iranica* (Vol. IV, pp. 257-261). London; Boston: Routledge & Kegan Paul.

Saleh, A. P. (1976). *Cultural ties between Iran and the United States*. Tehran: Sherkat-e- Chapkhaneh Bistopanj-e Shahrivar.

Sasaki, M. (2000). Effects of cultural schemata on students' test-taking processes for cloze tests: A multiple data source approach. *Language Testing, 17*(1), 85-114.

Schayegh, C. (2009). *Who is knowledgeable, is strong: Science, class, and the formation of modern Iranian Society, 1900–1950*. Berkeley: University of California Press.

Schrodt, P. (2006). Development and validation of the Stepfamily Life Index. *Journal of Social and Personal Relationships, 23*(3), 427-444.

Shackley, M. L. (2006). *Atlas of travel and tourism development*. Boston: Elsevier.

Shahghasemi, E. (2009). How do Iranian bloggers view the American people. *iCom 2009*. Melaka.

Shahghasemi, E., & Heisey, D. R. (2009). The cross-cultural schemata of Iranian-American people toward each other: A qualitative approach. *Intercultural Communication Studies, XVIII*(1), 143-160.

Shahghasemi, E., Heisey, D. R., & Mirani, G. (2011). How do Iranians and U.S. citizens perceive each other: A systematic review. *Journal of Intercultural Communication*(27).

Shahidi, H. (2007). *Journalism in Iran: From mission to profession*. London; New York: Routledge.

Sharifi, R., Shahghasemi, E., & Emamzadeh, Z. (2017). Cross cultural schemata Iranian women have of Americans. *Art of Communication*. Warsaw: Interdisciplinary Research Foundation.

Shatzmiller, M. (1993). *Crusaders and Muslims in twelfth-century Syria.* New York: Brill.

Shavit, D. (1988). *The United States in the Middle East: A historical dictionary.* New York: Greenwood Press.

Shedd, M. L. (1918). *Mary Lewis [Mrs. W. A.] Shedd papers.* Union Theological Seminary: Finding Aid.

Shedd, M. L. (1922). *The measure of a man: The life of William Ambrose Shedd, missionary to Persia.* New York: George H. Doran Co.

Shedd, W. A. (1904). *Islam and the Oriental Churches: Their historical relations.* Philadelphia: Presbyterian Board of Publication and Sabbath-school Work.

Shmuel, R. b. (2011). The Western missionaries and the revival of the Neo-Aramaic dialects. *Simtha, 5*(18), 6-13.

Shuster, W. M. (1912). *The strangling of Persia; A record of European diplomacy and oriental intrigue.* New York: The Century Co.

Sick, G. (1985). *All fall down: America's fateful encounter in Iran.* London: Tauris.

Sicker, M. (2001). *The Middle East in the Twentieth Century.* Westport, Conn.: Praeger.

Siew Ming, T. (1997). Induced content schema Vs induced linguistic schema—Which is more beneficial for Malaysian ESL readers? *RELC Journal, 28*(2), 107-127.

Simon, H. A. (1976). Discussion: Cognition and social behavior. In J. Carroll, & J. Payne, *Cognition and social behavior* (pp. 253-269). Hillsdale, NJ: Erlbaum.

Slade, S. (1981). The Image of the Arab in America: Analysis of a Poll on American Attitudes. *Middle East Journal, 35*(2), 143-162.

Smith, E., & Dwight, H. G. (1834). *Missionary researches in Armenia : including a journey through Asia Minor and into Georgia and Persia, etc.* London: Watford Field House.

Sokolowski, R. (2000). *Introduction to phenomenology.* Cambridge, UK; New York: Cambridge University Press.

Southgate, H. (1840). *Narrative of a tour through Armenia, Kurdistan, Persia and Mesopotamia: with an introduction, and occasional observations upon the condition of Mohammedanism and Christianity in those countries.* New York: D. Appleton & Co.

Speer, R. E. (1911). *The Hakim Sahib, the foreign doctor: A biography of Joseph Plumb Cochran, M.D., of Persia.* New York: Fleming H. Revell Co.

Spellman, K. (2004). *Religion and nation: Iranian local and transnational networks in Britain.* New York: Berghahn Book.

Stockwell, P. (2003). Schema poetics and speculative cosmology. *Language and Literature, 12*(3), 252-271.

Strickland, D. H. (2003). *Saracens, Demons, and Jews: Making Monsters in Medieval Art.* Princeton: Princeton University Press.

Stümpel-Hatami, I. (1999). Christianity as described by Persian Muslims. In J. Waardenburg, *Muslim perceptions of other religions: A historical survey* (pp. 227-240). New York: Oxford University Press.

Sullivan, W. H. (1981). *Mission to Iran.* New York: Norton.

Tadayon, K. M. (1982). The changing image of Iran in the United States: Open-ended format surveys before and after the hostage crisis. *International Communication Gazette, 30,* 89-95.

Tavassoli, S. (2011). *Christian encounters with Iran: Engaging Muslim thinkers after the Revolution.* London: I. B. Tauris.

Taylor, G. (2005). *Fever And thirst: Dr. Grant and the Christian tribes of Kurdistan.* Chicago: Academy Chicago Publishers.

Taylor, S. E., & Crocker, J. (1981). Schematic bases of social information processing. In E. Higgins, C. A. Herman, & M. P. Zanna, *Social Cognition* (pp. 89-134). Hillsdale, NJ: Lawrence Erlbaum Associate.

Terror Free Tomorrow. (2007). *Polling Iranian Public Opinion: An unprecedented nationwide survey of Iran.* Washington: Terror Free Tomorrow. Retrieved October 12, 2013, from http://www.terrorfreetomorrow.org/upimagestft/TFT%20Iran%20Survey%20Report.pdf.

Tigay, J. H. (1982). *The evolution of the Gilgamesh epic.* Philadelphia: University of Pennsylvania Press.

Van Gorder, C. (2010). *Christianity in Persia and the status of non-muslims in Iran.* Lanham: Lexington Books.

Walker, W. O. (2002). Narcotics policy. In A. DeConde, R. D. Burns, & F. Logevall, *Encyclopedia of American foreign policy / Vol. 2, E-N* (pp. 455-472). New York: Charles Scribner's Sons.

Ward, S. R. (2009). *Immortal: A military history of Iran and its armed forces.* Washington, D.C.: Georgetown University Press.

Waring, E. S. (1807). *A tour to Sheeraz, by the route of Kazroon and Feerozabad : with various remarks on the manners of the Persians to which is added a history of Persia.* London.

Warne, A. (2013). Psychoanalyzing Iran: Kennedy's Iran Task Force and the Modernization of Orientalism, 1961–3. *The International History Review, 35*(2), 396-422.

Werner, C. M., Rhodes, M. U., & Partain, K. K. (1998). Designing effective instructional signs with schema theory: Case studies of polystyrene recycling. *Environment and Behavior, 30*(5), 709-735.

Westwood, A. F. (1965). Politics of distrust in Iran. *Annals of the American Academy of Political and Social Science, 358*(1), 123-135.

Wishard, J. G. (1908). *Twenty years in Persia: A narrative of life under the last three shahs.* New York: Fleming H. Revell Company.

Woods, L. (1833). *Memoirs of American missionaries, formerly connected with the Society of Inquiry Respecting Missions, in the Andover Theological Seminary: Embracing a history of the Society, etc., with an introductory essay.* Boston: Peirce and Parker.

World Public Opinion. (2009). Iranians Favor Diplomatic Relations With US But Have Little Trust in Obama. Maryland: *World Public Opinion.*

Yekta Steininger, M. (2010). *The United States and Iran: Different values and attitudes toward nature; scratches on our hearts and minds.* Lanham, MD: University Press of America.

Yeselson, A. (1956). *United States-Persian diplomatic relations, 1883-1921.* New Brunswick, N.J.: Rutgers University Press.

Zajonc, R. B. (1989). Styles of explanation in social psychology. *European Journal of Social Psychology*, 19(5), 345-368.

Zaki, J., & Ochsner, K. (2011). You, me, and my brain: Self and other representations in social cognitive neuroscience. In A. B. Todorov, S. T. Fiske, & D. A. *Prentice, Social neuroscience: Toward understanding the underpinnings of the social mind* (pp. 14-39). Oxford; New York: Oxford University Press.

About the Author

Ehsan Shahghasemi, PhD
Assistant Professor
University of Tehran, Tehran, Iran
Email: Shahghasemi@ut.ac.ir

Ehsan Shahghasemi was born in Rostam, south west of Iran. He was mainly raised in Nourabad, Shiraz and Tehran. In 2002, he graduated in Mechanics of Agricultural Machinery from the University of Shiraz. After serving in the Iranian Army from 2003 to 2005, he entered the MA program in Communication at University of Tehran. In 2009, he started his PhD in Communications at the University of Tehran and graduated in 2014. He is now a Professor at the Department of Communications, University of Tehran. Ehsan Shahghasemi has published on different subjects including intercultural communication, cyberspace, and media philosophy and technology. He is interested in international collaboration and he has published works with scholars from different parts of the world.

INDEX

#

19th century, 39, 45, 47, 48, 49, 52, 54, 57, 65, 67, 73, 74, 254
300 (movie), 7, 8

A

Abdollahyan, Hamid, vii
Abrahamian, Ervand, viii, 45, 84, 86, 88, 90, 92, 97, 98, 100, 103, 245, 252
Afghanistan, 79, 102, 103, 149
Ahmadinejad, Mahmoud, 103, 123, 160, 196, 197, 198, 199, 200, 229
airborne warning and control system (AWACS), 98, 99
Alabama, 121, 133, 150, 154, 179, 180, 188, 193, 194, 214, 225
Alaska, 121, 132, 139, 142, 150, 179, 182, 199, 205, 206, 214
Alborz College, 56
American Board of Commissioners for Foreign Missions (ABCFM), 40, 42, 43, 44, 45, 61, 71, 245
Anglican, 45
Arizona, 118, 121, 126, 131, 145, 150, 158, 167, 170, 171, 177, 179, 180, 182, 188, 189, 194, 196, 197, 198, 201, 206, 208, 222, 230
Arkansas, 121, 140, 158, 166, 169, 186, 188, 193, 203, 218
Assyrian, 46, 47, 50, 57, 59, 60, 61, 171, 255
Axis of Evil, v, 1, 28, 103, 251
Azerbaijan, 79, 83

B

Bakhtiari, 16, 87
Bashir, Hassan, viii
Baskerville, Howard C., 50, 73, 85
Bateson, Mary Catherine, 21, 22, 247
Benjamin, Samuel Greene Wheeler, 13, 82
Berger, Arthur Asa, viii
Bonaparte, Napoléon, 5
Boston, 40, 44, 48, 58, 137, 245, 250, 253, 254, 256, 257, 260
Bourdain, Anthony, 34, 251
British, 26, 41, 45, 50, 64, 66, 70, 71, 72, 78, 79, 80, 81, 83, 85, 86, 87, 88, 94, 95, 102, 104, 250, 254

C

California, 1, 105, 121, 129, 131, 132, 133, 135, 140, 143, 149, 150, 151, 153, 154, 163, 164, 168, 170, 171, 175, 179, 182, 188, 194, 203, 205, 206, 207, 208, 212, 213, 220, 221, 222, 225, 233, 246, 252, 257

Caribbean, 6

Carter, President Jimmy, 5, 6, 24, 98, 100, 101, 194, 195, 198, 228, 247

Central Treaty Organization (CENTO), 95

China, 27, 51, 61, 92, 94, 95, 134

cholera, 48, 49, 50, 54, 59, 70

Christian, viii, 15, 27, 43, 44, 45, 51, 52, 55, 61, 62, 63, 65, 67, 70, 72, 73, 79, 81, 85, 104, 154, 171, 173, 189, 200, 246, 250, 259

Christianity, 22, 43, 45, 46, 52, 60, 65, 66, 71, 72, 73, 252, 259, 260

Coan, Rev. F. G., 14, 46, 49, 248

Cochran, Joseph Gallup, 44, 46, 48, 52, 53, 55, 68, 259

cognition, 107, 109, 110, 111, 120, 245, 246, 250, 255, 256

Cold War, 94, 102

Colorado, 121, 139, 142, 145, 161, 165, 171, 172, 174, 185, 187, 204, 210, 215, 217, 218, 219, 224

Connecticut, 121, 127, 131, 135, 136, 139, 145, 149, 151, 171, 176, 180, 204, 219, 225

Cooper, Merian C., 16

cross-cultural schemata, 30, 246, 257

Crusades, 4

D

DAESH, 1

decolonization, 6

Delaware, 121, 142, 146, 153, 179, 199, 200, 218, 233

Douglas, William O., 18, 249

Dwight, Harrison, 9, 10, 41, 42, 44, 45, 61, 67, 94, 258

E

ecclesiastics, 55

Egypt, 3, 6, 40, 45, 92, 162

el-din Shah, Mozafar, 83, 84

el-din Shah, Naser, 83

English, 5, 15, 26, 44, 62, 66, 67, 68, 71, 72, 115, 153, 209, 216, 232, 237, 247, 254

European, 5, 7, 10, 13, 15, 18, 21, 22, 37, 68, 70, 71, 79, 180, 204, 247, 258, 261

evangelical, 39, 65, 79

evangelization, 62, 64, 67

exotic, 3, 4, 5, 6, 7, 36, 217, 218

Eyre, Alan, 242

F

F-14, 97

F-4, 97

F-5, 97

famine, 51

Fiske, Fidelia, 44, 49, 55, 64

Florida, 121, 125, 126, 127, 131, 154, 158, 161, 166, 167, 168, 170, 171, 174, 177, 181, 182, 186, 195, 196, 202, 206, 210, 211, 212, 216, 219, 222, 223, 224, 227, 247

G

Gable, Richard W., 19

Gastil, Raymond, 19

Georgia, 121, 127, 158, 162, 171, 176, 196, 201, 216, 258

German, 12, 14, 62, 87, 90, 252
globalization, 2, 7, 22, 253
Goodrich, Samuel, 13
Google Drive, 118
Grant, Asahel, 11, 48, 51, 64, 68
Great Satan, v, 1, 28, 251
Greek, 3, 40, 41, 78, 144

H

Hamedan, 46, 47, 53, 54, 79
Hawaii, 121, 158, 196, 206, 212
Heisey, D. Ray, vii, viii, 114
Herman-Chomsky, 36, 251, 255
Herodotus, 3
Homo sapiens, 107, 109
Huntington, Samuel P., 241

I

Idaho, 121, 140, 153, 161, 166, 168, 169, 176, 182, 207, 217, 223
Ifilm, 243
Illinois, 121, 132, 135, 139, 141, 150, 167, 171, 174, 178, 198, 201, 223, 232
Indiana, 45, 121, 128, 142, 143, 144, 150, 151, 162, 165, 166, 168, 169, 170, 177, 185, 190, 191, 193, 217, 218, 227, 228, 231
Iowa, 121, 126, 143, 158, 165, 166, 168, 184, 193, 194, 196, 197, 200, 212, 223, 238
Iranian Americans, 29, 207, 256
Iran-U.S, 1, 2, 73, 78, 89
Iraq, 16, 25, 27, 32, 50, 87, 95, 102, 103, 128, 134, 137, 145, 146, 180, 196, 199, 208, 228, 238
Islam, 4, 21, 25, 32, 60, 61, 62, 65, 66, 73, 104, 146, 150, 171, 180, 182, 189, 193, 200, 201, 236, 246, 250, 252, 258
Islamic Revolution, vi, 37, 74, 100, 104

Israel, 69, 90, 100, 133, 134, 147, 192, 195, 227, 252
Izadi, Foad, vii

J

Jackson, Abraham Valentine Williams, 16
Jordan, Samuel Martin, 57

K

Kansas, 121, 128, 138, 140, 148, 153, 161, 162, 165, 168, 171, 172, 174, 177, 178, 182, 183, 184, 186, 191, 200, 201, 207, 208, 212, 223, 226, 228, 232, 239
Kennedy, John F. President, 96, 248
Kentucky, 121, 126, 140, 144, 153, 158, 166, 168, 172, 175, 183, 184, 189, 190, 193, 194, 200, 204, 206, 207, 223, 226, 228, 229
Kerman, 87
Kermanshah, 22, 46, 54, 79
Keshishian, Flora, viii, 27, 37, 101, 252
Khatami, Mohammad, 102, 214, 241

L

Labaree, Rev. Benjamin W., 50, 60, 84
Lazarist, 45, 59
Llewellyn-Jones, L., 4, 7, 52, 253, 255
Louisiana, 121, 143, 145, 165, 167, 178, 189, 192, 200, 212, 222, 223, 233

M

Maine, 121, 127, 135, 180, 217
Majles, 85, 86, 88, 94
Malinowski, Bronislaw, 6

Maryland, 121, 126, 127, 136, 141, 150, 155, 162, 166, 175, 177, 182, 190, 196, 197, 204, 214, 220, 223, 228, 230, 260
Massachusetts, 44, 121, 126, 127, 138, 143, 144, 145, 155, 158, 169, 171, 175, 176, 204, 210, 213, 216, 219, 220, 225, 230
Merrick, James Layman, 12
methodology, viii
Michigan, 122, 127, 136, 138, 139, 141, 150, 167, 171, 172, 174, 176, 179, 183, 185, 194, 197, 199, 201, 208, 209, 214, 217, 218, 224, 230, 232
Middle East, 1, 7, 8, 31, 40, 41, 54, 65, 73, 78, 83, 87, 98, 141, 143, 160, 171, 172, 173, 175, 176, 179, 181, 184, 185, 186, 191, 193, 208, 241, 242, 247, 248, 250, 251, 253, 254, 255, 258
Millspaugh, Arthur Chester, 17
Millward, William G., 21, 255
Minnesota, 122, 131, 138, 139, 140, 141, 146, 168, 185, 188, 190, 198, 199, 201, 202, 204, 209, 212, 213, 218, 222, 225, 233
missionary, 9, 11, 12, 13, 14, 39, 40, 42, 44, 45, 49, 50, 51, 52, 54, 56, 57, 59, 60, 61, 65, 66, 68, 70, 73, 74, 78, 82, 251, 254, 255, 256, 258
Mississippi, 122, 126, 144, 150, 167, 169, 170, 172, 178, 183, 193, 221, 223, 226
Missouri, 122, 127, 128, 139, 141, 145, 150, 151, 153, 166, 168, 169, 170, 172, 177, 178, 184, 185, 186, 191, 192, 207, 208, 212, 217, 224
Mobasher, Mohsen, viii, 24, 27, 32, 34, 36, 255
Montana, 122, 142, 148, 163, 172, 209
Mosaddegh, 78, 93, 94
Murre-van den Berg, Heleen, viii, 66

N

NATO, 94
Nazi, 90, 104
Nebraska, 122, 126, 142, 148, 149, 162, 166, 172, 178, 180, 183, 184, 185, 186, 194, 207, 209, 227, 232
Nestorian(s), 10, 11, 41, 42, 44, 45, 47, 48, 49, 52, 55, 56, 62, 63, 67, 68, 69, 73, 78, 250, 253, 256
Nestories, 50
Nevada, 1, 122, 130, 154, 178, 188, 209, 218, 225
New Hampshire, 122, 158, 189, 212, 215, 223, 238
New Jersey, 88, 92, 121, 122, 125, 131, 137, 141, 144, 151, 153, 158, 161, 169, 180, 181, 186, 191, 195, 197, 219, 221, 222, 225, 253, 256
New Mexico, 122, 125, 127, 138, 140, 143, 152, 163, 192, 200, 210, 212, 217, 235
New York, viii, 25, 40, 48, 60, 88, 122, 128, 131, 135, 140, 148, 150, 153, 154, 163, 169, 176, 178, 192, 193, 194, 197, 202, 204, 205, 210, 213, 214, 215, 218, 221, 234, 237, 245, 246, 247, 248, 249, 250, 251, 252, 253, 254, 255, 256, 257, 258, 259, 260, 261
Nixon, President Richard, 96
North Carolina, 122, 129, 133, 143, 145, 148, 150, 158, 163, 170, 172, 194, 195, 197, 198, 202, 203, 204
North Dakota, 122, 125, 132, 138, 139, 142, 144, 150, 154, 163, 164, 172, 176, 186, 187, 192, 194, 201, 213, 214, 223, 224, 234, 235
North Korea, 27, 94, 103, 134, 245

O

Ohio, 32, 122, 126, 132, 144, 145, 148, 149, 150, 151, 166, 172, 184, 193, 200, 202, 206, 215, 219, 225, 251
Oklahoma, 122, 138, 143, 144, 149, 163, 176, 178, 179, 192, 193, 194, 197, 198, 202, 210, 212, 215, 217, 220, 224, 236, 239
Operation Ajax, 94
Operation Eagle Claw, 102
Oregon, 122, 125, 127, 132, 138, 143, 149, 163, 167, 170, 178, 181, 183, 194, 198, 199, 203, 210, 212, 215, 217, 236
Ottoman, 41, 64, 78, 87, 92

P

Parsons, Levi, 40, 255
Pennsylvania, 45, 116, 122, 127, 137, 143, 145, 148, 151, 171, 173, 177, 180, 189, 195, 210, 214, 217, 222, 223, 226, 231, 259
Perkins, Justin, 10, 42, 44, 49, 58, 61, 63, 68, 69, 256
Persian, 3, 4, 7, 9, 10, 11, 14, 15, 16, 17, 18, 21, 25, 30, 31, 37, 40, 41, 42, 43, 49, 54, 57, 59, 61, 63, 65, 67, 69, 79, 80, 81, 84, 85, 86, 87, 88, 89, 93, 98, 99, 100, 105, 118, 127, 128, 144, 167, 168, 169, 170, 173, 200, 202, 204, 208, 210, 211, 214, 217, 221, 231, 232, 237, 238, 242, 256, 259, 260
Persian Gulf, 79, 80, 81, 87, 93, 98, 100, 242
Plague, 49
Pope, Arthur Upham, 18, 105
Presbyterian, 13, 42, 45, 47, 50, 51, 52, 53, 56, 63, 78, 82, 85, 249, 251, 253, 258
Prosser, Michael H., viii, 123

Public Affairs Alliance of Iranian Americans (PAAIA), 29

Q

Qajar(s), 64, 70, 72, 73, 79, 80, 82, 84, 87, 88, 90, 246, 248, 249, 251, 255
Qavam, 93

R

Rabiei, Ali, vii
Rasht, 46, 54, 56, 79, 86
religion, 9, 10, 12, 20, 24, 32, 56, 60, 61, 62, 71, 74, 78, 128, 130, 145, 150, 170, 172, 173, 174, 183, 185, 190, 208, 233, 235
respondent, 118, 156
Rhode Island, 122, 130, 148, 170, 187, 188, 205
Russian, 45, 59, 65, 70, 79, 83, 85, 88, 93, 104

S

Sahrifzadeh, 32
Saied, Reza Ameli, vii, 101
Schwarzkopf, Col. H. Norman, 92
Shah, Muhammad Ali, 84
Shah, Reza, 57, 67, 73, 88, 90, 91
Shahabi, Mahmoud, viii
Shahghasemi, E., viii, 30, 34, 115, 223, 246, 257, 263
Shedd, John H., 44, 46
Shedd, William Ambrose, 14, 44, 47, 50, 56, 60, 67, 258
Sheean, Vincent, 17
Shuster, William Morgan, 16, 85, 86, 87, 258

South Carolina, 122, 129, 137, 148, 150, 154, 164, 173, 187, 202, 204, 213, 214, 224, 236
South Dakota, 122, 135, 176, 177, 183, 188, 213, 220, 223
Southgate, 11, 62, 258
Speer, Robert E., 14
stereotype, 21, 26, 27, 113, 142, 144, 164, 173, 193, 219
Stoddard, David Tappan, 55, 58
Syria, 40, 45, 77, 245, 258
Syriac, 41, 48, 57, 58, 59, 63, 65, 66, 68

T

Tabriz, 11, 41, 42, 45, 46, 47, 50, 52, 54, 59, 61, 79, 83, 85
Taliban, 102, 103, 146, 193, 242
Tehran, v, viii, 13, 14, 22, 25, 29, 32, 34, 45, 46, 47, 53, 54, 56, 57, 59, 62, 69, 72, 79, 80, 82, 83, 85, 86, 87, 88, 90, 93, 99, 100, 101, 102, 140, 169, 195, 196, 197, 206, 227, 238, 246, 249, 251, 257, 263
Tennessee, 122, 132, 135, 153, 169, 182, 193, 195, 198, 202, 210, 213, 217, 237
Texas, 1, 32, 121, 122, 125, 127, 128, 129, 132, 133, 135, 138, 142, 153, 154, 167, 168, 170, 175, 177, 178, 179, 183, 186, 189, 192, 195, 200, 209, 210, 213, 217, 218, 220, 225, 226, 231, 238, 239, 255
Torrence, 46, 53
Tudeh party, 94
Turkish, 9, 14, 50, 59, 63, 68
Turkmanchai, 79

U

United States (US), v, viii, 1, 2, 6, 8, 16, 22, 23, 24, 25, 26, 27, 28, 33, 34, 37, 41, 42, 44, 48, 54, 65, 67, 68, 71, 77, 78, 80, 81, 82, 83, 87, 88, 89, 90, 91, 92, 93, 94, 95, 96, 97, 98, 99, 100, 101, 102, 103, 104, 105, 116, 117, 120, 121, 122, 123, 124, 125, 127, 131, 132, 135, 145, 148, 154, 155, 161, 169, 170, 174, 176, 180, 190, 193, 199, 203, 205, 212, 213, 215, 220, 222, 228, 241, 242, 245, 246, 247, 248, 251, 252, 255, 257, 258, 259, 260
University of Tehran, vii, 30, 114, 117, 246, 263
Urmia, 10, 14, 42, 44, 46, 47, 48, 49, 50, 52, 53, 55, 56, 57, 58, 59, 60, 61, 64, 67, 72, 82, 255
Utah, 122, 131, 133, 139, 148, 152, 163, 173, 177, 182, 201, 208, 235, 237

V

Van Duzee, C. O., 46
Van Duzee, M. K., 46
Vathek, 5
Vermont, 122, 144, 193, 214
Vietnam, 97
Virginia, viii, 122, 123, 132, 136, 145, 148, 150, 154, 165, 170, 171, 179, 187, 192, 193, 196, 198, 205, 207, 216, 218, 221, 222, 223, 226, 228

W

Washington, 83, 88, 93, 96, 99, 104, 122, 135, 138, 139, 142, 144, 150, 158, 165, 179, 180, 185, 188, 189, 190, 203, 206, 212, 218, 220, 223, 232, 259, 260
Wassmuss, 87
weapons, 81, 91, 96, 98, 102, 103, 189, 198
West Virginia, 121, 122, 145, 148, 158, 203, 213
Western, 1, 7, 14, 18, 28, 31, 46, 58, 64, 68, 69, 70, 75, 84, 87, 98, 100, 115, 163, 173, 212, 214, 243, 246, 248, 251, 258
Westwood, Andrew F., 20

Wisconsin, 122, 132, 135, 138, 140, 141, 143, 167, 169, 170, 171, 178, 185, 191, 193, 201, 204, 214, 220, 221, 225, 229
Wishard, John G., 14, 47, 72, 82
Wright, Austin H., 59
Wright, Dr. Hamilton, 89
Wright, Elizabeth Washburn, 89
Wright, Rev. J. N., 46
Wyoming, 121, 122, 153, 158, 170, 199, 203

X

Xenophon, 4

Z

Zagros Mountains, 16, 96
Zahedi, Fazlollah, 95
Zahrire d-Bahra, 59, 60
Zogby International, 29
Zoroastrian, 45, 169

Iran and Iraq: Human Rights Reports

Editors: Kyle T. Hunt and Alfred Ferguson

Series: Human Rights: Background and Issues

Book Description: This book on human rights practices chronicles dramatic changes and the stories of the people defending human rights in the countries of Iran and Iraq; with a focus on providing lawmaker's decisions on foreign military and economic aid.

Hardcover ISBN: 978-1-62257-418-6
Retail Price: $130

Iran: U.S. Concerns and Policy Responses

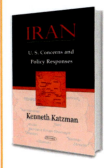

Author: Kenneth Katzman

Book Description: Iran's human rights practices and strict limits on democracy have been consistently criticized by official U.S. and U.N. reports, particularly for Iran's suppression of political dissidents and religious and ethnic minorities.

Softcover ISBN: 978-1-60456-845-5
Retail Price: $45

Iranian Foreign Policy: Context, Regional Analyses and U.S. Interests

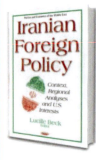

Editor: Lucille Beck

Series: Politics and Economics of the Middle East

Book Description: This book begins with an examination of Iran's policy motivators and instruments of Iran's foreign policy before moving on to deeper analyses of Iranian foreign policy as a whole and by region.

Hardcover ISBN: 978-1-63484-817-6
Retail Price: $145

Iran's Nuclear Program, Sanctions Relief, and Associated Legal and Legislative Issues

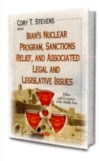

Editor: Cory T. Stevens

Series: Politics and Economics of the Middle East

Book Description: This book discusses Tehran's compliance with international obligations. It also examines the interim agreement on Iran's nuclear program; the economic sanctions and the authority to lift restrictions in Iran; and the Iran sanctions.

Hardcover ISBN: 978-1-63321-460-6
Retail Price: $172